Opposite the Cross Keys

Also by S.T. Haymon:

Death of a God
Stately Homicide
Ritual Murder
Death and the Pregnant Virgin

Maud Fenner with Maisie and Sylvia

OPPOSITE THE CROSS KEYS

S.T. Haymon

St. Martin's Press
New York

Library of Congress Cataloging-in-Publication Data

Haymon, S.T.
         Opposite the Cross Keys / by S.T. Haymon.
                p.   cm.
     ISBN 0-312-01803-7
     1. Haymon, S.T.—Biography—Youth. 2. Authors, English—
20th century—Biography. 3. England—Social life and customs
—20th century.   I. Title.
PR6058.A9855Z47 1988
823′.914—dc 19
[B]   87-38239
                                                            CIP

First published in Great Britain by Constable & Company Ltd.

First U.S. Edition

10 9 8 7 6 5 4 3 2 1

To my husband

Prologue

THE bicycle was a dowager of its kind: a Hudson, black with a yellow stripe outlining its tubular bits and pieces. The upper half of its rear wheel was obscured by a skirt guard made of black and yellow strings twisted together, waspish.

The handlebars were set square on to the frame, no nonsense of sportiness, with grips made of a Neanderthal plastic, liable, when grasped, to shed prickles which embedded themselves in the palms like ticks, requiring a penknife to pry them out. The brakes were programmed to respond only to large hands which wouldn't take no for an answer.

The bicycle belonged to my sister Maisie, who was grown up and gone to work in London. It was to be mine as soon as my legs were adjudged long enough by those who had the power to decree what was long and what was short – which was to say, when you came down to it, Maud. Maud, with that insufferable smirk of hers which drove me barmy, said that my feet did not reach the pedals. I protested that they did; and it was a fact that, quite often, when practising on my own on the Hippodrome forecourt, I was able to sit on the saddle and control the bike with complete sang-froid for minutes at a time. Seconds, anyway. The maddening thing was, that whenever she came out to check up on my progress, my legs shrank yards and I would find myself faced with the choice of either having to stand up on the pedals – a practice for some reason considered only slightly less reprehensible than wetting one's knickers – or dismounting altogether.

It was, I suppose, something to be grateful for that we lived in St Giles, a few doors away from the Hippodrome, and that Mr Fitt, its owner, was a friend of my father's. As such, he gave me permission to practise my cycling on his forecourt, which was kept railed off with chains during the day to prevent anyone parking there before it was time for the first house in the evening. Whilst I was deeply sensible of the favour, the truth was that I was never in my best cycling form there. The splendidly stuccoed building with its twin domes and its pediment between, surmounted by an Ancient Greek lady holding aloft an electric light with deep suspicion, was overawing, out of scale. My scale, that is. It made me feel smaller, my legs shorter, than my nine years.

Though the façade of the Hippodrome was emblazoned with the words 'Grand Opera House', it was, in 1928 at any rate, a music hall. On that day which I have, for good reason, selected out of all the days upon which I practised my cycling there, I was overlooked on one side of the carriage sweep, by a larger-than-lifesize poster of Max Miller, the Cheeky Chappie, and, on the other, by a male impersonator in top hat and tails and a bust like a ski slope. It was hot and half-term and only four miles away lay St Awdry's and the Fenners, appropriately opposite the Cross Keys, the keys to heaven. It was more than flesh and blood could stand to possess the transport to Paradise and still be denied my chariot of fire.

The Cheeky Chappie leered down at me in friendly derision, daring me to do something about it. There scarcely seemed room in the forecourt for me and the bicycle and the male impersonator's bust. It overhung the two of us like an impending avalanche. In the nick of time, more reflex action than naughtiness, I dragged the bike under the spiky chains, and got us both away.

The bicycle was little easier to push than to ride, but I had more sense than to try and ride it along the winding streets which were my way out of Norwich. Not until I reached Hellesdon pond, well out on the Aylsham road, where some carters had driven a quartet of shire horses into the water to have a cool-off – and where, sweating and already weary, I could happily have joined them – did I venture to mount my conveyance, finding the pedals sufficiently often to keep it more or less on its way along the straight and level half-mile that ended at Horsford Point.

At Horsford Point the road forked, the left fork sheering off towards places of no interest, the right-hand one beginning its serpentine meander up to St Awdry's. At the tip of the V, closing in the approach, was a heavy post, upon which, as if by magic, a huge wooden square balanced itself on one corner. A gibbet could not have been more instinct with mystery and threat.

Long before I reached the Point I began to mutter to myself the words which alone could get me safely past. '*Ma gerto o ca!*' I mumbled breathlessly.

When I actually arrived, I got off the bike, wheeled it on to the grass verge, and propped it against the hawthorn of the hedgerow. Making sure nobody was looking, I bobbed the curtsey we were taught to do in school when greeting persons of consequence. I looked up at the great shape, its constituent planks warped by the passage of centuries, and recited once more the password painted there in letters all but erased by time; the cryptic formula without which all who travelled further down that road must unfailingly perish, their crow-picked bones whitening in the ditches. '*Ma gerto o ca!*'

The fact that, even as I pronounced those syllables of power, one part of me knew quite well that the legend on the signboard, long abandoned and uncared for, had once read MANN EGERTON FOR CARS in no way lessened the dread and doom of Horsford Point. I bowed deeply, wheeled the bike back into the road, and remounted, with a sense of dark forces appeased.

A Riley sports car which came whizzing round a bend on two wheels gave me – and no doubt its owner equally – a bad moment, but the pony-and-trap encounter really shook me. Its driver, as confused as his pony over the best way to get past a machine which was lolloping all over the road, lashed out at it with his whip and plucked the front lamp off its little bracket on the steering column. The bad-egg smell of carbide overlaid the sweetness of the May hedges. The man, shouting oaths, did not stop to apologize.

I dismounted: it was not quite a falling off. With trembling legs I wheeled the bike along, astonished that a road which seemed quite level when travelled over in our Morris Oxford tourer should present such a mountainous face to traffic of a humbler kind.

Two men who were unloading some telegraph poles from a lorry on to the grass at the side of the road looked at me kindly. One of them inquired, 'Got yerself a puncture then, have yer?'

I explained that my bicycle was the least bit on the large side.

'Want me to let down the saddle for you?'

I explained that the saddle was already let down as far as it would go.

'Oh ah. Going far, then?'

'Only to St Awdry's.'

Only!

The two men looked at each other. Then the one who seemed to be in charge said, 'Drop you off, if you want. The bike can go in the back.'

My legs felt like jelly, but I had been conditioned from babyhood never to accept lifts from strangers, so I replied politely, 'No, thank you.'

'Please yerself,' the man said. I didn't blame him for sounding huffy. He and his mate went round to the front of the lorry, got into the cab, and drove off without saying goodbye. I sat down on the pile of telegraph poles. The rest and the scent of pine were restorative, and I only got up when the poles began to stick to my bare calves, when I discovered that there were broad stripes of tar down my socks and the back of my legs.

For honour's sake I mounted the bicycle to ride into the village High Street, standing on the pedals and the hell with it; past the triangle of green at the crossroads; past the brick and flint of the churchyard wall, the brick houses, the village store. Not that there was anybody about to watch me, except for Ellie Fenner, who didn't count. Even when I had to stand outside the Cross Keys for an age, waiting to wheel the bike across the road, she gave no indication of having noticed me.

She sat, as usual, her loose body loosely draped in a faded wrapper, on a kitchen chair set out on the rudimentary pavement of gravel and beaten earth which insulated the terrace of four cottages known collectively as Opposite the Cross Keys from the highway. As usual, she had out the enormous comb whose rapacious teeth did not repay inspection, and she was combing her hair, which was stringy and lustreless, but long enough to sit on. Ellie spent a lot of time outside on the pavement demonstrating that she could indeed sit on her hair.

It was on the strength of this talent, I imagine, that she was designated by the Fenners their family beauty, an icon too precious to go out to work like the rest of them. My difficulty – and, looking back, I am sure that Ellie sensed it, though not a word was spoken; that it was the source of the glum disregard with which she invariably favoured me – was that I truly found her, not merely not beautiful, but downright ugly. If Ellie were beautiful then Maud, who was her sister and had a slight cast in her right eye and a wart on her nose like Oliver Cromwell, was Clara Bow and Greta Garbo rolled into one.

When I had got myself and bicycle safely across to Opposite the Cross Keys, Ellie stopped combing; raised her bum sufficiently to let her hair drop down to its full length, and resumed her seat, this time sitting on hair and bum together.* She said with undisguised satisfaction at disappointing me, 'Ma's up at Randall's, plucking.'

'Oh.'

'Stratton Strawlers, you want to go up there. Reckon she could do with a hand.'

Why don't you go and give her one yourself, then, you lazy mauther,** I thought but did not say. Ellie knew very well how much I hated plucking, I had proclaimed it often enough. Even so, for the pleasure of Mrs Fenner's company I would gladly have pressed on to Stratton Strawless, another two miles, if only my legs had been that tiny bit longer.

As it was, I suddenly felt at the end of endurance. I leaned bike and myself against the cottage wall and closed my eyes: then opened them again as, out of the corner of one, I became aware of a coloured rag dangling in the heat.

It was then I saw the Union Jack.

---

* That word 'bum'. For the reader's benefit I have to explain that, in St Awdry's, bottoms were always bums, a word which, so far as I was then aware, did not even exist in St Giles. St Awdry's being a different country, it seemed to me quite unremarkable that it should possess its own language.

** Mauther: St Awdry's for a girl, especially a great lump of one.

The four cottages which made up Opposite the Cross Keys were arranged as follows. At either end lived, respectively, the Harleys and the Leaches, the latter in the largest one, at the end of the row furthest away from Norwich. The Fenners' place was next to the Harleys'. In between the Fenners' and the Leaches' was a derelict cottage which was only kept up at all by the support of the dwellings on either side. At one time it must have been some kind of shop, because the ground-floor window was a good deal larger than the mingy little front windows of the other three cottages. The window panes were all gone, however, replaced by flattened petrol cans which, oxidized to purples and peacock blues of a barbaric intensity, lent the frontage an appearance that was distinctly unwelcoming.

There were children in the village who said that the old man – the old josser as everyone called him – who was the last person to live in the ruined cottage had died sitting in his chair in front of the fire, and that he was such a filthy old devil nobody had bothered to fetch him out and get him over the road and into the churchyard, which was why the landlord had never thought to do the place up and rent it out again. The grown-ups said that was ridiculous; but they, no more than the children, ever thought to put a foot to either the front door or the back one – both of them rotting on their hinges – to settle, once and for all, what was the truth of it.

When I stayed with the Fenners, my bed was the old horsehair sofa which was pushed up against the wall dividing their cottage from the derelict one, and at night the noise of the rats on the other side of the partition was horrendous. Gyp the dog, who slept on the opposite side of the room from me, on the rag rug in front of the fire, never so much as stirred in his snuffly sleep except for an occasional exasperated tail-thump when the sound rose to a double-forte, but I found it dreadfully disturbing. What could the rats find to eat in that empty house? I reckoned they must long ago have finished all that was edible of the old josser, so what next if not me, so conveniently to hand? I lay awake straining for the gnawing through lathe and plaster which would mean they were on their way.

When at last I mentioned my fears to Mrs Fenner, she only laughed. Rats were no fools, she said. They knew which side their bread was buttered. If they ran out of grub next door it

[14]

stood to reason they would start on the further, the Leach side. Mr Leach was something in an office over Catton way and went to work every day in a collar and tie, the stuck-up bor.* The Royal Family would open their eyes at what Mrs Leach spent at the Co-op every week. Catch rats wasting their time on the Fenners when they could have the freedom of the Leach larder!

Somebody had removed several of the flattened petrol cans from the window of the derelict cottage. There was no breeze to set the Union Jack waving. It hung limply from its stick which rested on the ruined window sill.

In my exhausted state I puzzled the meaning of this sign. Ellie was looking at me with that simpering expression of hers which signified 'I know something you don't, Miss Clever Dick!' Suddenly, to my astonishment, her purse-faced gaze melted, the little pleats round her mouth opening out like a drawstring bag when the ties are unloosed. With a lumberingly coquettish gesture she rearranged her wrapper over her large breasts as the front door of the derelict cottage opened, and a man came out.

He was a man of medium height, compactly built; wearing black trousers and a waistcoat over a black-and-white shirt without a collar and with its sleeves rolled up to above the elbows. He was powdered all over with what looked like plaster dust, dust which had settled on the hairs of his bare arms, giving them a bloom like the bloom on a peach. On his head he wore a black cap, from under the back of which little black curls stuck out. He needed a haircut and no mistake.

Either the curls were dusty too, or he was going grey. It was hard to tell the age of the brown face in which white teeth flashed under a natty little moustache like John Gilbert's or Ronald Colman's.

He came out of the derelict cottage in a cocky, confident way, holding his arms forward, hands opened out, like one of the Russian Ballet dancers I had been taken to see on my last visit to London; making his entrance and circling the stage as much

* Bor: all-purpose word for anybody, male or female, but mostly meaning 'man, fellow'.

[15]

as to say, 'Here I am – the one you've been waiting for. *Now* you'll see something!'

The cloth of his clothes was the usual horrid stuff that only the poor wore, and his cap the kind you could see hanging in bunches outside the cheap shops in Magdalen Street, his boots the stiff casings that made you wonder sometimes if the feet of working-class men weren't a different shape from one's father's feet, high-arched and narrow in their polished leather. Frosted with white, he nevertheless looked dirty and unshaven; yet, with it all, possessed of a slim-waisted elegance not to be denied.

His eyes were black and bright with mischief.

'Hello, 'ello!' he said. 'You must be that Sylvie gal Ma Fenner's always on about.'

I roused myself out of my terrible fatigue enough to exclaim automatically – the first thing Maud had taught me was that the people low down on the ladder must be accorded their proper respect: it was their only wealth – '*Mrs* Fenner!'

'*Mrs* Fenner!' the man repeated, with a mocking emphasis. 'She warned me you were a proper little madam.' He came over to where I drooped limply against the wall and, eyes screwed up against the sun, took a closer look at me. He smelled, of course. Everybody at Opposite the Cross Keys smelled; but a new combination I would have to get used to.

'Too much to suppose Lady Godiva here'd get off her arse an' make you a cup of tea.'

Ellie, who had freed her hair from its durance vile, and gone back to combing it with the unspeakable comb, said, 'She knows where the kettle's kept.'

'Bleedin' angel of mercy!' the man exclaimed. Ellie giggled and blushed all over her face. To me he said, 'Don't go away, darlin'', and slipped back to the derelict cottage, re-emerging a moment later with a wooden crate in one hand and a chipped enamel mug in the other.

The mug, half-full, contained standard Opposite the Cross Keys tea – the cheapest, dustiest leaves, boiled up three times and laced to a revolting sweetness with lashings of condensed milk. Tom Fenner, the elder of Mrs Fenner's sons, who worked for Mr Theobald, the dairy farmer, was allowed a billycan of milk every day as part of his perks; yet never, in all my time at

[16]

the Fenners', did I see a drop of natural milk pass any lips other than Gyp's and those of a couple of hedgehogs who used to wander into the scullery on summer evenings for a sup out of the dog's bowl.

Back home in St Giles, I would assuredly have thrown up at the mere sight of the contents of that mug, let alone the taste. At Opposite the Cross Keys, perched on an empty orange box, I drank deeply, and was revived. The tea was tepid, a tin spoon still sticking up in it, and I guessed that the man had been engaged in drinking it himself when I had arrived. The mug was so stained there seemed no point in speculating as to whether he and I had, or had not, drunk from the same side.

'Made it on me Primus,' the man said, as if boasting of the last word in kitchen gadgetry, at the same time explaining a taste of meths in place of the usual sulphur from the Fenners' coal fire, their sole means of heating water, and indeed of all cooking. 'Plenty for seconds, if yer ladyship feels so disposed.'

'I wouldn't say no,' Ellie put in, before I could answer one way or the other.

'Did the wind speak?' the man demanded, looking about him in a merry, exaggerated way.

'Ellie said she would like a cup of tea,' I supplied helpfully.

'Ellie can get her own fuckin' cup.' Ellie, her little eyes half-closed, said nothing. She went on dragging the comb through her hair as if playing some musical instrument with a tone range beyond the reach of the human ear. 'It's you I was asking.'

'I've had all I want, thank you, Mr –' I hesitated. 'I don't know your name.'

'Chicken.'

'Mr –' Again I hesitated, it sounded so improbable. 'Chicken.'

'Not Mr Chicken,' the man corrected. 'Chicken, as in which came first, the chicken or the egg.'

'Please – I mean – is Chicken your Christian name or your surname?'

'Either or neither.'

'It has to be one or the other!' Names, in my book, were not things to be treated lightly. 'You have to be either Mr Something Chicken or Mr Chicken Something.'

[17]

'Like Mr Roast Chicken, you mean, or Mr Chicken Soup?'
'No, of course not! Like –' I improvised wildly. 'Like Mr
Alfred Chicken, for example, or Mr Chicken Jones –'
'Do I look like an Alfred Chicken or a Chicken Jones?
People'd bust their sides laughing!' He stooped over me again.
I tried not to flinch at the still unfamiliar smell. 'Feelin'
better, are you?'

I nodded gratefully. I was feeling much better. 'Have you
come to live here in St Awdry's?' I asked.

'Your guess is as good as mine.' He took hold of my hand. His
own was very hard, with splayed fingertips. 'Come an' see what
I bin up to.'

He led me into the derelict cottage, handing me over the
shattered door sill with a parody of old world courtesy. Inside,
splicing the gloom, white dust sprinkled with red revolved in
the sunbeam which came through the pushed-out window
panes. The air was thick with plaster and pulverized brick.

What the man had done – what Chicken had done (I
reminded myself that I must get used to the ridiculous name
which, somehow, once put to use, did not sound so ridiculous
after all) – was to pull down the entire wall between the front
room and the scullery, making one long, low room.

'Weren't room enough to swing a fart!' he explained. 'I can't
abide not having a bit o' space about me.' He looked about him
with shining eyes. 'Not bad, eh?'

Flattered by the way Chicken sought my approval – something grown-ups, in my experience, seldom bothered to do – I
nodded eagerly. 'Except the ceiling looks a bit saggy.'

Deprived of the dividing wall, the ceiling looked dangerously
saggy. Discreetly, so as not to give offence, I moved from
beneath the saggiest part.

Chicken said indifferently, 'I'll get something to hold that up,
when I get round to it.' Looking young and enthusiastic: 'Jest
you wait till I get this muck out, an' you'll see something!'

I remembered the rats and asked what he had done about
them.

'Oh, them! Tied their fuckin' tails together, two at a time, an'
showed 'em the door.'

If he'd told me that he had put down poison I'd have thought
nothing of it. Poison, in those days, was standard fare for rats as

well as for black beetles and the murdered wives who filled the pages of the *News of the World*. But tying their tails –!

'Oh!' I cried. 'That's cruel!'

The white teeth flashed in the brown face.

Chicken said, 'I'm a bad man.'

Out in the air again, I asked the bad man where he had come from.

'Nosy, aren't you?' was the reply. 'I don't ask where you come from.'

'But you know where! Mrs Fenner must have said.'

'You know where, too. Everywhere that isn't here.'

'But that means anywhere!'

'So it do!' A bright, congratulatory smile. 'What matters is where you are, not where you ain't.'

Chicken's words made me aware with a sudden awful certainty that, on the contrary, where I wasn't at that moment – to wit, on the Hippodrome forecourt, cycling round and round like a good little girl – was of the greatest importance. I hurried over to the cottage wall, took hold of the handlebars and wheeled the bicycle to the edge of the pavement. Even as I did so, I knew there was no way I was going to be able to get the contraption home. My legs had never felt shorter.

Chicken asked, 'You got that saddle down far as it'll go?' I nodded dumbly. 'That Maud o' yours must be daft as Ellie here to let you out on the road on that ol' four-poster.'

Ellie scowled. She hated Maud to be classed her equal at anything, even daftness. For me, though, even in my extremity I couldn't bear to hear Maud blamed for my wrongdoing.

'She didn't let me out! I let myself out! I'm not supposed to go riding till my legs are long enough.' Tears welled up in my eyes.

'No bawlin'!' the man commanded sharply. 'An' we'll see if we can't figure out some way to get you home again. There's a bus along in half an hour –'

Trying not to cry: 'I haven't any money, and they won't take the bike anyhow.'

'Ferget what it costs. We can always take it out of Ellie's piggy bank, eh, sweetheart?' Ellie gave no indication that she had heard: lifted her bum ponderously and sat down on her hair again. 'This bloody bedstead can go up wi' the carrier Saturday –'

[19]

'But then they'll know!' The floodgates opened and I wept copiously. 'They'll know!'

'Fer Chrissake!' Chicken surveyed my agony with disgust. 'So what? What'll they do you – clap you in irons? Make you walk the plank?'

'Don't be silly!' I wailed. I could not explain that my parents' soft-voiced regret at my breach of trust, and, even more, Maud's contemptuous silence, would be worse than any physical punishment. The baby, the family pet, I could not bear not to be loved.

'Want my opinion?' said Chicken, proferring a considered alternative. 'Do you a power of good. Terrible thing to be trusted. Might as well tie a sodding millstone round yer neck an' be done wi' it!'

When I patently found no comfort in this counsel, he rolled his eyes up at the sky, ejaculated 'Kids!' and came over and took the bicycle out of my hands.

'All right!' he commanded. 'Turn off the water taps an' le's get on with it!' And when I continued to stand, staring stupidly, 'Get on behind, barmy! An' keep yer ruddy feet out of the spokes if you're going to need 'em tomorrow an' the day after!'

We came back from Salham St Awdry with incredible speed. In no time at all, or so it seemed to me, we were past the pile of telegraph poles, and the bend where the bicycle and the horse and trap had had their little confrontation. The remains of the bicycle lamp lay embedded like fossil remains in the sun-warmed tarmac.

Horsford Point with its Mann Egerton sign positively whizzed past. No need for magic when you had the magnet of home to draw you safely to sanctuary. My bottom corrugated with the indentations of the narrow grid intended for the conveyance of a schoolbag or music case, my legs aching with the effort of keeping them stuck out at a safe angle from the wheel, I was nevertheless so wracked with happiness that it was itself a pain, an overflowing of love out of a vessel inadequate to contain it.

The very bicycle was happy, skittish with a youth it had

thought had passed it by. The three of us sailed down the long slope to St Augustine's in a glorious breeze of our own making. As soon as I realized that I would be back at the Hippodrome with time to spare – Maud never came out looking for me unless I was late for tea – sorrow intertwined itself sweetly with the joy. The ride, alas, was almost over. When Chicken took the bike over St George's Bridge with a verve which lifted both wheels off the ground as we soared over the hump in the middle, and brought it to a stylish halt on the further side, I could, without understanding why, have cried again.

'Time to love you an' leave you.' Chicken held the bike until I had disembarked. 'You wouldn't want any of yer posh pals to catch an eyeful o' me an' ask, who that mucky ole tramp I seen you with yesterday arternoon?'

'I wouldn't mind!' I protested fiercely.

'Yes, you would, though.'

It was true. I hung my head in shamed, if belated, admission. Norwich and St Awdry's were different worlds. In Norwich I could have turned up in the company of one of those women who wear sticks through their noses and their ear lobes half-way down their chests, and elicit less comment. *They* were natives, educational. Whatever else Chicken was, he wasn't that.

St George's, thankfully, wasn't a 'good' street, which was probably why Chicken had chosen to stop where he did, before the 'good' streets began.

'You better mind yourself,' he warned. 'When Ma – when Mrs Fenner come up to market Saturday, full o' the lovely bloke what's moved in next door, don't you go letting on you've already had the pleasure of makin' my acquaintance.'

'Ellie –' I began.

'Her!' Contemptuously. 'Too busy looking for nits to think of anything else. *She* won't say nothing.'

I said, both concerned for him and anxious to speed him on his way – with every passing moment I grew uneasier about running into somebody I knew, 'You'll have to go over to Magdalen Street to get the bus back.'

'Don't fret about me!' Chicken returned. 'I'll find my own way home, never you fear!'

He went off in his brisk, balletic way, though his boots looked even more awful in the city, disappearing over the hump of the bridge before I could say either thank you or goodbye.

I pushed the bicycle the rest of the way home; uphill going, through Bridewell Alley and Swan Lane, along London Street to the Market Place, and so to St Giles, the last hill of all and the steepest. On my left the Market stalls clung to the slope, skeletal, awaiting their Saturday resurrection, when the pyramids of apples and oranges would rise again, cauliflowers coy in their necklets of green, canaries tweeting, tortoises crawling sadly over lettuce leaves. Chips frying, and the heavenly smell of the whelk stalls; funny men selling crockery as if on the bill at the Hippodrome; and Mr Marcantonio who always, because he had long cherished a hopeless passion for Maud, gave me a tuppenny ice-cream boat for a penny.

The clock outside H. Samuels, the jewellers, said ten to four. How well everything had turned out! Whether it was indeed a miracle, or whether Chicken's weight on the saddle had depressed the overall height of the bicycle that vital bit extra, I found, once back at the Hippodrome, that I could actually keep my feet in place on the pedals without slipping. I swooped about the forecourt with an aplomb which astonished the Cheeky Chappie and the male impersonator. I could see their painted eyes popping.

On the dot of four, Maud came out to summon me indoors for my tea.

'What sewer they dredged you out of, then?' was her dour greeting, as she eyed the tar on my legs, the plaster in my hair, my general air of dishevelment. 'Mr Fitt ought to be ashamed of himself and I'll tell him so tomorrow, see if I don't!'

'Maud!' I cried, brushing aside her strictures in the euphoria of the moment. 'I can ride it! I truly can!'

I sprang to demonstrate: but whether my exertions had finally overtired me, or whether miracles of their very nature (would the wine at Cana have gone back to water if you'd asked for a second glass?) have a short shelf-life, my legs had shortened again, and after a wavering yard or so, the bicycle and I fell over together, taking the skin off my right knee.

It didn't hurt to speak of, but it seemed politic to cry; tactics that paid off. Maud enfolded me in her arms in that exasperated way of hers which was infinitely more comforting than the tenderest embrace from any other quarter.

Bathed and clean, I lie in bed and think how lucky I am to have a great day like today happen to me when I am old enough to appreciate it: not like some other great days, such as being born, which happen when you are too young to understand what is going on. As always, when I am clean, St Awdry's seems a long way away.

Over my bed hangs a picture of a boy with his arms full of toys – so many of them that a box of lead soldiers, a teddy bear and a game of Snakes and Ladders have spilled on to the floor. One of the soldiers, who has lost his head in the fall, will never be the same again. Underneath the picture is written, in letters dripping with unction, *He who grasps at too much holds nothing fast.*

In fresh pyjamas, between crisp sheets, I grasp at too much; confident that, never mind how it is with stupid boys, my arms can safely contain Norwich and Salham St Awdry alike, to say nothing of the world, the universe, infinity. No lead soldiers are going to break in pieces at *my* feet.

I lie in bed and think about Chicken.

PART I

The way there

Chapter One

B EING born, in my case, was chiefly remarkable for what
happened six weeks later.
Maud came.

She was sixteen and she came as a nurserymaid, my family,
whilst modestly prosperous, not being in the nanny class –
engaged, I imagine, because my mother, who had considered
her family complete, had flinched at the prospect of a new baby
after ten years pregnancy-free. In the days when I was not (so I
was told), the household chores, child-minding and all, had
been performed by one Eliza, a devoted household retainer for
many years.

By the time I first remember Maud – and I cannot, I think,
have been much more than a year old when I came to a
realization that the universe revolved round a tall, gaunt
woman with a doughy face and hair done up in a bun which
leaked in wisps over her lace collar – Eliza had long since
departed; driven to the lunatic asylum, my father asserted, by
Maud's machiavellian machinations.

'What's machiavellian machinations?' I asked, when I was
of an age to get my tongue round such questions. Naturally
I asked it of Maud, not my father, who whilst not un-
intelligent was, unlike Maud, not the fount of all knowledge. When asked something, he quite often answered that
he did not know, which was upsetting, contradicting as it
did all one's perceptions of the adult world. Whereas
Maud always knew. So: 'Maud – what's machiavellian
machinations?'

'Scotch motor bike,' Maud replied without hesitation. 'One
of them kind with a side-car.'

'And did you really drive Eliza to the lunatic asylum in one?'

'Don't be daft! They come and took her in a van.'

Proof that Maud, young as she was at the time, established her ascendancy over the household with a truly astonishing speed is provided by a photograph* taken when I was coming up to three months old. It was taken by Mr Ballard, who, it was said in the town, had been a Court photographer until the day when, having drink taken, he had goosed Queen Mary whilst arranging her in a pose in her Garter robes; something he always denied on the grounds that Her Majesty, in her armour-plated corset, was ungoosable.

Whatever the truth of the story, it was almost certainly true that never before had Mr Ballard been commissioned to take a studio portrait of a domestic. People in the Twenties simply didn't shell out good money to have their servants photographed. Their families, their lovers, their dogs, yes: but not their maids.

Yet there is Maud, no more than three months in my parents' employ, sitting with me on her lap, my sister Maisie at her side, having her photograph taken.

There are other things about that photograph which are revealing. Look at the apron. See how creased it is, despite the importance of the occasion. My sister and I are immaculate – well, I am: my sister's socks could have done with a pull up, her shoes with a coating of Blanco. But then, Maisie was part of Eliza's left luggage.

But how to explain that crumpled apron? From our house to Mr Ballard's studio in St Benedict's was no more than ten minutes' walk. And anyway, the creases are not the creases of use, but of poor ironing, or even of no ironing at all. Who would deliberately choose to turn up for the first professional photograph of her life wearing an unironed apron?

Maud.

Maud hated ironing, and I take the photograph as further evidence that in this, as in so much else, she was already at work rearranging our lives.

* See frontispiece.

[28]

Since Eliza's departure, the only other help in the house had consisted of a Mrs Hewitt, who came every Monday to do the washing. She was a small woman but immensely strong, capable, unaided, of lifting large tin baths filled with household linen bubbling away in boiling water off the kitchen range, crossing the kitchen floor with them, and up-ending them in the sink. Her salient features, in my imperfect recollection, are obscured by the clouds of steam which, like the cloud which interposed itself between the Israelites and the Egyptians, accompanied all her comings and goings.

Once Mrs Hewitt had got the washing hung out on the clothes lines in the yard, her job was done. Its taking down, when it had reached its ideal condition of slight dampness, its ironing, airing, and putting away, was Maud's business.

And Maud hated ironing.

The ironing was done with a set of flatirons of varying sizes and weights, first heated up on the range and then, as needed, slid into a steel shoe which ensured no soot or iron rust was left on the fresh linen. Eliza, it seemed, had managed very well with these primitive implements, which were the norm for their time, but then Eliza, as Maud frequently reminded my mother, had had a screw loose. I fancy Maud must have been taken aback when, anxious to keep her new treasure propitiated, my mother, one day, brought home one of the new electric irons which were becoming all the thing. It wasn't what she had had in mind at all.

Like most houses at that period, ours had no power plugs. We did not feel deprived for lack of them. As my mother said, the house was riddled enough with electricity as it was. Prepared for this attitude of mind, manufacturers of the early electric irons provided them with a cord and a pronged end which married with the slots of ordinary electric light fittings: as simple as putting in a bulb.

Maud accepted this triumph of technology from my mother's hands, still in its box; and, still in its box, it stayed unopened on the kitchen table week after week, until – I must have been a good six months old by then, and the creased apron already enshrined in its photograph for posterity – Maud convinced my mother that, what with my having to be taken out into the fresh air every day, leaving her with no possible time into which the ironing could be fitted, the sensible thing was for Mrs Hewitt to come in on Tuesdays as well, to finish up the job she had begun the day before. The only surprising thing about this story is that my mother held out as long as she did.

A coda, however. This was not one of Maud's undiluted victories. When I finally began school – I was almost six and Maud had run out of reasons why I was not yet ready to go – my mother gently but firmly pointed out that, as there was no longer an infant to be taken walkies, there was now plenty of time in the afternoons for Maud to do the ironing. Mrs Hewitt was demoted back to washer-woman *tout simple*, the electric iron disinterred from the cupboard where Maud had buried it. My mother bravely announced that one really must move with the times. The electric iron *must* be used.

'Well, Maud,' she inquired, after the first Tuesday had passed without complaint. 'How did you get on with it?'

'Not so dusty,' Maud replied with surprising good humour. 'On'y thing was the cord. Bothersome, the way it dangled about.' Finishing meekly: 'Still an' all, once I cut it off, it heated up on the range pretty much as well as the others.'

I don't know how Mr Ballard contrived to make Maud look so plump in that photograph, and so nearly pretty. Perhaps at sixteen she had a brief blooming I was too young to catch. On the other hand, I don't quite know what it was that made her so plain, either. Her wart, after all, was the same colour as the rest of her skin, not brown and obtrusive, like some. You could really only appreciate it in profile, when it lent an interesting outline to what was otherwise a deeply uninteresting nose. The slight cast in her right eye didn't count for much, either. I can only conclude that my confident apprehension of her essential unattractiveness arose from her own deep conviction of it.

I don't know, either, how it was that I knew she was on my side, since she practically never praised anything I did, and her usual tone to me was shot through with a mockery only carelessly disguised: simply that I knew it and that, safe in her love, I was unconquerable. She dressed me, fed me, attended to my most intimate needs with a lack of tenderness which was a wonderful antidote to the anxious adoration lavished on me by my besotted family.

One of the few books she had read was *The Pilgrim's Progress*, given her as a prize for Good Conduct and kept wrapped up in a brown paper cover on which she had printed, each letter in a different colour crayon, MAUD MARY ANN FENNER, A PRIZE. She was fond of telling me that I was the burden Christ had seen fit to put upon her, one of which, like Christian's in the story, she could not hope to divest herself until the Celestial City was in sight, if then.

'Knowing you,' she said, with that familiar mixture of mockery and complaint, though this time it wasn't clear to whom exactly the complaint was addressed, 'once I get through the pearly gates what's the odds the first thing I'll hear 'll be a certain little voice piping up, "Maud, can I try out your wings? Maud, can I have a go on your harp? Pleeease. Maud –" a passable imitation of myself in the wheedling mode – "can I?"'

'At least,' I pointed out, 'it'll mean I must have been good enough to get to heaven myself.'

'You good! Artful, you mean. Slipped in when Peter had to go and do a Number Two.'

Apart from the family, who, in her book, were put on earth to serve my needs, Maud hated everyone who was so much as civil to her charge. Even the milkman, whose dashing good looks always set Maud's face aflame when he strode up to the kitchen door looking like Tom Mix except that the wide leather belt swaggering about his hips was hung with the pint and the half-pint measuring mugs instead of pearl-handled shooters, was punished with the withdrawal of his weekly sweetener of Woodbines after the day he took me for a ride in his milk chariot, among the clanking churns. Her chief enemy was May Bowden, our neighbour, a spinster who would have been dumbfounded had she been able to plumb the depths of Maud's hatred for her.

May Bowden, who, being rich, was said to be a little eccentric – as distinct from being soft in the head, a condition which only afflicted the lower orders – often proclaimed her intention of leaving me her fortune when she died.

'That'll be the day!' Maud would mutter, not very inaudibly.

*

The only other person allowed unrestricted access to my favours was Mrs Fenner, who, as Maud's mother, was, one might say, a mere extension of Maud herself; the only other Fenner I knew until I went to Salham St Awdry.

Mere!

Mrs Fenner was the blooming miracle who, once a week, erupted into our pleasant, but bland, existence. She was a large, handsome woman with polished apple cheeks, whose abundant flesh, electric vitality, and sheer animal high spirits appeared all three indifferently restrained by the Edwardian corset and costume of antique mode which, summer or winter, were her best for a day in town. There was scarcely a Saturday, out on the Market Place, when one or other of the pearl buttons which marched in formation down the front of the close-fitting, three-quarter length coat did not pop off, a small explosion, to be scrabbled for by me under people's feet, or among the trash accumulated beneath the stalls; sometimes to be found, more often not, which was why none of the buttons quite matched, the spaces being filled in, upon our return for tea, from the nearest my mother's sewing box could provide. How Mrs Fenner laughed whenever a button took off! Often enough to launch a second mini-missile upon the Market Place air.

Nature's overflowing cornucopia – that was what my father said you thought about when you looked at Mrs Fenner; heard her rich, Norfolk voice and her laughter which stirred the lees of mirth. Maud, inordinately proud of this prodigy which was, so improbably, her progenitor, was at the same time, in our kitchen especially, a little afraid of it, as of a large, friendly lioness who might yet, with a carefree swish of tail, bring the plates crashing down from the dresser. As soon as dinner was cleared away, she vanished upstairs to her attic bedroom to change into the dim *toilette* of excruciating refinement which was *her* best, the navy coat and skirt which were, in fact, her nurserymaid walking-out uniform, together with the navy hat – straw in summer, felt in winter – which went with them. On Saturdays, to signify that despite what the raiment might seem to indicate, her services were not available, Maud pinned to the hat a bunch of red cherries interspersed with some other fruit she always asserted were medlars, but which, at a much later date, I was able to identify positively as testicles. The fruit on the hat was the equivalent of the red flag on the breakwater which tells you it is forbidden to swim. Once the fruit was hoisted, it was no earthly use asking Maud to pick up so much as a paper of pins for you, since she was going to be in the Market anyway.

It was her afternoon off.

Once Maud was out of the way titivating herself, Mrs Fenner and I got down to business. Mrs Fenner had never been to school. She could neither read nor write; and every Saturday – so soon, that is, as I myself had mastered those skills – she would ask me to read to her extracts from the previous Sunday's *News of the World*, saved for that purpose, to say nothing of old favourites cherished in a biscuit tin until they fell apart along the creases.

'Read me that one again,' she would demand admiringly, ''bout the feller what chopped up them women an' buried the bits under the hen run. You read it so lovely!'

Newspapers, in our household, were issues of the day in more ways than one, my father as an addict subscribing to several, of varying degrees of seriousness and political complexion. He had been known to rise at the crack of dawn in order to stand at the front door, ready to commandeer the lot the moment the delivery boy arrived – before, that is, Maud could get her hands on them. On days when he had overslept, you might find him in the drawing-room with the carpet rolled back, absorbed in the news-sheet spread out under it to discourage moths; or else, down on his hands and knees, with his head in the cupboard under the stairs where we kept the Wellington boots and galoshes, studying, between the mud marks, a page of the *Daily Chronicle* which Maud had whisked away before he had had time to do more than glance at it.

'You'd never think newspapers were made to be read,' was his constant lament; and indeed, if you lived in our house, actually reading a paper came pretty low in our – or rather, Maud's – list of priorities. They were made to bear away the cold ashes of the fires, and to be laid artfully crumpled under the kindling and coals of the new ones awaiting the liberating match. They were made to protect freshly scrubbed floors, or the scrubbed deal table in the kitchen. Newspapers were in never-ending demand for lining knife boxes and silver boxes, shoe-cleaning boxes and polishing boxes, and the box reserved for the cleaning rags. My poor father, who was always intending to cut out this article or that to preserve for some ill-defined future purpose, and then forgetting to do it until the article in question had vanished from human ken, could think of no better counter-measure than to add yet another newspaper to the list; knowing in his heart of hearts that the newcomer, like all its companions, was doomed to disappear with the rest.

So far as I was concerned, once I had learned how to manage a pair of scissors, the day of the week when newspapers came into their own was Friday. Every Friday, after tea, Maud and I would sit at the kitchen table, reducing the Thunderer of Fleet Street and all its satellites impartially to Fenner toilet paper. Unlike the unfortunates at St Giles, who had to make do with rolls of polished stuff, chill to the skin and about as flexible as quarry tiles, the Fenners of Salham St Awdry wiped their backsides on great events, cut into fine, generous squares. Every Friday Maud and I cut a week's supply for Mrs Fenner to take back with her on Saturday, Maud wielding a skewer to pierce the completed pile with a hole through which, with an enormous sense of achievement, I threaded a piece of string which I knotted and finished with a loop so that it could hang on the nail knocked into the Fenners' lav door.

Once, greatly daring, I abstracted a piece ready for bunching, and retired with it to our lavatory; but, there, could not bring myself actually to use it. It seemed a kind of blasphemy, seeing it had a picture of Lloyd George on it.

However, as I had already crumpled it, I couldn't hope to return it, undetected, to the kitchen. Needing to get rid of the evidence, I dropped it in the pan and pulled the chain. Horror of horrors – plumbing in St Awdry's must have been different (It was. I later discovered there was none) – it *would* not go down. That is, it did at last, but not before I had learned never again to get ideas above my station.

When I came back downstairs, Maud, who had heard the cistern filling, emptying and refilling, looked up dourly from her scissoring to remark, 'What you been doing up there, then? Cannon-balls?'

Chapter Two

THE Saturday afternoon which, of all the Saturday afternoons I spent on the Market Place with Maud and her mother, I select from my treasury, was a day mellow as honey, one of those autumn days you sometimes get in East Anglia, the memory of which keeps you going through the months when Arctic gales sweep down from the North Pole, and the damp of the Broads corrodes your very soul. I was just six years old, in my first term at Eldon House School, and looking very chic, I congratulated myself, in my new school uniform – double-breasted navy overcoat with a dinky little half-belt at the back, hat of plushy velour with a badge in front embroidered with EHS, and a hatband striped in black, purple and white, the school colours; knee-high white socks, black lace-up shoes and navy gloves, knitted ones, with a narrow edging of black, purple and white which showed that they came from Green Brothers, the officially appointed school outfitters, not any old shop. To be seen out on the street in your school uniform not wearing your gloves was, if not the sin against the Holy Ghost, the next thing to it.

Was it OK to take them off for eating? I hadn't been at Eldon House long enough to be sure. I was already a bit uneasy about the gloves even before I bumped into the Saunders girls – the younger one was in my form – out with their mother. I had purchased a pennyworth of locust beans, or 'lokusses', as they were called by the *cognoscenti*, something purportedly vegetable with the texture and taste of varnish and the further advantage that neither Maud nor her mother could stand them, so that I could safely pass them round. I was very fond of them, though I had to admit, that particular Saturday, they did not taste quite as good as usual, stuck all over with glove fluff.

'Take your gloves off, fathead!' Maud commanded: and when I explained that to do so was against school rules, she made a face, not having yet forgiven them, whoever 'them' might be, for removing me from her jurisdiction for the better part of the day, and said, '*They* tell you to go jump in a barrel of cowpats, you'd do it!'

I had been on the point of compromising by removing one glove, when I suddenly remembered that eating out in the street whilst wearing your school uniform was an even worse offence than taking your gloves off in public.

And that wasn't all.

Mrs Fenner had bought a chamber pot. It was pink, with *Evening Exercises* inscribed about its ample girth in letters of gold – 'Genuine twenty-two carat,' swore the man at the crockery stall – Gothic script, visible at a hundred paces.

No one gave wrapping paper in the Market, and as we moved on to the fruit and the vegetable stalls we all had a good laugh as Mrs Fenner, in her exuberant progress, explained loud enough for all to hear that she had made her purchase because her old man liked his tea out of a real big cup. Even Maud permitted her lips to twitch slightly, and, as for me, I was quite weak from laughing. When Mrs Fenner bought a bunch of celery and stuck it inside the chamber pot with the explanation that she had always wanted a pot plant for her window sill, I could have died.

And when I bumped into Mrs Saunders out with Vera and Amy, I almost did.

Eldon House, you have to understand, was one of the poshest schools in the city, if not *the* poshest. It didn't take just anybody; though how Miss Boothby and Miss Chandos, the joint Principals, decided who was and who wasn't just anybody I couldn't, and can't say. They took boarders as well as day girls, and two of the girls were Honourables.

I had yet to prove myself worthy of such exalted company.

It was one of those seminal moments which, if they do not exactly alter the course of one's life, alter the world in which one breathes and moves. In that moment I – an 'I' sprung that instant into being, like Minerva from the brow of Jove – saw the Fenners for the first time for what they were: a pair of grotesques who, with their preposterous clothes, their wild, anarchic humour and their brazen disregard of convention, could have nothing to do with a little lady in an Eldon House uniform.

To put it another way, without dressing it up in highfalutin' excuses: I was suddenly ashamed of them.

'Hello.'

'Hello.'

The girls and I greeted each other decorously. I had already taken the precaution of moving a little distance away from my companions. I shook hands with the mother, who looked a little disconcerted at the stickiness of my glove, and did the little bob which was the first, if not the only thing Eldon House ever taught me. As I curtsied, I sent up a desperate prayer that the Saunders' hadn't noticed who I was with.

I reckoned without Mrs Fenner.

Surging forward, she thrust the chamber pot, greenery and all, into my protesting arms.

'Your turn now, gal Sylvie!' she boomed. 'Blamed if I'm goin' to carry a jerry about all arternoon jest in case *you* get caught short!'

To this day a haze of misery descends between me and the reality of that moment and the next few hours – at least, it seemed like hours, if not the remorseless reaches of eternity – during which I was made to carry the chamber pot the length and breadth of the Market Place. Sometimes, reliving it, I almost succeed in convincing myself that the misery consisted in my horrified, if belated, awareness that, silly little snob that I was, I had antagonized the two people who meant more to me than anyone else in the world, and not in the fact that there were several other Eldon House girls and their mothers who saw me, to say nothing of Miss Whistler, who taught English and Needlework, and who had to put on her pince-nez before she could believe her eyes.

Though her expression abated not a whit of her customary sunny humour, Mrs Fenner was pitiless. If any passer-by missed the significance of my burden, she did not hesitate to

[37]

enlighten them. Through it all, Maud pressed her lips together the way she did when she was annoyed, but, apart from an occasional sniff which made her wart wobble, made no other comment until we passed by Mr Marcantonio's ice-cream cart, where she turned aside without a word and bought a cornet. Not a boat, so it couldn't be for me.

When she had paid for it, she rounded on me abruptly.

'I reckon people ashamed to be seen out with people won't be wanting to come out on the Market Place with people any more.'

My response, the inevitable one, was to burst into noisy crying, to which she listened for a while with the air of someone trying to put a name to a familiar tune. Then, as if the performance had begun to bore her, she handed the ice-cream to Mrs Fenner to hold and brought out a man-size handkerchief in whose folds she nipped my nose painfully between her thumb and forefinger.

'Blow. Again.'

When I had complied, she polished the reddened organ as if it were the knocker on our front door, returned the handkerchief to her pocket, and, relieving me of the chamber pot – which I had not dared to drop in the midst of my keening, though the thought had flashed through my mind – handed it back to her mother.

'Here, ma. She'll fill it up for you if she goes on much longer. I reckon she's learned her lesson.'

'What lesson's that, then?' Mrs Fenner inquired innocently. 'Iggerant ole cow like me can't hope to teach anything to the likes of her.'

'All right, ma. Put a sock in it.' Repossessing herself of the ice-cream which it seemed, wonder of wonders, was intended for me after all – though a cornet, not a boat, a subtle distinction Maud knew would not be lost on me – she snapped, 'For heaven's sake, take those gloves off! That school o' yours 'll probably put you in solitary for a week for it – but there! Give us all a rest!'

I licked the ice-cream and felt better, though it was one of the mysteries of life how the same ice-cream could taste altogether different according to whether it came in a cornet or a boat. Mr Marcantonio, who, being Italian, was very emotional, leaned over the edge of his little cart and murmured, '*Coraggio*, little one!' which nearly set me off again. I was in no mood for *bel canto*.

'No need to put *your* spoke in, thank you very much!' Maud said ill-humouredly, at which Mr Marcantonio's dark little monkey face with its twirled moustaches screwed up as if he were about to burst into tears himself. Maud would probably have been kinder to him if she hadn't known that he had seven children at home and another on the way inside his fat little Italian wife.

My mother happened to be in the kitchen when we got back home. She looked with concern at my reddened nostrils and eyelids.

'Oh dear!' she said. 'I hope Sylvia isn't coming down with one of her colds.'

'Wouldn't be surprised,' was Maud's answer. 'She *would* take off those new gloves of hers, no matter what.'

Chapter Three

I was seven and a half, I calculate, when I first set foot in Salham St Awdry. That is to say, I had seen the village many times before then because Cromer was my mother's favourite choice for our Sunday outings to the sea, and St Awdry's was on the main Cromer road.

We never got out, though: just that my mother would invariably say, as we drove through, 'This is where Maud comes from,' and I would peer about in all directions, wondering which was the Fenners' house, and hoping vainly for a sight of Mrs Fenner.

My brother Alfred did the driving on these occasions – indeed, upon every occasion: the thought that my father might himself learn to drive had never occurred to him. He and my brother had come to an arrangement which suited us all very well. In return for acting as family chauffeur on Sundays, Alfred had the use of the car for the rest of the week, when he and his friends, on summer evenings, would cram into it with their ukeleles and drive away singing and laughing, just when it was time for me to go to bed.

The weekday Morris, decorated with pretty girls with red lips and long cigarette-holders, and young men in plus-fours or Oxford bags, was quite a different car from the Sunday one, which was sedate and very blowy because my father was a believer in fresh air as a cure for almost everything, and it had to be hailing, snowing or pouring cats and dogs before he would agree to having the windscreens put up, or the hood.

As the windscreens – made of a kind of celluloid with a border of black belting – were kept under the back seat when not in use, a call upon their services meant that rear passengers had to disembark whilst the back seat was moved aside and the screens retrieved. Each one had two fingers of metal protruding from its base which had to be slotted into the holes prepared for their reception in the thickness of each door or, in the case of the rearmost screens, in the top of the coachwork. This operation always took time because, for some reason we did not understand but accepted without question, all six windscreens were slightly different: only one fitted any one door. We were always meaning to mark them in some unmistakable way, but somehow never got round to it.

What with one thing and another, then, we were usually wet through before we had got the windscreens in place; the interior of the car likewise, since the screens had to be positioned before the hood could go over. When at last the latter was ready to be raised, my father and my brother, with many an 'Over to you' and 'Over to *you!*' exchanged on a rising note of exasperation, would finally get the heavy fabric unconcertina-ed, and bedded down in the sockets provided at either side of the front windscreen.

By the time we had succeeded in making all shipshape and Bristol fashion, quite often the sun had come out again. Quite often, too, having proceeded to our destination seated on wet upholstery in wet clothes, we – to my father's sorrowful but ill-concealed satisfaction – arrived back home sniffing and sneezing. What else could we expect, he demanded, if we insisted on huddling together like pigs in a sty, breathing in each other's carbon dioxide instead of the good fresh air, excluded on the inadequate ground that it was, for the moment, a little on the damp side? None of this would have happened if only we had kept the hood down.

The day I first set foot in Salham St Awdry, however, was a glorious day in June. The picnic basket was strapped to the luggage rack. My bucket and spade were in the back of the car, together with towels and bathing costume and sand shoes, and my brother's tennis racquet. To my disgust, he had a date to play tennis with some of his Cromer friends – which meant that a rather boring day loomed ahead of me. My parents were really too elderly to enjoy building sandcastles or making sand pies. Although occasionally, just for the devil of it, I had both of them down on their knees digging and tunnelling, I was usually merciful and allowed them to sit peacefully in their hired deckchairs, immersed in the Sunday papers. To be truthful, I wasn't much of a castle and sand pie person myself, and, as we prepared for our departure, the prospect of the day stretched ahead, infinitely expendable.

It was Maud's own doing, not any uppishness on the part of my parents, that we never offered her a lift to St Awdry's when we happened to be going that way ourselves. She could not, she asserted, get off with an easy mind if she didn't tidy up after we had left and before she took her way down to the bus station in Recorder Road. She was sure no one wished to come home to a pigsty.

This used to puzzle me, since the house patently wasn't a pigsty, until, years later, I came to the conclusion that her last-minute scuttling around, smoothing bedspreads, folding pyjamas, replacing the breakfast cloth on the dining table with the embroidered runner which was its usual dress between meals, was the equivalent of her adamant refusal to let me out of the house wearing a liberty bodice with a button missing.

'I'll be late for school!' I would wail. 'You can sew it on tonight. Nobody will know the difference.'

'And suppose you have an accident, Miss Clever, and they cart you off in an ambulance to the Norfolk and Norwich? What are *they* going to think then, eh?'

'I could always say it came off in the accident.'

'Liars go to hell,' was the reply, delivered in a tone which indicated Maud was half-inclined to leave me to my just deserts. But it was no good. The other half invariably won, and I would have to wait for the button to be sewn on before I was free to go.

And so, I think, it was with the house on Sundays. Suppose it caught fire whilst we were away, what would the firemen think when they saw the mess we'd left the place in? I believe that if she had anticipated a burglary, her chief worry would have been that the silver could have done with a polishing.

On that never-to-be-forgotten day, my brother, by the happiest chance, had trouble getting the car to start. When the so-called self-starter failed to bring the engine to life, he was forced to bring out from that repository under the back seat a large implement with a kick like a mule which, upon being thrust through a hole at the base of the radiator, hopefully engaged with the engine when the handle was turned. By the time he discovered that the root of the trouble lay in his having forgotten to switch on the petrol supply, he needed a fresh shirt and flannels and Maud had had ample time to leave the house in a condition she had no cause to be ashamed of, whatever disaster might befall in our absence.

Accordingly, my mother offered her a lift, which she accepted with moderate enthusiasm, her scepticism about my brother's driving ability, I believe, tempered only by the éclat of being seen arriving in her native village *en voiture*.

I sat between her and my mother on the back seat, Maud in her navy costume, on her knees the leather handbag my mother had given her on her last birthday. She wore her blue straw hat with the off-duty insignia pinned to it.

As we got under way and into that turbulence which invariably filled the rear of the car at speeds in excess of twelve miles per hour, the cherries and those other strange fruit plopped against each other like castanets. Myself, bareheaded, sat happily enjoying the wind rushing through my hair: my mother, a seasoned traveller who had not thought to warn a beginner of the hazards of motoring al fresco, had tied a scarf over her hat and under her chin.

'What the hell's that noise?' called out my brother, out of sorts after his earlier argument with the car.

'It's only Maud's cherries,' I answered for her.

'Tell her to shut them up, then. They're driving me batty.'

Maud, hanging on to her hat with both hands as the wind schemed to send it skimming over the hedgerows, went red in the face. 'Tin't me making this here wind! Turn it off an' they'll stop!'

Obviously, her worst fears about my brother as chauffeur were being borne out. Alfred slowed down enough to reduce the hurricane to a mere gale, but Maud was unappeased. When he came into St Awdry's he brought the Morris to a halt outside the Cross Keys, and asked winningly – he was a sweet-natured young man and, I am sure, regretted his momentary lapse – 'Opposite the Cross Keys – that's right, isn't it?'

Maud, unforgiving, replied sarcastically, 'That's on'y to have the postman on. Opposite the Swan, actually.'

[43]

'Look here – I said I'm sorry, didn't I?'

'Not so's I heard it!'

Maud straightened her hat, feeling tenderly to make sure the cherries were still in place, picked up her handbag from the floor. My parents, as was normal when any unpleasantness was in the air, pretended they were admiring the scenery.

Quite deliberately, I looked out at the ugly brick public house with its swinging sign and asked in my little-girl voice, 'And is *their* address Opposite the Fenners?'

Suddenly, whilst everyone, even Maud, was laughing as intended, a much better, a stupendous, idea struck me.

'Can I stay with Maud? I don't really want to go to Cromer. I'd much rather stay here with Maud. Can I, Maud – can I?'

With a child's unconscious cruelty, I had appealed to where power lay. Still, it was my mother who answered, taking no apparent offence.

'You can't possibly do that, dear! It's Maud's day off. It isn't fair to ask her to work on Sundays.'

'But I'm not *work*!' I cried, outraged to be put in the same category as sweeping out the yard.

Maud interjected abruptly, 'She can do what she likes, far as I'm concerned.'

'That's very kind of you, Maud.' But my mother protested, rather pathetically, 'Except that we've got a picnic –'

'I could pull off a leg or a wing –' Maud, having prepared the feast the evening before, knew exactly of what it consisted – 'if it's her dinner you're worried about.'

'Of course I'm not worried about that,' my mother came back quickly, though looking as if she had suddenly realized that perhaps she ought to have worried. What kind of meal could the Fenners, so poor, so primitive, provide for her darling? The cottages opposite the Cross Keys must be all right, if Maud lived there; but none of the four exteriors was such as to instil confidence in what lay behind their façades of crumbling brick. One of them even appeared to be derelict, with its windows filled in with flattened petrol cans.

My father tore himself away from his contemplation of the scenery to say gently, but firmly, 'Maud will take the whole chicken and whatever else she fancies to her mother with our compliments. See to it, Alfred, would you mind?' And, to my

[44]

mother, 'You and I, my dear, will lunch at the Cliftonville – all right? I can't tell you how glad I am to be spared chicken with sand flies down on Cromer beach.'

Alfred obediently opened the car door on his side and got out into the road.

'Best thing,' he suggested, 'would be if they took the whole hamper. We can pick it up when we pick *them* up on the way back.'

Maud said, admitting no contradiction, 'We'll be taking the bus, thank you very much. We won't want to have to lug that with us.' I could see that she was still bursting to tell my brother what she thought of his driving. Instead, she said to my mother, 'You won't want to be worrying about the time on account of *her*, and *we* won't need to be kept hanging about waiting for *you*.'

'If you're sure . . .' My mother was looking childishly pleased at the prospect of Sunday lunch at the smartest hotel in Cromer. She loved treats and being taken out. 'I hope Sylvia's properly grateful, that's all – you giving up your day off to her . . .'

'I'm not giving up anything,' Maud returned. 'And by the time the day's over, she'll be sorry she asked.'

My mother laughed, a little anxiously. She fumbled in her handbag and brought out half a crown to cover my fare home. Maud, whose total weekly wage consisted of four of those same half-crowns, accepted the coin with the cool acknowledgement, 'Three-pence ha'penny, half-price single. It'll be enough.'

She stood up to get out of the car. Alfred, who had disinterred the roast chicken and a bag of fruit from the picnic basket, appeared from the rear and handed her down from the running board with a slyly exaggerated old world courtesy. If St Awdry's were indeed looking on – and, though there wasn't a soul in sight, later experience convinced me that it was, with a curiosity not far short of passion – he did her proud. She took over the food and rewarded him for his gallantry with, 'I reckon all you need is a bit more practice.'

I kissed my parents goodbye and followed Maud out.

My mother admonished me fondly, 'Be a good girl, now!'

'Some hope!' said Maud, but not until my brother had set the Morris Oxford on its course again, my mother waving until the road curved just by the Swan, and hid them from our sight.

[45]

Chapter Four

I stood outside the Cross Keys feeling the way I imagine the Pope feels when he arrives in a new country and the first thing he does is go down on his knees and kiss the ground: humble and at the same time triumphant.

Every Sunday Maud went home for the day, something I resented bitterly. It wasn't that I couldn't live without her. On the contrary, the peace that descended upon the household on Maud's day off, the lack of reprimands, sarcasms, orders to do this, that and the other, was something precious to be savoured. Frequently, on Sundays, my mother and father took me to see ruins which, for some reason, they seemed to prefer to buildings with window panes and roof properly *in situ*; or we went to have tea with friends who made a delightful fuss over me and, unlike Maud, let me eat as many cakes as I wanted and no three pieces of bread and butter first. Life without Maud was perfectly acceptable so long as I was the one who chose to be without. For Maud to go off and leave me without so much as asking my permission was quite another kettle of fish.

But now, I had actually arrived!

Waiting for a gap in the coast-bound traffic, Maud gave me the bag of fruit to hold. She hoisted the box containing the chicken under her arm. Awkwardly, thus impeded, she began to fiddle with her hat. I grew afraid that she was going to take off the bunch of cherries, but all she did was remove the two hatpins, one at the front, one at the back.

'Oh goody!' I cried out in my relief. 'Then I'm not work after all!'

'Work?' echoed Maud, already gone over to her native tongue. 'Oh no! Bloody hard labour!'

My astonishment at hearing from those lips a word which

was never, never uttered in St Giles – or if it sometimes seemed to me to have been uttered, then, no matter how much I insisted to the contrary, I must have misheard it – was as nothing to my astonishment at what happened next.

Maud took off her hat.

I suppose I must have seen her bareheaded before, when I was too young to have noticed. I cannot believe that even Maud would have pinned her cap on before picking me up for my 2 a.m. feed and nappy change. I only knew that, consciously, I had never before seen her with head bare, noting for the first time that the centre parting in her hair was not quite straight. There was a little wiggle just above the point where it disappeared into the bun, which appeared larger than it usually looked peeping from under her headgear.

Nothing could have made me more aware of the uniqueness of the occasion; and when Maud went further, actually handed me the hat to carry, I received it as I might have received the Holy Grail.

'Just one thing afore we cross over –' Maud spoke as if the road were the Jordan, as, in a sense, it was – 'St Awdry's in't Norwich, so don't you go thinking it is. Anything that don't suit your ladyship, you'll have to lump it. No turning your nose up, if you know what's good for you.'

'I won't turn my nose up, I promise!' Because of the hat and the bag of fruit I could not, as I wanted, fling myself at her out of sheer happiness. 'I *do* love you, Maud.'

A sniff. 'Tell me the old, old story.'

The rule was to hold hands crossing a road but, again, the hat prevented it. Instead, Maud put her free arm round my waist. Did I imagine that she held me tighter than was strictly necessary to secure my safe passage? Held me lovingly?

Mrs Fenner was waiting for us with her front door open, filling the narrow aperture so that I could not see the room behind. It being a day when everything was new and wonderful, I wasn't surprised that she hadn't a hat on either, and was wearing a dress instead of the old-fashioned costume which, up to then, was all I had ever seen her in. It was a pretty awful dress, made like a coat with buttons down the front, and gaps, through which some kind of greyish undergarment was visible, between one buttonhole and the next. The dress had short sleeves. I had never seen Mrs Fenner's bare arms before, strong and freckled and friendly.

'Well, I must say!' she greeted me. 'Look what the wind's blown in.'

Maud said, 'She *would* come. Think you can put up with her a full day?'

'I reckon.' Mrs Fenner did not kiss me. She put her hand on my head and stroked my hair as if I were a young animal. 'If she can put up with us.'

'Oh yes!' I promised fervently.

'Better not speak too soon!'

Maud said with a touch of hauteur, 'We come in the car.'

'I saw. You still talkin' to us?'

'Oh ma!' Maud burst out laughing. Another first. I had not dreamed she harboured a laugh like that inside her, a laugh almost as good as her mother's, and felt momentarily aggrieved. She had no business keeping such secrets from me. 'We got some things for you. Take that hat, will you, afore Sylvie takes a bite out of it. Everyone home?'

'Charlie's off somewhere.' Mrs Fenner relieved me of the hat and led the way indoors. Heart beating, I followed, along a shaft of sunlight, treading on tiles that looked as if piddocks had been at them, the room otherwise so dark I could hardly make out anything after the brightness outdoors. The one small window was all but blocked with geranium plants growing every which way, all leg and leaf, no flower.

In that narrow shaft of light I saw the horsehair-covered sofa, the stuffing poking through in several places, which later was to be my Salham St Awdry bed. It had a carved back with whose every curlicue, every rich little pocket of dust, my probing fingers, in that blissful interval between bedtime and sleep, were to become lovingly familiar. On the wall above the sofa hung two large sepia photographs framed in a vaguely sacramental way, the wood beading extended at each corner to form little crosses.

Whilst my eyes were readjusting themselves, the sofa and the photographs were all that I saw with any clarity. The smell, on the other hand, hit me with an immediacy explicit and

[48]

overwhelming. Soot and cheap tobacco, the day's – the past year's – cooking, farmworkers' clothes encasing farmworkers' unbathed bodies, rag rug on which had taken their ease uncounted generations of dog: in time I was to analyse with precision, even affection, the components of the Opposite the Cross Keys smell. On my first encounter with it – oh the shame of that moment! – my chest heaved, my breakfast rose up out of my stomach like Leviathan from the deep. It was as if, upon reaching heaven, the goal of all his striving, Christian's first reaction to the odour of sanctity was to throw up.

Which I did, copiously, filling the little piddock holes with my sick.

'Too much excitement,' pronounced Maud, as calmly as if I were sick every day of the week. She bent my head forward, manipulating me gingerly so as not to get vomit on her best costume, whilst Mrs Fenner disappeared through an inner door, returning with a dwile* and a galvanized bucket spilling over with water. Maud herself then vanished through a smaller door at the side of the fireplace, papered over with the baskets of roses and lilacs which covered all the walls. I heard her footsteps ascending an uncarpeted stair and even noted that the ceiling billowed a little as she moved about the room above.

I cried, needing her.

She was back in less time than it seemed to me, having taken off her best clothes and changed into a dress very like her mother's, except that hers was flat all the way down, with no gaps between the buttonoles. The arms emerging from the short sleeves were thin and wiry, without a single freckle.

'Now, then,' she said, and propelled me smartly in the direction her mother had taken to get the water; across a kind of scullery where most of the floor space was taken up by a brick copper, out of the back door into a garden more correctly described as an area of rough land which stretched impartially behind all four of the Opposite the Cross Keys cottages without hedge or fence to divide it.

In the middle of this shaggy place was a pump with a bucket hanging on its iron spout; and here Maud stopped and carefully removed my soiled dress, which she put to one side. From

* Norfolk for a floorcloth.

somewhere she produced a bar of soap, a towel and, most amazing of all, another of my dresses, an old one, a favourite, which I can only think she had packed in the car against some mishap with sea or sand, and retrieved – hidden in her handbag or concealed among the roast chicken – following our change of plan.

'You want to pump?'

It was the completion of the cure. In my world water came out of taps or geysers. Only in fairy tales did it manifest itself out of pumps, usually operated by goose girls who turned out to be princesses under a spell.

The sound of that first splash into the tin bucket was pure enchantment. I forgot the embarrassment of being sick in somebody else's house, and – a close second – of being out of doors where anybody might see you, clad only in vest and knickers. I pumped water for me to wash in, water for Maud to wash in, and then I pumped water all over the dress I'd been sick in, sluicing all the horrid little bits away in a glorious cascade.

I pumped until Maud, doubting sourly that enough water was left in the pump to keep the inhabitants of Opposite the Cross Keys from dying of drought, made me desist. By the time she had slipped the second dress, the old favourite, over my head and combed my hair with a comb produced providentially from her pocket, the awfulness of what had happened had receded into oblivion, swallowed up by renewed happiness; nothing remaining but my dress drying on the clothes line, and a dampness slow to disappear on the piddocked floor.

The room to which we returned still smelled awful; probably, after my contribution, worse than before. But it no longer signified. I was immune, initiated. I came in from the open air without even having to catch my breath.

The room, as I now saw, was dirty. Not, be it said, 'dirty' uttered as a moral judgment, but purely as a style of interior decoration. With a father who was an architect *manqué* I had, even at that age, come to know a lot about architecture and household furnishings. I knew about round Norman arches and pointed Gothic ones. I could recognize Jacobean and Palladian and Victorian and point out the differences between them.

Now, with an instant and instinctive understanding, I added

to my infant expertise a style in which my father had neglected to instruct me, though its characteristics, once identified, were as unmistakable as any Regency striped satin, or the marble and ormolu of Louis Quatorze.

It was called Poverty.

The room was dirty because, as I was later to discover for myself, the fire of coal dust which burned day-long in the mean little grate smoked when the wind was in any direction. When there was no wind, it stopped smoking but instead, every few minutes, with the regularity of a striking clock telling the quarters, let out a fart of pure sulphur. When that happened, Gyp, the smelly old mongrel who spent most of his day stretched out on the rag rug in front of the hearth, would raise his head, growl petulantly, and fart back before sinking afresh into his geriatric trance.

The walls of the room, as I have already mentioned, were covered with a wallpaper which had a pattern of baskets of roses and lilacs set between panels of trellis where small birds perched, their tails cocked, their throats opened wide in song. The trouble was that the walls, full of strange bumps and hollows, were not really suitable for papering, and the roses and lilacs, the trellises and songbirds, flapped loosely over large areas, or else curled up at the seams. It could have been that the dirt acted as a kind of adhesive, for otherwise it was hard to understand what kept the paper up at all. As for its original coloration, that could only be guessed at, for all was now reduced to a uniform khaki, except over the fireplace, where it had turned coal black.

The low ceiling – once, at a guess, distempered white – was a paler shake of khaki, except for a ring of dense brown sited over the table which took up a good part of the room. Until I found out that this was caused by the oily deposit which ascended from the paraffin lamp which was the sole lighting, the circle appeared to me mysterious and frightening. When I came to know that room after dark, its daytime Poverty style converted into a velvety richness which enfolded everything except for the people seated round the table, their faces lovely in the lovely lamplight, it seemed even more mysterious, a sign planted on the ceiling as it might be a rainbow: a promise of grace.

The furniture at Opposite the Cross Keys matched the décor

with an exactness to gladden the heart of the perfectionist. Apart from the sofa and the table, it consisted of a number of kitchen chairs, an old rocking chair which had long ceased to rock, and a high chest of drawers made of some yellowish wood. It had knobs, of which several were missing, instead of handles, and three bun feet, the place of the missing fourth being taken by a small pile of *Old Moore's Almanacs*. The mantelshelf was draped with a swag of green plush finished off with bobbles, every fold heavy with enough coal dust to bank up the fire for the night.

As for what are known in the trade as decorative items, these consisted of a pair of green glass vases painted with a design of a pierrot and a pierrette, and, in the centre of the mantelshelf, a model of a WC in white ceramic with, on the open lid, the legend: *When you're passing, do drop in.* Variously disposed about the walls were several out-of-date calendars displaying pictures, mostly of simpering children holding simpering cats and dogs. The only other pictures were the two large photographs over the sofa.

There were three people in the room I had not met before.

Mr Fenner sat in the rocking chair reading *Old Moore's Almanac*. He was a small man with blue eyes and a lively look almost eclipsed by a wide-brimmed trilby hat, black but so misused by time as to look, in the dim light, greenishly iridescent. When Maud brought me over to him, he said, without waiting for an introduction, 'I heard a lot about you, gal.'

Good or bad? I longed to ask, but didn't dare.

Mr Fenner poked a finger at the open page of his *Almanac* and went on without waiting for me to say anything.

'Ma's always on about how you read her the paper a treat. What you make o' that, then? There!' Handing me the *Old Moore's* with another poke to make sure I knew where to look.

Though the sight of his black-nailed forefinger distracted me, the words themselves presented no especial difficulties: I had been reading since I was four.

'"May 25th to 27th,"' I read aloud. '"An explosion on board a large passenger ship will result in its sinking with

[52]

considerable loss of life. A Welsh climber will break all records for —"'

'Bugger the rest,' said Mr Fenner, which I took to be instructions to stop. He took his *Almanac* back. 'What you say to that? I never heard o' no ship goin' down in May. An' now we're well into June. You see anything in them papers o' yours?'

I shook my head. I had seen nothing. Mr Fenner observed gloomily, 'Never knew Old Moore to get it wrong afore.'

'It doesn't say an *English* ship,' I pointed out, trying hard to be helpful. 'They might not bother with putting foreign ships in the paper.' And indeed Mr Fenner brightened up considerably. Jolly little puckers appeared at the corners of his eyes.

He reached up to the mantelshelf and selected a clay pipe from among a number lying there. It was hardly used, with only a small stain of yellow down one side.

He thrust it towards me.

'You know how to blow bubbles? There's something for you to blow bubbles with.'

'After she's had her dinner!' Maud peremptorily interposed a hand, confiscating the gift, which she placed on top of the chest of drawers. But I could see she was pleased I had hit it off with her father.

Ellie Fenner, in a discontented voice, from the other side of the room, asked, 'You forget my bonbons?'

'When do I ever forget your bonbons?' answered Maud, in a tone from which I immediately deduced that, bonbons or no bonbons, Ellie Fenner and I were destined to be rivals, if not outright enemies.

In a sense we were that already, before we had ever met. Every Saturday, on the Market Place, Maud paid out four-pence for a quarter of cream bonbons, which were brown, sausage-shaped sweets rolled in something white – icing sugar, perhaps, or ground rice. I never did know exactly what, because I was strictly forbidden to eat any of the candies piled up in gorgeous abundance on the Market sweet stalls. 'Flies!' Maud would pronounce, if the suggestion was made that a pennyworth of jujubes or pear drops would not come amiss. 'Germs!'

Yet there was Maud herself, Saturday after Saturday, buying

her quarter of cream bonbons regular as clockwork! Why? For Ellie, I was told: for Ellie, the beautiful sister, who specially needed them, and the Market Place was the only place you could get them. I was given the impression they were vaguely medicinal, and that when Maud bought Ellie's weekly supply it was the equivalent of going to Boots the Chemists and getting a prescription filled.

When Ellie spoke, therefore, I was not surprised to see Maud open her handbag and take out the bag which contained the sweets. I expected her to put it on top of the chest of drawers next to my clay pipe. '*Not before dinner!*'

Instead, to my chagrin, she handed the bag over with the kind of smile I hated to see her wasting on others. Ellie snatched it without so much as a thank you, peered inside as if seeking a particular cream bonbon, and finally settled on one which to all outward view differed in no way from its fellows. This, to my amazement, she did not pop into her little round mouth for a suck and a chew, as I, salivating jealously, had expected, but – with the aid of a small hand mirror which she produced from somewhere – proceeded to rub vigorously over her cheeks and up and down her pudgy nose. It took a little while to realize that Maud's fourpennyworth was the snip of the week: not only sweets but face powder. It took three of them to coat Ellie's face and neck to her satisfaction, after which the de-powdered sweets were returned to the bag to await their final ingestion.

It might have been expected that, unsympathetic as I was from the start to the very idea of the lovely Ellie, the belle of Salham St Awdry, I would have been cockahoop to discover there was no such animal, only this blowsy creature with drab hair. On the contrary, it distressed me greatly. I felt guilty and inadequate at what I took as a failure of my own perceptions, that I could not perceive a beauty which – it was plain from the others' admiring homage – was there to be acknowledged by anyone else with eyes in his head. What was the matter with mine?

Ellie admired herself in the mirror, turning her head on its short neck. She looked across at me with contempt, and demanded, 'Can you sit on *your* hair?'

Since my hair, cut short with a centre parting and fringe, barely covered my ears, it was not really a question calling for an answer. Nevertheless, I answered in a small voice, 'No. I'm afraid I can't.'

'I thought not,' remarked Ellie, sitting back, well satisfied.

Tom, on the other hand, the elder of Maud's two brothers, *was* beautiful; or would have been, if something – as a child I had no idea what it might be – had not happened to him.

That night, on our way home on the bus, nestled blissfully between Maud's left arm and her bony hip, I asked sleepily, 'Why is Tom like that?'

Maud drew away, making me sit up, pouting.

'Like what?'

Me, faltering as I perceived that once again, all unmeaning, I had put my foot in it: 'Like the way he is.'

Maud repeated fiercely, 'What you mean, the way he is? He's the way he is like everyone's the way they are. Why are you the way *you* are, little Miss Swankpot, I'd like to know?'

Tears of disappointment welled up in my eyes. Up to that moment it had been such a lovely day.

'I didn't mean anything –'

'It's that nose of yours!' Maud looked sideways at the offending organ as if she couldn't stand the sight of it. 'It's turning up again, I can see it.'

'It isn't! It isn't!'

Maud appeared not to have heard.

'If you had the sense to use the eyes God give you 'stead of that stuck-up nose of yours, you'd 'a seen what coat he was wearing.'

'I *did* see it, so there! An old Army one.' Comprehension dawning: 'You don't mean he was in the War and got wounded, and that's what it is?'

Maud answered cryptically, 'People who know how to put two an' two together an' make four, wouldn't need to ask.'

'But the War was so long ago. I didn't think –' I dropped that line quickly as Maud's face began to darken again, and anyway being quite unequal to figuring out how old Tom would have needed to be to have fought in the Great War. Instead, I asked placatingly, 'Did he get gassed like the man who sells matches outside Woolworth's? Is that why he's like that?'

Maud's wart quivered, a dire portent.

'There you go again! Like what?'

I could not bear the day to peter out in ill will. Out of the bus window, behind my reflection and Maud's, I could see that we were just coming up to Horsford Point, where the mighty lozenge was doing its balancing act against the setting sun.

'*Ma gerto o ca,*' I mouthed silently, knowing it was hopeless, but hoping just the same.

'Like *what?*' Maud repeated ominously.

'Like – an angel,' something made me say. Something magic.

Chapter Five

Tom had a face like an angel in a medieval picture except that it was unfinished. It looked as if the painter had got so far – only a very little further to go – when he put his brush down. Perhaps the glory had suddenly become too much for him. All the usual features were there and in their accustomed places – two eyes, a nose, a mouth, a chin with a cleft down the middle – but the outline was smudged, it lacked definition. Something was missing, just as something was missing from the way Tom's arms and legs were joined to his body, the way he moved, the way he spoke.

At first, that first day, except for 'Sylvie', which he sang rather than spoke, I couldn't make out a single word he said. Nobody else seemed to have any such difficulty as the table talk went on between the absorbed business of eating, Tom's mouth opening, now to take in vast shovelsful of food, now to let out sounds whose significance escaped me. My contribution was to smile and nod my head vigorously to show I was taking it all in. Every now and again I caught Tom looking at me puzzled and a little pitying, as well he might: one of those cracked city folk, sitting there grinning like an idiot, with a brain to match.

I sat facing the two photographs, the old men on the wall over the sofa. One of them particularly – the other looked sad but accommodating – regarded me sternly over the top of his high, stiff collar. I dropped my eyes and tried to get on with my dinner, which wasn't easy. I am sure now that Maud, knowing my finicky ways, had deliberately selected for me the most chipped and crazed plate out of the motley pile she had placed on the table. It was a kind of test, like the gritty cabbage, potatoes and bits of gristle she spooned out of the soot-caked saucepan which had been simmering on the fire, dumping the mess on top of my portion of roast chicken and thus, from my point of view, rendering the whole inedible. The whole day was a kind of test.

Maud wasn't even looking at me, but the old man on the wall over the sofa did. I didn't like the way he looked at me at all; and just to spite him, I picked up the awful old knife and fork with which Maud had provided me, took up a mouthful of food, and ate it.

To say that I did not enjoy it is an understatement, but I got it down somehow, and after that the going was easier. Not because the second and the following mouthfuls were any more to my taste than the first, but because, though nothing in her face showed it, I could feel Maud's approval radiating like sunlight through my entire being. Inconspicuously, and as though I were licking a morsel of food off my upper lip, I put out my tongue at the old man. Tom said, and I understood every word of it, 'Want me to catch you a toad this arternoon?'

'Oh, yes please!' I exclaimed, before I realized the wonder of it, the miracle. 'Yes, please!'

Tom said, 'I know where there's a good toad, if no one's bin an' got there first.'

Tom not only kept his cap on at table, as his father did his trilby hat, he kept on his coat as well: in fact, all the time I knew him I never saw him not wearing it. It was a khaki greatcoat which had lost most of its buttons and acquired, with age, the look of bark covered with lichen.

Tom put his hand into one of the pockets and brought out a large snail, which he placed among the plates and food on the table.

'You can have him too, if you want.'

As it happened, I had been afraid of snails ever since Dorothy Coulton, a girl at Eldon House, had shown me how, if you poured salt on to the opening in their shells when they were curled up inside, they frothed like Eno's Fruit Salts and died, except that the froth was green, or sometimes prussian blue. So I was relieved when the snail, which was waving its eyes about in a way which boded no good to anyone, moved towards Mrs Fenner's plate, not mine.

If it had been Dorothy Coulton, iron-nerved as she was, sitting there in my place, she would undoubtedly have seized the packet of Saxa Salt which stood on the table, and sprinkled the little monster without a qualm, but I was made of weaker stuff. How many tests, I wondered agonizedly, did you have to pass before you were given the freedom of Opposite the Cross Keys?

Fortunately for me, Mrs Fenner exploded in one of her enormous laughs and exclaimed, 'Sylvie don't want no truck wi' that rubbish! What you think we are, bor, Frenchies?' She picked up the snail, went and put it in one of the flower pots on the window sill. 'There!' she announced, returning to the table. 'That'll keep him happy till you've finished your dinner.' To me, she said, 'You heard the Frenchies eat 'em, han't you, jest like winkles? Funny ole world, in't it?'

Charlie Fenner, the youngest of the family, came in just then, and hung his cap on a peg on the door into the scullery. It was a surprise to see a he-Fenner bareheaded. Small and strong-looking, he was a younger edition of his father, only less good-humoured: no crinkly lines at the corners of his bright blue eyes.

He was dressed nattily for a working man: navy blazer and grey flannels such as my brother Alfred often wore, yet not at all the same, really. An apology for a badge on the blazer, and trousers of that horrid thick cloth which seemed at permanent odds with the human form. Even though it was immediately obvious that we had got off on the wrong foot – all unknowingly, I was sitting in his place – I couldn't help feeling sorry for him for being such a poor imitation of Alfred.

When Mrs Fenner said, as one announcing good news, 'We got gal Sylvie here for the day,' his only acknowledgement was a querulous 'Oh ah?' He gave me an irritable once-over and went into the scullery for a stool which turned out to be much too low, only there wasn't any other. His chin practically touched the table.

'You're late.' Maud plumped his plateful down so that he nearly stuck his nose in it. 'Where you been, then?'

Charlie did not answer; tucked into his dinner hungrily, though with no appearance of enjoyment. Mrs Fenner intervened mockingly, 'What you mean, where's he bin, on the

Lord's Day? Singing the praises o' the Lord, tha's where he's bin – eh, Charlie?'

Maud looked surprised.

'You been to Chapel? You never!'

'Wrong Lord,' said Mrs Fenner. 'Doreen, Mrs Lord's little angel, over past the mill. Holds an organ service Sundays an' every night o' the week.'

Charlie looked up from his food, suddenly cheerful and good-natured.

'Give over, ma. Didn't you an' pa never go courtin'?'

'Me an' your pa?' Mrs Fenner's laughter rocked the room once more. 'Picked him up under me arm an' wouldn't let him down till he said "I will!"'

Mr Fenner smiled across the table.

'Tha's right . . .'

The two smiled at each other contentedly.

When dinner was over, Tom went over to the geraniums, retrieved his snail with little soothing sounds, and dropped it back in his pocket. In a voice full of happy importance he said to me, 'Better see about that toad afore somebody else gets his paws on it,' and hurried out.

As soon as he had gone Maud stated baldly, 'If you're thinking of taking a toad back to Norwich, Miss, you've got another think coming. One dumb animal's as much as I can manage.'

'Oh! But Tom –'

'Never mind Tom. We'll put it down somewhere he don't see, before we catch the bus. No waterworks!' she commanded, seeing from my face that I was getting ready to turn on the stopcock. 'Where you keep a toad in St Giles?'

'I'm sure May Bowden would let me keep it in her garden. I could always go and play with it there.'

Maud's brow darkened as it always did at any mention of her rival.

'That one! Wouldn't trust her with a grasshopper! And anyway, wild animals ain't for playing with.'

The toad question remained unresolved. Whilst Mrs Fenner put away the leftover food, using the rusty old range in the scullery as a larder, I helped Maud wash up. She poured sooty water from the kettle into a basin from which most of the enamel had vanished, adding cold water from the pail on the floor. I did the wiping with what looked like a piece of old sheet, absorbent enough but shedding bits of lint on to the plates which Maud handed to me still a little greasy and speckled with soot. In Norwich she'd have gone through the roof to see plates washed up like that, but in St Awdrey's it obviously didn't matter. What a glorious place it was!

I took the plates back to the living room a few at a time. Charlie had gone and Ellie had taken a chair outside. She had left the front door open, and through it I could see her sitting in the sun, chewing a cream bonbon and combing her hair with a languid rise and fall of fleshy arm. She had done nothing to help with the clearing away. 'The lazy mauther!' I muttered under my breath, broadening my vowels and savouring the saying of it. I went back to the scullery and said to Maud, 'Gimme a dwile, bor, I'll gi' the tablecloth a lick.'

'Who you taking the mickey out of?' The tone was truculent but I could see Maud was pleased to hear me speaking the native lingo. She handed me a smaller piece of sheet, first wringing it out in the washing-up water. I went back and wiped over the oilcloth, guiding the crumbs and bits of this and that into my hand. My hand wasn't big enough and several bits fell on the floor, which didn't matter. *O glorious St Awdrey's, where such things didn't matter!*

I brushed the bits off my hand into the fire, where they raised little points of flame that lasted less than a second. Mr Fenner was back in his non-rocking rocking chair at the side of the hearth, wearing wire-rimmed half-spectacles and reading his *Old Moore's Almanac*. He needed the spectacles because he was engulfed in a cloud of evil-smelling smoke which rose from his clay pipe. It was so thick I couldn't think how he could see to read, even so.

He peered out of the smoke and told me I was a good gal. My ma must be pleased to have a good gal like that to help her in the house. I didn't think it politic to admit that she didn't; that it was Maud who cleared away the St Giles crumbs and anything else that needed clearing up, me particularly.

Mr Fenner sucked in his cheeks and blew out a great blast of cloud. It didn't smell anything like the way my father's tobacco smelled.

[61]

'Made it myself' – gently boastful. 'Grew it, an' picked it an' cured it, none of your shop rubbish. What you think of that?'

Eyes watering, I mimed surprise and admiration.

'I expec' you notice it smells a bit different from your ordinary shag?'

I nodded through the haze. Mr Fenner's tobacco smelled a lot different from anything.

Lowering his voice as if he feared to have his secret stolen by spies sent out by the tobacco companies, Mr Fenner explained, 'Threepennyworth of rum poured over afore you shred it, an' left for a week to sink in.' He offered charmingly, 'I don't mind giving you a bit, if you like, to take home to your pa.'

I answered, truthfully, that my mother didn't like my father smoking a pipe.

'Oh ah?' With sympathy for the put-upon male: 'That kind, is she?' Mr Fenner withdrew into his private smog, savouring his home-made tobacco and the knowledge, I felt sure, that *his* wife wasn't one of that kind.

We went down the garden, Mrs Fenner, Maud and I, following a path trodden between tall grasses and poppies, and accompanied on our way by two pairs of butterflies, one pair cabbage, one, small tortoiseshell. Bees swerved about their business, grasshoppers chirped. The grasses tickled my bare legs.

It was a lovely way to go to the lav.

The privies stood in a row at the bottom of the garden, looking like bathing huts on a shore from which the sea had long since retreated. The one between the Fenners' and the Leaches', like the cottage of which it was a dependency, tottered in a state of dereliction, the roof stripped of its pantiles, the door hanging by a single hinge. Under the sagging lintel crowded several little clay cups of house martins' nests; and it was clear that a further colony of the birds was housed within, for the air was busy with the non-stop twitter of nestlings, and the tireless comings and goings of the parent birds.

When Mrs Fenner opened the door into our own kingdom I was delighted to discover that one pair, preferring privacy, it may be, or simply finding standing room only next door, had

taken up residence in an angle of the Fenner lav. As we entered
– all of us together! What new experience was in store? – a flash
of black and white shot ahead of us like an arrow, and, in an
instant, was on its way out again, back to the insect-rich
outdoors.

The privy doors were not privy at all, beginning some
eighteen inches above the ground, and ending at least as much
below the lintel; in addition to which, each had an unglazed
porthole, the shape of a playing-card club, gouged out of the
centre. You could see that someone was in the Leaches' lav,
which was the only one which was painted; spick and span like
the polished black shoes and the grey socks with fancy clox
which showed under the door.

'Mr Leach,' said Mrs Fenner, making no effort to keep her
voice down. 'Known him to be there of a Sunday from dinner
till tea.' The black shoes scuffed each other self-consciously.
'You got to hand it to him, poor bugger. He do keep trying.'

New smells. Horrible new smells, but with such compensa-
tions they might have been flower fragrances. Not only a nest of
real live birds to watch while you were doing your business, but
company! Suddenly the whole boring business of evacuation
was transformed: a social event, a lav party, as it might be a
Christmas or a birthday one, for which you might send out
invitations, with spaces to fill in the date and the times, and
RSVP at the end. No stupid games like My Friend's Chair and
Pin the Tail on the Donkey. Just you and two best friends –
there were never more than two people you *really* wanted to
invite, the rest were just make-weights, there to make up the
numbers – sitting at peace with the world.

There were three holes in the wooden seat at Opposite the
Cross Keys, three holes of different sizes – one for Daddy Bear,
one for Mummy Bear, and one for Baby Bear. Marvellous!
Though I couldn't help being glad that Baby Bear's – my – hole
was at the other end of the seat from the birds' nest, where the
wood was distinctly splodgy.

'Mucky little bastards,' Mrs Fenner observed affectionately.
She brushed some segments of regurgitated bluebottle on to the
earth floor before pulling down her bloomers and getting on
with it.

We didn't talk much. There was no need. The sense of

[63]

companionship was all. I felt quite sorry for poor constipated Mr Leach in his grey socks and polished shoes stuck there two doors away, all on his own.

The porthole in the door was too high up for me, seated, to see anything but the sky. I sat happy and mindless until Mrs Fenner said, at exactly the right moment, 'All good things have to come to an end. Pass us a bit o' paper, Sylvie, there's a good gal.'

Chapter Six

MAUD said it was time for my walk. I didn't know how this intelligence was revealed to her and did not dare to ask. Mrs Fenner, looking as if the very idea of a walk in St Awdry's was something novel, not to say barmy, demanded, 'Walk? What bloody for?'

'Sylvie needs the exercise. We can go round by the Swan, and up as far as the fields.'

'Oh ah.' Mrs Fenner received the suggestion without enthusiasm. 'Fields. What you want to go an' look at them fer?'

'Oh, ma!' exclaimed her daughter, who, after seven years in the city, had evidently acquired some of the townee's chronic sentimentality about the countryside. 'You know yourself it's nice up there.'

'Nice for cows.' But Mrs Fenner came along cheerfully enough.

We walked in single file along the narrow pavement until, just before the public house, where the signpost said Norwich one way, Cromer the other, and nowhere at all up the little lane Maud intended us to follow, we came to the pond. That is, so I was told: I was expected to take the pond on trust. All you could actually see from the road was a tangle of rushes and yellow flags, hog bean and water forget-me-not.

'Can't we go closer and take a look?'

No, we could not. Closer was dangerous. One Saturday night a couple of years ago, after some louts in the Swan old enough to know better had put away more beer than was good for them, they had gone outside and turned the signpost round, so that the sign which said to Norwich pointed straight into the bog. And a young man and a girl in an Austin saloon, who had also drink taken, had driven off the road, crashed through the bulrushes, and ended up in the pond.

Or the car had, anyway.

Mrs Fenner finished, 'Last summer, when we had all that dry weather, you could just see the roof showing. They never did get it out. Tin't the water, you see, it's the mud. Goes down to Australia. Sucked it in before any one of the great gowks got enough wits together to go for a rope.'

'But the young man and the girl –' The lovely secret place had become suddenly full of dread.

'Don't worry. They wasn't as drunk as all that. Jumped clear, both on 'em, afore the car hit the water. All they needed was a good bath.'

But I had seen the look Maud gave her mother over my head. Was I being fobbed off? Were the young man and his girl still sitting there in the car, under the still, secret water, packed solid with mud, the young man's hands still clutching the steering wheel?

'There you go again,' said Maud, interpreting my expression with her usual accuracy. 'Ask your brother Alfred if you don't believe what my ma just said. That Eric Woods he knows, the one that plays the piano, he knows the two of 'em. So no nightmares, young miss, if you know what's good for you!'

'So why did you look at your mother like that?'

'Like what? I got to ask your permission, now, how I look at my ma?'

I persisted. 'As if there was something you didn't want me to know.'

'Couldn't be that, could it? You who know everything!'

Maud's tone was jeering, but again I sensed an underlying unease. Suddenly I knew without being told that Charlie had been one of the great gowks old enough to know better.

I also knew that I must never say that I knew.

My fears lifted, leaving only a residual regret. The pond had become less doomful, but also less interesting. A sudden skitter and splash made us all three jump, until we saw it was only a pair of mallards taking off from the hidden water.

Nobody in St Awdry's ever took a walk. In a world geared to the plough, the hoe, to cows to be brought in for milking, putting one foot in front of the other for pleasure was a daft idea

[66]

if ever they heard one. There seemed to be hardly anybody but us alive in the village. At the side of one of the cottages which straggled along the unmetalled lane, a boy was looking for a bicycle puncture, moving the inner tube round in a basin of water, watching for bubbles. A black and tan dog, rolling on its back in the sandy roadway to get rid of its fleas, lifted its head to see who was coming along, sensed no threat, and went back to its rough and ready grooming. In a front garden a woman with a net over her hair and wearing a black cardigan in spite of the heat was cutting sweet williams.

'Arternoon!' Mrs Fenner greeted her politely, receiving in return what might or might not have been a nod.

'Stuck-up bit o' bacon!' remarked Mrs Fenner when we were past, but not sufficiently past not to be overheard. 'Acts like she's the Queen o' Sheba on account she used to work in the kitchen at Sandringham. Just because King Edward, bless him, once pinched it on the back stairs, don't mean we all got to bow down an' kiss her arse.'

The houses petered out and the fields began, boring, exactly as Mrs Fenner had intimated. There did seem to be an unnecessary amount of green in the world.

Mrs Fenner took out a handkerchief and wiped the sweat from her face. 'How long's this bloody walk goin' on?' she wanted to know.

Maud didn't answer. As ever, she knew what she was about. She led the way across the first field and a second, to a stile between hawthorn hedges where, after a quick survey of what lay beyond, she turned and waited for us to catch up. She was looking very pleased with herself.

'Get an eyeful o' that,' she commanded, when we arrived, hot and bothered. 'The same like always, year after year ever since I was Sylvie's age, *and* younger.'

The third field was less green than gold. Not the common gold of buttercups, but an orange shimmer, a gold that seemed to pulsate in the hot sun, that *was* the sun. The air was good enough to eat, heavy with the fragrance of apricots.

'Cowslips,' Maud instructed me, as she helped me over the stile. 'Thought you might like to take a few back to your ma.'

A few! Surrounded by that sweet-scented treasure I ran about like one possessed. The stems yielded easily, a little juice

[67]

exuding from the broken ends, enough to make my fingers sticky. I picked cowslips until I could hold no more, until I dropped as many as I picked, and still I went on picking.

Maud and her mother watched me unmoving, leaning on the stile side by side and apparently uninfected by my manic greed. Only when I ran to them and gave Maud my gatherings to hold, preliminary to beginning all over again, did she yank me back with a hand on the skirt of my dress.

'Leave some for somebody else, greedy guts!' She thrust the flowers under her mother's nose. 'Smell nice, don't they?'

I said, 'They smell of apricots.'

'Don't talk daft!' said Maud. Then, 'What do *you* say, ma?'

Mrs Fenner sniffed judiciously before pronouncing.

'Armpits? No. Tripe an' onions? No.' She buried her nose so deep in the flowers that golden pollen flecked her rosy cheeks. Then, with a radiant smile of recognition, 'Cowslips! Tha's what they smell like. Cowslips!'

How happy I was!

Mrs Fenner took a penknife and a piece of string out of her pocket, and sat down on the step of the stile. 'Gimme those.' Whilst I watched anxiously, afraid she was about to set all my effort at naught, she divided up the big bunch of cowslips into smaller bunches, cut some stems so short there was little left but the nodding flowerets, left others as I had picked them. She saw my eyes on her and sent me to an oak tree which grew in the hedge by the ditch, to see if I could find a nice little pincushion of moss, not too big, not too small, and no bloody bugs in it either.

I found the moss without difficulty. When I brought it back, she rammed the bright green pad into the heart of the cowslips; knotted the string, cut it, made a loop big enough to get your hand through in the piece that was left: felt for a hairpin in her hair to make a kind of anchorage at the other end. A lock of hair plopped down on her neck, which made us all laugh, and made me feel suddenly sure that my cowslips were going to be all right after all.

'Ma!' Maud exclaimed, her voice vibrant with love. 'You are a one!'

Mrs Fenner had made a cowslip ball, a small sun brought down to earth. She slipped the loop of string over my wrist. Its

[68]

beauty was beyond words and I bore it back to Opposite the Cross Keys, myself made beautiful by the bearing of it.

When we were back in the scullery, Mrs Fenner made me dunk the ball in the bucket of water, just once, and then she hung it up to drain on a nail over the range, the excess water puddling the floor. Maud brought the kettle in from the living-room and filled it from the same bucket, taking no account of the ants and other small insects which were floating there. The difference between Maud's Salham St Awdry and her Norwich standards of hygiene enchanted me.

While she cut great doorsteps of bread and marge as against the paper-thin bread and butter for which my mother's tea table was justly famed, I slipped out of the back door and down to the privies. I didn't need to go, and if I had needed to, I would have held it in until I had company. I just wanted to see if Mr Leach's shoes and socks were still there.

They were; only just at that moment a woman came out of the Leaches' cottage and shouted 'Bert!' in a voice that shattered the sweet contentment of the place, the grasses, the nodding poppies. A moment later, a man of medium size, dressed in grey trousers, a white, long-sleeved shirt and a black, grey and red-striped tie that went well with the shoes and the socks with the fancy clox, came out of the Leach privy and hurried up the path. He was youngish, I thought – so far as, in my judgement, any grown-up was anything but bowed under the weight of years – even though the hair on the top of his head was thinning. His rounded shoulders, his nose advancing, chin retreating, gave him a sad and fretful look. He did not look as if he had accomplished much, down at the lav or anywhere else.

I wished I had the nerve to tell him about senna pods, which May Bowden swore by. Or that I were like Mrs Fenner who, I felt, would certainly have called out, in her rich, warm voice, 'Better luck next time, bor!' As it was, we both saw and pretended not to see each other.

At tea I sat on the sofa, underneath the photographs of the two old men. It was uncomfortable to the point of agony. How could horses, who looked so smooth and glossy, be so prickly when made up into furniture? Perhaps it was their way of taking revenge.

Tears came into my eyes – not of pain, but pride. Now, I kidded myself, munching the clodhopper bread, drinking the horrible sweet tea with a dead ant, which I went out of my way to swallow, floating in the cup, my thighs and calves chafed, I too knew what it was to be poor. It seemed to me an accomplishment for which I deserved praise, like mastering the present tense of *être*. *Je suis* poor, *tu es* poor, *il est* poor, *elle est* poor. It wasn't until years later, when my father, out of the blue, happened to mention that Salham St Awdry had once been known for its horsehair weaving, that up to the Great War there had been between forty and fifty horsehair weavers working in the village, that I knew for certain what I had known instinctively ever since that first day at Opposite the Cross Keys: that St Awdry's was the place where they had manufactured poverty, weaving it thread by thread, warp and woof, on a loom.

Tom came in for his tea full of a secret – not so secret – glee. I immediately guessed, by the way he kept smiling at me, winking and nodding, that he had got me a toad, only I wasn't supposed to know. It was to be a lovely surprise. With conspiratorial glee he patted the right pocket of his greatcoat, to let me know where the surprise was located.

Tom ate his bread and marge and drank his tea with an enjoyment that involved his whole body; twisting about as he chewed, smacking his lips loudly and moving the bread round his mouth as if he wished to present it, another lovely surprise, to every nook and corner of his digestive system. Ellie put away just as much, but did it in mean little nibbles, as if she only ate the stuff because she had to, to keep body and soul together. Perhaps, I don't know, she was acting the lady for my benefit.

Mr Fenner chose not to come to the table. Maud took his tea and bread and marge over to where he sat, still crowned with smoke, in the rocking chair. He put the tea on the mantelshelf while he ate the bread and drew on his pipe alternately. When he had finished the bread he spat a hissing gob of phlegm into the fire, knocked out his pipe, and settled down to his cup of tea.

'Maud gal –' he smiled at his daughter when she came to relieve him of the empty cup – 'I reckon King George hisself weren't served a better cup 'n that.'

'Speakin' of royalty,' said Mrs Fenner, who had taken her

chair over to the window – the cars were beginning to come back from the coast, and she enjoyed watching them go by – 'we saw her Ladyship o' Sandringham up the lane. Couldn't dirty her lips wi' passing the time of day with the likes of us, o' course.'

'She in't so dusty, ma.' Mr Fenner sat back comfortably, surveying his family with affectionate satisfaction. 'Can't all be lucky like us. Tin't her fault she's such a misery, hubby done a bunk, and young Gordon on the War Memorial, missing.'

'I'd go missing if all I had to come back to was a ma like her,' Mrs Fenner insisted, unrepentant. 'No flies on that Gordon. Holed up over there wi' some Mamselle from Armentières, I shouldn't be surprised.'

'Ma!' cried Maud. It seemed to be an expression she felt called upon to use often, invariably in a tone of admiration mingled with laughing reproof. 'You *are* a one!'

Tom unbuttoned the pocket of his army greatcoat with exaggerated care, and took out the toad. He held it out over the table so that I could get a good look at it, but holding on to it firmly, not inviting me to take it into my own hands.

I was grateful for that because, although the last thing I wanted to do was hurt Tom's feelings, I was uncertain how I felt about toads. I wasn't exactly afraid of them, but I wasn't exactly unafraid either.

Because I could see that was what Tom expected of me, I exclaimed with enthusiasm, 'A toad!'

'I said I'd get you one, didn't I?' Tom bounced up and down in his seat, his angelic, unfinished face wreathed in smiles.

'And you did.' Seeing how pleased with me Maud was looking, I added, in my best little-girl voice, 'You *are* kind!'

Tom, red with pleasure, said that the toad's name was Pillow. I looked at Pillow and Pillow looked back at me with such bright-eyed trustfulness that I was quite won over: or would have been, if, at that moment, it hadn't needed to blink. A thin, semi-transparent membrane flicked down over the eyes and up again in a way to make the blood run cold.

'Hello, Pillow,' I managed nevertheless.

'Go on – stroke it,' Tom commanded, and when I shrank away, unable to disguise my aversion, he stroked the toad's

[71]

head himself with one of his large, scarred hands. The little creature all but purred, its eyes rolling upward in ecstasy.

It looked so absurd that I had to laugh, and, laughing, came to terms with the alien life-form. I had to have a go myself. The toad's skin, I was thankful to find, was dry and cool to the touch, an agreeable roughness.

'He likes you,' Tom assured me. 'Pillow likes you. I can see that.'

'How can you tell?'

'If he didn't, he'd 'a spit in your eye.'

Maud went into the scullery and came back with a tin which had criss-crossed Union Jacks and Danish flags printed on the sides, and on the top, portraits of King Edward and Queen Alexandra. The portraits were a good deal the worse for wear already, so that it didn't matter when she took a metal meat skewer out of the chest of drawers and punched several holes in the lid.

She had lined the tin with some newspaper crumpled up, only that didn't suit Tom, who first buttoned Pillow carefully back in his pocket and then went out into the garden and came back with a handful of grasses and poppies to serve in its place. He also brought back a large worm the colour of mahogany which he sliced up on one of the plates and tipped into the tin in case Pillow felt peckish on the journey to his new home.

I could tell by the look in Maud's eyes that there was going to be no question of leaving the toad behind at the bus stop. How clever Tom was! Anyone could get rid of a toad, so long as that was all it was, a toad. But once give it a name . . . ! To abandon Pillow would be tantamount to abandoning a newborn infant on the steps of the Norfolk and Norwich.

When his preparations were complete, Tom placed Pillow gently in his makeshift nest and quickly shut the lid. One of the skewer holes had gone right through the middle of King Edward's nose, making him look very silly. Maud let out a sigh, and said it was time to get ready to go. She went upstairs, through that mysterious door at the side of the fireplace, and came down changed back into her navy costume, with her straw hat on. The sight of her, returned to her St Giles self, brought home to me as nothing else that the day was really and truly over, that there would never be another day like it.

Old as I was for such carryings-on, I began to cry and cry for the perfection that would never come again. Mrs Fenner remarked, with moderate sympathy, 'Put a cork in it, gal Sylvie. Tin't the end o' the world.' But it was, and I went on crying. Tom's eyes, too, were wet with tears, but that might have been for Pillow, not me. He could have been regretting his generous impulse in giving away such a toad of toads.

Charlie came in, looking glum; this time with his cap on, which made him look different, lumpish. His mother poured him out a cup of tea, and cut some more bread for him.

'No jam?' He took a discontented bite out of the bread and looked down at the peculiar wetness on his plate. 'Wha's that?'

'Oh, that? Tom just cut up a worm.'

'Christ!' But it didn't stop him from finishing the bread, swilling it down with the brewed tea. Perhaps he knew his mother was joking. Perhaps she was.

He looked at me with small curiosity. 'Wha's she going on like that for?'

Maud said, 'She don't want to go home.'

Charlie said, 'She must be mad.'

'You're in a lovely mood,' Mrs Fenner observed. 'What you bin up to now?'

'Playin' pontoon at Jacko Brown's, if you want to know. Lost ninepence.'

'More fool you.'

'You wouldn't say that if I'd 'a won.'

'True enough,' Mrs Fenner conceded. 'But you didn't, bor. Wha's the good o' talking if?'

What indeed was the good of talking if? Or of crying over it? The living-room at Opposite the Cross Keys had grown darker as the sun moved round, shadowy; and the Fenners too seemed to have grown shadowy, borne away on the turning world. Mrs Fenner kissed me, and when, with my St Giles manners, I went over to the rocking chair to shake Mr Fenner's hand and say thank you for a lovely day, to my surprise he bent down and kissed me too, and told me to be sure and come again. His moustache was much pricklier than my father's. It could easily have been horsehair.

Charlie gave me a nod, and Ellie a poker-faced stare. Tom was not somebody you said goodbye to.

[73]

Chapter Seven

BACK in Norwich, at my insistence we called in at May Bowden's before going home. I was anxious for Pillow, shut up in the tin. Maud's attempted reassurance, that toads could see in the dark, only deepened my anxiety. How doubly awful to be able to see in the dark and find that there was only the dark to see!

Maud was in a good mood. We hadn't bumped into anyone we knew on the longish walk from the bus depot to St Giles: no one had seen me in my mucky Salham St Awdry state, so that although she would rather have procured me a bath and fresh clothing before tackling May Bowden about taking Pillow in as a lodger, she gave in to my importunings without too much fuss. It was, after all, only May Bowden, who didn't know clean from dirty.

May Bowden was out in her garden, which, to tell the truth, wasn't much of a garden at all, being mostly cobblestones, beach pebbles tedious to walk on and death to ladies' high heels. One corner was taken up by a construction which looked more like a pile of rubble left behind by the builders than a rockery, which is what it was supposed to be; another by what Maud called May's mosquito nursery, a small pool which, every spring, covered itself with slime and an occasional lily pad, never a water-lily.

The house, Virginia creeper-clad, with two single-storeyed wings projecting at right angles from its main bulk, surrounded the garden on three sides. Under the dining-room window, in the centre, was a large rose bed where, in season, debilitated roses bloomed consumptively. Due to the way the house was built, in one of the old Norwich courtyards – courts, as they are called locally – surrounded by tall houses of earlier and later construction, few sunbeams found their way into the garden, where such as did collapsed exhausted, at the end of their range. Ferns were what grew there best, laurels, and some other vegetable matter of dubious pedigree, of which the best that could be said for it was that it was at least green.

Looking at the garden with eyes unaccustomedly critical, I worried about what Pillow would think of it, after what he had been used to. However, I didn't worry too much, because I was a great believer in the power of love. I was convinced that my loving care would more than make up for the wide open spaces of St Awdry's.

May Bowden smiled when she saw us coming, which, whilst it boded well, was aesthetically a pity. It was not her best expression. Her false teeth were so large and shiny, with such a lot of pretend gum showing, they would have made her look like the Wolf in *Red Riding Hood* if it hadn't been for the rouge on her cheeks and the lipstick on her lips. As it was, she looked like a raddled old woman with more money than sense.

I was practically certain May Bowden did not get her face powder off cream bonbons bought in the Market Place, because when she bent down and kissed me, which she did from time to time, she didn't smell of vanilla, but of Parma violets. Sometimes, when she kissed me, some of the powder got on to the front of my dress, and I could smell it for a long time afterwards. I once invited Maud to have a sniff, it smelled so nice, but all I got back was, 'Lucky she didn't smear you with her hair. We'd 'a had a fine job getting *that* out!'

May Bowden's hair was a bright red which Maud said came out of a bottle; but my father said he remembered old Mr Bowden, and he had had red hair too, so it couldn't have: to which Maud's dour retort had been to the effect that in that case they must both have used the same bottle.

Old Mr Bowden, who died before I was born, had been a boot-mender who had been so good at his trade that he had ended up owning a boot and shoe factory which he had sold to a large company for a lot of money. The company had stuck a new front on to the factory, but round at the side you could still read, shadows on the dingy bricks, *Bowden & Co. Quality Footwear for Ladies, Gentlemen, and Infants. Artisans' Boots. Only the Best Suffices.*

With the money from the sale of the factory Mr Bowden had

built a lot of horrid little rows of houses in the streets down by the river, and named them after the women in his life, such as Ivy Terrace and May Terrace, named after his wife and his daughter. Nobody knew who Daphne Terrace and Sophie Terrace and Beryl Villas and Millicent Villas were named after, but, as my father said, you had to give a man the benefit of the doubt. When Mr Bowden died, his wife having predeceased him, he left all the houses, and all the rents that came out of them, to his daughter May.

Maud said that he had ground the faces of the poor, to say nothing of making them ill by putting in bad drains, and no good would ever come of money got in that way. As May Bowden had promised to leave all her money to me when she died, I hoped it was only Maud being niggly: that the money hadn't been got as sinfully as she made out.

May Bowden came to the garden gate, pinning a lock of her bright red hair back into place as she came. She wore her hair in a style I was familiar with from old photographs, flat on top as though permanently squashed by the wearing of heavy hats. She leaned over the gate to look at the cowslip ball and the tin with King Edward and Queen Alexandra, both of which I was carrying in the box in which the roast chicken had been packed.

'You dear child!' she trilled, showing all the false teeth at once. 'You've brought me cowslips!'

It was embarrassing to have to explain that the cowslips were spoken for. 'But I'll be sure to bring you some back next time,' I promised, looking sideways at Maud. Mr Fenner, after all, had invited me to come again soon. But all Maud did was to say brutally, 'They'll be over by then.'

'Things are always over when it's my turn.' May Bowden spoke without self-pity, but I felt awful. I put the box down on the ground, picked up the tin, and held it out to her.

'I've brought you back something much better than cowslips!'

May Bowden was in no hurry to take my gift. The stare she directed at King Edward with a hole skewered through his nose held none of the respect she was accustomed to accord royalty.

She said coldly, 'I'm not short of tins, thank you.'

'Not the tin! What's inside!'

Carefully, as Tom had done, I raised the lid of the tin, just enough to get my hand inside, and pressing lightly on the toad's back so that it couldn't make a sudden leap for freedom. Despite the discomforts of the journey, it still felt cool and contented. Its head popped up between my thumb and forefinger, so sweet, so good-humoured, that May Bowden was instantly conquered.

'A frog!' she exclaimed. 'Just like in the fairy stories!'

Maud sniffed. 'If you think that one's going to turn into a prince you've got another think coming! It's not a frog. It's a toad.'

'His name's Pillow,' I intervened hastily. 'I thought he could live in your garden and eat up all the bad insects and things. Adding unwisely, 'And I could come and visit him, being just next door.'

May Bowden withdrew the hand which had been about to lift Pillow out of his makeshift nest. Her countenance had become narrow and suspicious.

'Let's get one thing straight, young lady. Is it your toad or mine? Or are you simply proposing that I should let you use my amenities for your own purposes?'

I gulped. Maud opened her mouth to speak, and shut it again without saying anything. Put on the spot, I assumed my most endearing smile and said, 'It's yours. I already told you.'

'Let him choose where he wants to be.'

May Bowden lifted Pillow out of the tin and placed him tenderly on the cobblestones. The toad's bright eyes rolled from side to side. He took in his new quarters and made a quick decision. Finding the beach pebbles, apparently, a lot easier going with four legs than human beings with two, he bounced over to the rockery and, after another brief pause for inspection, clambered over a giant conch shell and a couple of broken bricks to disappear into a clump of fresh young ferns which had not yet unfolded all their croziers.

'No time lost making himself at home!' May Bowden's voice vibrated with satisfaction. She hugged me to her beaded bodice, gave me another of her Parma-violets kisses. In so doing she must have caught a whiff of Salham St Awdry, because she straightened up abruptly. 'You need a bath, child.'

[77]

Maud said, 'Come on, Sylvie. She's got her present. You don't have to stay to be insulted.'

'Sylvia knows how grateful I am,' May Bowden responded with dignity. 'She also knows I know that when she smells like a manure heap it's not her who's to blame.' Her delight in the gift getting the better of her malice: 'He shall be my watch toad. I shall teach him to croak when anyone comes to the door.'

'Not that sort you won't,' Maud returned with satisfaction. 'All that sort o' toad does is make a kind of cough.'

'In that case I shall buy him some cough drops.' A sudden anxiety: 'I suppose there *is* enough food here in the garden to keep him properly nourished?'

'If there isn't,' Maud suggested nastily, 'feed him a couple of black beetles or a few maggots. Whatever you happen to have in the house.'

May Bowden ignored the affront. She kissed me again, despite the smell, which made Maud hopping mad. So mad that she couldn't wait to lam into me the moment we were away, crossing the courtyard towards our own back door.

'A fine thing!' she exploded. 'My brother go to all that trouble to get you a toad –' she made it sound as if he had scaled Everests, swum Hellesponts – 'an' first chance you get, you go and give it away to that old bag of rubbish.'

'I didn't!' I hissed, keeping my voice down in case May Bowden had her antennae raised. 'All the time I was saying "It's yours" I kept my fingers crossed.'

'You old artful, you!' I preened at her admiration. She put an arm round my shoulders and gave me a small hug. 'Tha's all right, then.'

My parents were not yet back. The house was dark. Maud hung the cowslip ball on the hallstand, to surprise my mother on her return.

Perhaps doubly put on her mettle by May Bowden's aspersions, she not only supervised my bath as if I were still a baby, but insisted on washing my hair, which I could well have done without. When at last I was allowed into my bed, hair damp, my clothes whisked away for laundering before my mother could see them, she brought me, as custom dictated, a book for bedtime reading, for once not consulting my wishes in the matter. The book was *The Frog Prince*.

[78]

I was, however, too sleepy, and said so. What I didn't say was, that for all her soaping and shampooing, I could still, when I turned my nose into the hollow of my upper arm, smell Opposite the Cross Keys on my skin: the sweet-sour smell of poverty.

Between waking and sleep, I could not decide whether to feel glad or sorry I wasn't poor. True, it meant I shouldn't inherit the kingdom of heaven (by 'poor in spirit' I understood too poor even to afford the bottle of Johnnie Walker my father kept out on the sideboard to offer visitors). But whilst it would be galling, on the Last Day, to find the gates of the Celestial City closed against me, I should at least have had May Bowden's money on earth by way of compensation. Whether heaven was worth being poor for was a question which required further thought.

Maud came over to the bed to take *The Frog Prince* away. I reached up my arms, pulled her down and kissed her.

'I do love you,' I said.

Maud said, 'I love you too.' That is, what she actually said was, '*Now* what is it?' but I knew what she meant.

I first went to Salham St Awdry to stay, not just going there for the day, more than a year later, in July, when I was getting over chickenpox. In those days, children who had contracted the disease were deemed infectious so long as any scabs remained in place, so that although I felt, and was, perfectly well, I was forced to stay away from school and forbidden all companionship of my own age, the only permissible alternatives either to stay indoors or else be smuggled out, hat pulled down over face to conceal the tell-tale evidence, to deserted places like Mousehold Heath on the edge of the city, where there was nothing to do but sit and listen to the gorse pods popping in the heat of the summer afternoon.

It was intolerable, and so was Dr Parfitt, a foolish old man whose yellow-stained moustache completely hid his mouth and came down to his chin, almost. He wore the moustache, he said, because it trapped the germs to which his profession particularly exposed him. Whenever he ran into my father, he invariably exhorted him, for his health's sake, to grow his moustache longer. He was, however, puzzled by his female patients, finding it hard to account for the fact that, although on the whole moustacheless, they tended to outlive his male ones.

My mother said it was Dr Parfitt who first mooted the desirability of getting me away to the country – presumably, contact with country children didn't count. It may have been he, or it may have been my mother, driven to distraction by my bored naughtiness; but I am pretty sure it was Maud's idea. What she wanted was to get me away from May Bowden.

May Bowden was my one refuge during this trying time. When I called on her she would take me into her dining-room and bring out several small cloth bags, drawn up at the neck with a cord, whose contents she would shake out on to the green chenille cover of her dining table.

There were buttons and brooches and all manner of small trinkets, some worthless, some, as I now think, of beauty and price. One morning when I pricked my finger on a hat-pin shaped like a dagger she took me into the kitchen to wash and bandage the wound. Because I had been so brave, she said – I carefully omitting to point out that I was years beyond fussing over such small mishaps – I might choose any one thing to take home and keep.

I chose a tiny carved mouse, curled nose to tail, no bigger than a button. And that was what it was, my father told me when I showed it to him, one of the Japanese toggles called netsuke. It was valuable, he said, and I ought to give it back, but my mother said May Bowden would only be offended, and it wasn't as if she couldn't afford it. What had begun to worry my mother a little – she spoke diffidently, for she had difficulty in speaking ill of anybody – was whether it was safe for me to be alone in the house with that dotty old maid.

It did not take much in the way of brains to discern behind this misgiving the fine Italian hand of Maud. Maud even tried to stop me visiting Pillow in the garden, asserting it to be cruelty to wild animals to treat them as pets, brushing aside my insistence that, on the contrary, the little creature looked forward to my coming. When none of her devices succeeded she changed tack, and began to speak of asking Tom whether he couldn't find a she-toad to keep poor lonely Pillow company. I was not deceived. What really moved her, I could swear, was a wicked desire to see her rival's garden awash with baby toads, a mini-plague such as, on a grander scale, had afflicted the Ancient Egyptians. I think she hoped that if only there were enough of them it might induce May Bowden to tell me, as Pharaoh had told the Israelites, get out of my sight for God's sake: never darken my door again.

Only two weeks remained of the summer term when it was decided that I was to go to St Awdrey's, returning to Norwich in September, hopefully a new girl. Terms were struck, Mrs Fenner paying me the compliment of offering to take me for nothing (which I overheard my sorely tried brother Alfred say was about all I was worth in my present frame of mind). Arrangements were made for the carrier to drop off extra supplies every Monday, Wednesday and Friday. Nothing was said about family visits, it being tacitly understood that a little respite from each other's company would be good for all of us. I was, after all, going to be no more than four miles from home, and Maud would be down every Sunday to report on how I was getting along and whether I needed anything.

That Maud, my handmaiden and footstool, was not coming with me was the biggest surprise of the whole arrangement. Unable to envisage any other life but one in which she was perpetually within call, I had not noticed, as I grew older, that her primary function of nurserymaid had been progressively subsumed by those of cook, housekeeper, Supreme Being. Mrs Hewitt still came every Monday and Tuesday to do the washing and the ironing, but the services of a dim creature called Edie, whose duties consisted principally of doing down the stairs and whitestoning the front step, had been dispensed with; Maud rising that little bit earlier to ensure that no one, not even the postman on his first round, should see one of her exalted status performing such a menial task.

Once I had got over the shock, the prospect of Opposite the Cross Keys *sans* Maud grew ever more delectable, though at the same time a little unnerving. The prospect of freedom, which I had been taught was a good thing, even though I was not quite sure what it was, nor what you did with it once you got it, excited me. Freedom that meant not having Maud telling you what to do, telling you what not to do. Freedom that meant, the reverse of the coin, having to tell yourself what to do, and taking the consequences.

[81]

One day after dinner, as Maud was changing her morning apron for her fancy afternoon one with lace round the edges, I put my arms round her.

'I do wish you were coming with me,' I said, meaning it just at that moment; and also, not meaning it. At that time of life, believing two contradictory propositions simultaneously presented no problems. Life was a thousand different roads along which one could travel at one and the same time.

'Mind what you're doing to that apron!' She unclasped my arms firmly, but her eyes were gentle. 'There's worse dangers at sea. You'll get used to it.'

'I won't, you know. I shall miss you dreadfully.'

'Tell us another!'

Two days before I was due to leave, something awful happened. My scabs fell off, all together. I woke up in the morning and there they were, on my pillow, dot, dot, dot. With them went the whole *raison d'être* for my visit to St Awdry's. I would be sent back to school. I wasn't infectious any more.

Dr Parfitt and his moustache were due after breakfast to pronounce finally on my fitness for the journey. It was a time for desperate measures.

With my right hand I delicately removed the shed scabs from the pillow, transferring them one at a time to my left palm which I kept extended flat in front of me. Choosing quiet floorboards which wouldn't inform Maud I was up, I tiptoed over to the dressing table and fished out the jar of glue I kept in one of the small drawers which flanked the central mirror.

The scabs were aggravatingly brittle, the glue maddeningly gooey, but I persevered. By the time the last fleck of scab had disintegrated into dust I had glued the greater number of them back in place. My face, scabby, infectious, smiled back at me in triumph even as I heard Maud's step upon the stair.

In fact, I looked scabbier than ever, thanks to frilly little edgings of glue which outlined the scabs rather as Maud's lace outlined her afternoon apron. Dr Parfitt looked at me thoughtfully, riffled through his moustache as if looking for his prescription pad, and prescribed his runny cream. He had two in his repertoire – one the consistency of dumpling batter, the other

[82]

more like a stiff pastry mix. Maud always contended that his selection of one rather than the other depended on what his wife had had over from dinner the day before.

One of the questions that gave me much thought in the days before I left for St Awdry's was, where was I going to sleep? Somehow I sensed I was never to be allowed through that door at the side of the fireplace.

'Am I going to take Alfred's camp bed, then?' I finally asked when I could contain my curiosity no longer. Maud looking surprised, I explained, 'For me to sleep on, I mean.'

'What you want that ole thing for? Wha's the matter with the sofa?'

'It's a very nice sofa,' I agreed placatingly. 'Only, it *is* a little prickly.'

'Should 'a thought of that before. Not too late to change your mind.'

'Oh no!' I protested, alarmed. 'I'm sure it will be beautifully comfortable, once I get used to it.'

Maud actually grinned. 'No call to overdo it! I warn't born yesterday. Mattress pad an' a couple of blankets 'll take care of the pricks. You'll sleep like a queen, see if you don't.'

There was indeed something queenlike about my departure for Salham St Awdry. My brother, who was to deliver me and my goods to Opposite the Cross Keys, had piled the car so high that, give or take a Morris Oxford in place of Tudor baggage carts, the resemblance to the Virgin Queen embarking for her royal progress of Norfolk in 1578 must have been very marked.

'Sure that's the lot?' he inquired caustically, having, with difficulty, wedged me into the front seat on top of a pile of pillows.

May Bowden came out to the car with her own contribution: a wooden painting case and an easel, items Alfred hadn't the heart to turn down, even though the easel had lost the pegs which held the canvas in place, and the case, when she tried to open it in order to display its incomparable contents (all May Bowden's benefactions were, in her own word, incomparable) proved immovably cemented with tubes of paint put away any old how on the last of the dear, dead days when she had been a young lady, genteelly sketching.

All in all, it wasn't an easy day for my poor brother. Arrived at Opposite the Cross Keys in the middle of a blazing afternoon, we found no sign of Mrs Fenner: only Ellie sitting outside in the sun, combing her hair. I went up to her and said, at my most winsome, 'Ellie, this is my brother Alfred.' And, 'Alfred, this is Maud's sister Ellie. I don't believe you've met.'

Over a pile of bedding, my brother's face, frank and handsome, smiled down at the woman.

'Sorry I can't shake hands,' he apologized. 'I'm a bit loaded, as you can see.'

'Please yourself,' returned Ellie, turning her back on him. 'All one to me.'

If Ellie was a shock to my brother, it was as nothing to his first sight of the interior of Opposite the Cross Keys. Inured by many visits since my first to its dirt, its smells, I hadn't thought to prepare him. I had forgotten how, that first time, I had been physically sick.

Judging by Alfred's sudden pallor, he wasn't far short of the same condition himself.

'Sylvia!' he hissed, keeping his voice down for fear of being overheard by Ellie, outside. 'You can't stay here! Impossible! If any of us had ever guessed how it was once you got inside –!' He took a firmer grasp of the blankets and pillows. 'I'm going to take these things straight back to the car. We'll think of some excuse.'

'You mustn't! You mustn't!' In my eagerness I grabbed at his burden and the pillows tumbled to the floor. Gyp waddled over, lay down on top of them, and scratched himself luxuriously.

'Get off, Gyp! Alfred, you mustn't!' I didn't care if Ellie heard me or not. 'You don't understand! It's lovely here, it really is! Lovely!'

'Lovely? This?'

'The loveliest place in the world.'

That stopped him. He stood goggling at me. After a little, he dumped the blankets on the sofa.

'This do?' He bent down and pushed Gyp off the pillows;

picked them up and placed them on top of the blankets. He kissed me. I hugged him tight.

'Oh, Alfred!'

'You're a funny little thing and no mistake.' He looked about him, taking in the room's gorgeous awfulness with a look of bafflement. 'I'd sooner spend my hols breaking stones on Dartmoor. And that sister of Maud's! What Chamber of Horrors did they dig her out of?'

My heart jumped with gratitude. The Fenners' calm acceptance of Ellie's beauty had always disturbed me; made me doubt whether I was capable of making a proper judgement. If I could be wrong about Ellie, I could be wrong about everything.

I covered up my relief with a giggle. 'The Fenners think she's beautiful.'

'Not Maud as well?' I nodded. 'And she's the one says May Bowden is barmy!' He moved back towards the door. 'I'd better get that food out of the sun.'

'Put it on the table,' I directed. 'Then Mrs Fenner will see it when she comes in.' I went over to my brother and looked up into his face, straining to put into my own all the strength of my feelings. 'Promise you won't say anything back in St Giles. Promise!'

A little wait, while he thought it over. Then – bliss! – 'OK. I won't say anything. Am I allowed, though, to tell Maud I saw her sister, and thought I'd never seen such a vision of loveliness in all my born days?'

Mrs Fenner came in. She had been over to Mr Fenner's allotment and she came in with a basinful of peas. Her face was sunburned, and she looked fat without her stays, but firm, not flabby like Ellie, and nice to touch.

She turned the peas out on to the table, and we sat together shelling them into a colander she fetched from the scullery, eating almost as many as we shelled, and throwing the pods back in the basin. It was a lovely beginning, precisely because it didn't seem like a beginning at all, but a continuation of something that had been going on already. Mrs Fenner's only comment on the three cartons of Norwich groceries was, 'You eat all that, gal, you'll blow up like a balloon.'

'It's not just for me. It's for all of us.'

'Oh ah?' Mrs Fenner commented, on a note of mild interest. Then: 'You sure us lot got the right teeth?'

I saw that we had done something dreadfully wrong. Why hadn't Maud warned us that it was dangerous to give things to people who couldn't give things back?

I managed, choking – what I actually said was that a pea had gone down the wrong way, 'You don't have to eat it if you don't want to.'

'Tha's a thought.' Mrs Fenner flashed me a brilliant smile. She didn't seem angry, that was something. 'You're a clever gal, Sylvie. I'm goin' to learn a lot from you, time you're here, I can see that. Only thing, where we going to stick it, out of the way? That Charlie come in, see anything in a tin, he thinks it grew in the Garden o' Eden. I know!' she exclaimed. 'We'll put 'em in next door, tha's what we'll do.' She hefted the largest of the cartons in her strong arms.

'The Harleys', you mean?' I felt confused. The Harleys in the end cottage were very clean, very old, very deaf, very silent. The Fenners didn't have much to do with them. Their son was a butcher in a good way of business who paid their rent and saw they didn't go short of anything.

'Don't talk daft! They don't need charity no more 'n we do. The other side!'

She levered herself sideways out of the front door, balancing the carton on one generous hip. In a moment I heard a creaking noise: a door being forced open on its rusty hinge. Whilst I waited, frozen to the spot, I could hear Mrs Fenner, through the connecting wall, moving about inside the derelict cottage. I distinguished the sound of the carton being dumped on the floor, jars and tins tinkling prettily.

'Scared of the ole josser, were you?' Mrs Fenner inquired jovially, re-entering. 'No cause to be afeard of him, poor ole bugger. Never hurt nobody, alive nor dead.' Hoisting a second carton into position: 'You don't have to come in there, if you don't want to.'

Miserably I blurted out what was on my mind: the arrangements made with the carrier.

'Tha's all right, lovey,' was the response. 'If yer ma wants to send you down something special, tha's different –'

'No, it isn't!' Unable to put into words that I couldn't stand being treated at Opposite the Cross Keys as if I were a different species, unable to digest the food of the natives, I took refuge in shouting. 'I'm going straight down to the Post Office and phone Maud up to cancel it!'

Mrs Fenner let her load down for a moment. She looked concerned.

'Phone? You sure you know how to use it? You be careful, d'you hear? You get one of those electric shocks, Maud'll have something to say. You let that Miss Lethaby get the number for you. Tha's what she's paid for.'

'All I have to do is ask them to reverse the charges.'

'I don't know nothing about that. You ask Miss Lethaby. If the ole bitch goes and gets herself electrocuted, tha's her business.' Taking hold of the carton again, she favoured me with that smile of hers which put all right between us. 'An' don't go an' get yourself run over crossing the road. That won't do me no good wi' Maud either!'

One bonus about sleeping on the sofa was that I couldn't go to bed until everybody else was ready to turn in for the day. After a supper of bread and jam and condensed milk tea, we took our chairs outside to the pavement – all except Mr Fenner, who preferred to stay by the fire reading his *Old Moore's Almanac* – and sat watching the cars and the traps, the carts and the bicycles going home to roost like the rooks still making a great cackle in the beeches at the back of the pond.

Happiness was all round me – something I knew, if I wanted to, I could reach out and feel under my hand. There I sat, secure, watching other people scurrying past, poor things, still seeking what only I, so far, had had the good luck to achieve.

I played games with Tom, counting how many black cars passed by, or how many brown horses. He was better with the horses than with the cars, and with neither if they came to more than ten. I soon learned to call an end to each game before that point was reached. Even Charlie, seemingly quite pleased to see me, joined in a game or two, until one of his pals came by and they went off to the Swan together.

[87]

Mrs Fenner warned him, 'You late, don't you wake up Sylvie.'

How lovely to hear in words that I wasn't to be packed off home at the end of the day!

In the long light of the summer evening I even saw one or two people I knew from Norwich: Mr Martin the butcher, driving his white van with the picture of a bull on one side and a sheep on the other – we were on the sheep side – and Mr Hooper, who cut my father's hair, driving with his wife in his Austin Seven, the first car he had driven in his life. Mr Hooper had told my father that the day before he collected the car from the dealer's, he had gone to St John the Baptist's, the Roman Catholic church at the top of St Giles, and vowed to the Virgin that he would never, so long as he lived, drive above twenty miles an hour. As he came round the bend by the Swan you could tell, by the line of cars bunched up behind him, that he was keeping his promise, and wouldn't need to go to Confession on that account at least.

There were several cars full of young people going the other way – to Cromer, probably, where, in the season, there was almost always a dance on somewhere; on the pier, or in one of the big hotels on the cliffs. As one of the cars went past, its driver went *honk-de-de-honk-honk* on his klaxon, putting the rooks in a frightful tizzy. I thought it must be one of my brother's friends, who had recognized me sitting there outside Opposite the Cross Keys. But it wasn't. Just high spirits and the general joyfulness of the evening.

I did see one young person I knew – coming away from the coast, though, towards Norwich. I could hardly say that she knew me. I knew her because she was beautiful and strange and she had a red Alvis car – you didn't see many red cars in those days – and also because her father was Mr Lee, who taught my father Chinese writing.

Mr Lee was Chinese, but Miss Lee his daughter was half-Chinese and half I don't know what. There didn't seem to be any Mrs Lee. When she went out she sometimes wore cheongsams and sometimes ordinary dresses, but the result was never ordinary whatever she wore. She looked gorgeous, but so fierce! She looked like the dragon on the vase my parents had bought in Mr Lee's curio shop. Her eyebrows were very black and came together in the middle, which was threatening.

[88]

I recognized the red Alvis before I recognized her, and I recognized her black eyebrows before I recognized the rest of her. She was driving fast. I wondered what was going to happen when she caught up with the queue behind Mr Hooper. She wouldn't like it one bit, I was sure of that.

We came back indoors at the beginning of dusk – one or two cars, no more, with their sidelights on – to find that, within, it was already night.

Mrs Fenner lit the lamp; a poor way for one who had never done anything to make light except press a switch on a wall to describe the absorbed ritual of preparation: the oil, the wick, the mantel, the shade, elements in an act of communion, as they might be the wafer and the wine. And at last the match, the flame, as on that first day when God said Let there be light: and there was light.

We sat round the table, quiet, bathing in the light as in a benediction. I believe it was done for me, an extravagance and a celebration. Left to themselves, I'm pretty sure, they would have made their preparations for the night, such as they were, in what was left of day, and gone to their beds in the gathering dark.

I was enchanted, but fearful. Mr Fenner had let the fire die down. The merest glimmer of red showed behind the bars. How was I, far from my own darling bed, to face the country night that lay in wait?

Mr Fenner and Ellie were the first to disappear through the door at the side of the fireplace. Their footsteps clumped upstairs, sounded overhead for a little, then silence. Mrs Fenner made up my bed on the sofa, then took me into the scullery, dipped my facecloth into the water bucket and, as if I were a baby, wiped over my face and hands. Nothing was said about washing my teeth, and I didn't like to ask.

In bed, I thought I felt the prickles of the horsehair, but that was probably only because I expected it. Mrs Fenner was very gentle in her jolly way. She tucked me in, and began to tell me stories about her two grandfathers, the old men in the photographs over the sofa who, I could take her word for it, would watch over me through the night. Guardian angels wouldn't do it better.

They were a pair, she asserted. Not on speaking terms, it stood to reason, they were so different. The one with the high collar and the muttonchop whiskers had been on the starchy side, but kind. He used to give her pennies for singing hymns. Once, would you believe it, he knitted her a pair of mittens. He always said no man who knitted would ever strike a fellow being in anger.

Mrs Fenner burst out laughing. Not even the memory of her revered ancestors could restrain her mirth. She was sitting at the end of the sofa, and made it shake as if it too were enjoying the joke.

'Didn't stop him sticking one of his ruddy needles up some bugger's backside. Never knew what it was about, I was too young, on'y he weren't the sort to bend a good knitting needle out o' true fer nothing!'

And the other one, the one with the dark curls, the goatee and the romantic, not to say moony, air? Don't let it fool you, Mrs Fenner said. He was a one, a gambler and a great one for the women. Always in trouble and always landing on his feet however far he fell. Married a widow with a nice little pub over Attlebridge way. Drunk himself to death, o' course, but did it in a warm bed and on the best liquor money could buy.

Mrs Fenner kissed me a resounding goodnight, and blew out the lamp, leaving me to the care of the two of them.

Years later – I must have been getting on for twelve – I came across pictures of Mrs Fenner's two grandpas in a school history book. The captions underneath said that they were Gladstone and Disraeli.

Shaken to the core, I rushed to Maud. She was sitting at the kitchen table, sewing.

'Look at that!' I thrust the book under her nose, furious that I had been made a fool of. 'D'you know who your mother's grandfathers really were? Two Prime Ministers of England!'

Maud never batted an eyelid; went on cobbling up one of my school stockings into the hideous pucker she called a darn. She completed her handiwork and bit off the thread before replying.

'What about it?' she said then. 'Yours in't the on'y family wi' brains.'

Chapter Eight

I must have slept, because I never heard Charlie come home. I was completely unaware that Gyp had left his smelly old rug to heave his ancient carcass on to the blanket covering my legs, though, given his girth and his age, the feat could not have been accomplished without a great to-do of scrabbling and snuffling.

Yet I do not remember sleeping and, once awake, could not imagine that I could ever have slept through the noise which came from the derelict cottage on the other side of the wall.

Despite its awfulness, there is something reassuring about a big noise – a thunderclap, say, an explosion. Whatever else it may be, it is one thing: it happens and is over. A single rat, on the other hand, makes a small noise, something between a squeak and a wheeze; and a colony of rats, an empire of them, still does not add up to a big noise, but to something far worse – to an infinite number of individual noises which do not blend into a whole but remain obstinately apart, each decibel insisting upon its own unique place in the brazen-throated universe. Hearing them, you do not simply screw up your face and think *Rats!* You begin counting the uncountable.

I found out, that first night, that there were rats who wheezed basso and rats who squeaked castrato; rats who played tympani, making their tiny feet drum out Tartar hoof-beats galloping off the steppes and up to the gates of Vienna. The noises sounded extremely bad-tempered, as if rats didn't like rats any more than people did.

By the end of the week – by which time I had learned to sleep through everything they could throw at me – I could have found this apparent absence of love in a rat's life pathetic. As it was, I stood up in my bed, much to the annoyance of Gyp, interrupted in the middle of a snore, and slapped the wall with all my strength.

'Shut up, do you hear! Stop it!'

The result was a momentary lull before the noises redoubled. I might as well have cried 'Encore!' Above me, invisible in the darkness, Mrs Fenner's grandpas vibrated to the blow.

Now it was the old josser's turn. There was a bang and a scooping sound, as of a cardboard carton being pushed over a rough floor. Tins and bottles rattled against each other. The old josser sounded as bad-tempered as the rats.

Gingerly, I let myself down, barefooted, from the sofa on to the gritty floor, on to those lowlier forms of life which, rightly or wrongly, I imagined to be scuttling about there. I felt my way to the chest of drawers and dragged open the drawer where Mrs Fenner kept her cutlery, such as it was, feeling around until I located what I wanted.

The next part was harder: back past the sofa to the front door, which I unbolted, and out on to the pavement. The night air was an unexpected balm after the smell within, but there was a loneliness about the country dark which set me shivering with more than cold. The only thing consoling was the road, the road that led home to St Giles, shining in the starlight like a ribbon of black taffeta.

From outside, the noises from the derelict cottage sounded distant, scarcely noises at all. I squatted down, gravel pushing up between my toes, and slipped Mrs Fenner's tin opener under the door.

I awoke to a drab half-light and Mrs Fenner cutting bread at the table. The fire was red, the kettle steaming on the hob. Four bottles of assorted shape filled with tea stood on the table.

I awoke with eyes stinging. Mrs Fenner was making onion sandwiches, thick-cut rings between the thick bread. She saw that I was awake and reached across the table with a slice of bread for me to take.

'Press it over yer eyes, it'll stop the watering. Then eat it up without messing about. It's all the breakfast you're going to get, if we aren't to get there too late. Way you were sleepin' I thought you were going to be there till Doomsday.'

I took the bread and followed her instructions. It did indeed make my eyes stop watering, even if it did make the bread soggier than I could have wished. I swung my legs out of bed, almost into the pink chamber pot with *Evening Exercises* printed on it in gold. The chamber pot had already been well used.

'Get on with it,' Mrs Fenner urged. 'Shy? You in't the on'y person with a bum.'

She went across to the fire, lifted the kettle off the hob and brought it over to the table, where she removed the lid and, with a spoon, fished about for half a dozen eggs which had been cooking inside. These she distributed, one to go with each sandwich, making up five packages wrapped in pages of the *Daily Telegraph*. The sixth portion she placed to one side, presumably for Ellie's dinner.

'You tell your pa, now, to go back to the *Daily Mail*. Can't get on with this what's-it-called. I always say you can't beat the *Daily Mail* for sangwiches.'

We went out into the early morning. On the other side of the road the Cross Keys was barely visible in the mist. Overhead the rooks sounded muted, bunged up with catarrh. Only the hardness of the road beneath my plimsolls was real, everything else was a dream, deeper than any which might engulf me on Mrs Fenner's sofa. I felt damp and chilled and breathless with happiness.

Breathless, too, with trying to keep up with Mrs Fenner, who was hurrying along at a great pace. We were going plucking, she informed me, over to Randall's at Stratton Strawless. Although no hands were actually taken on before eight o'clock, if you weren't there well ahead of time you might as well never have started. *They* would be there first, you could depend on it, grabbing all the places available.

'Not that there's a bleeding one of 'em plucks half as clean as we do, us from the village. Leave on enough feathers to trim a hat, that lot. We do that, we'd be docked an' no next time. But them – not a word said! It's that bloody foreman, silly ole fool. 'Fraid they'll put the evil eye on him if he says anything.'

I had no need to ask who *they* were. Only one kind of people in the vicinity of Salham St Awdry attracted that particular inflection, that curl of the lip. The gypsies. Their encampment, in a bit of scrubland half-way to Salham Norgate, the next village along the road, looked quite inviting with its brightly painted caravans, fires of sticks crackling under cauldrons, and the horses and ponies hobbled close by.

The men and women who lived there were less welcoming, regarding all outsiders with closed faces and, with a flaunting insolence that was next thing to a smack in the face, crossing to the other side of the road to avoid passing close by anyone not of the tribe. Even the gypsy children, tumbling down the road bright with laughter, evaporated through the hedges if they saw you coming.

'Hedge-rooters! Diddikoy! Pickers an' stealers!' declared Mrs Fenner.

On our way we had been conscious, in the thinning fog, the strengthening sun, of others taking the same road as ourselves, other village women, middle-aged, soberly pinafored, similarly off to a day's plucking. 'Morning,' we greeted them, not slowing down; and 'Morning,' they responded, showing no ill will when we pulled ahead.

After we passed the gypsy encampment the atmosphere was less amicable. The women on the road now were younger, wearing flowered headscarves and patterned aprons over voluminous skirts. Many of them carried babies, slung in a shawl in front of them or carried on their backs like Red Indian papooses. The babies were sallow and dark-eyed, not one of them so much as whimpering.

The gypsy women travelled in small groups, shouting to each other as they went. Whether it was the deadening effect of what remained of the mist, or the overwhelming strangeness of the little cavalcade, I could not make out a word they said.

'Are they talking English?' I asked Mrs Fenner.

'Double Dutch, I shouldn't be surprised.'

As we drew near to Randall's, in the narrow loke* which led to the plucking shed, things got distinctly nasty.

'Who you think you're shoving?' yelled a young woman who seemed bowed down with the weight of a fat boy-child with flaming red hair.

* loke: Norfolk for lane or narrow alley

[94]

Mrs Fenner, ready to use her elbows to guard our places in the queue, restrained herself nobly when she saw the size of the infant.

'That one looks big enough to carry *you*,' she commented, yielding ground, ''stead of the other way round.'

'Big enough to give you a poke in the kisser, you silly ole arse-hole,' was the gracious acknowledgement of the good deed, as the young woman forged ahead, unregarding.

Mrs Fenner went red. The gypsy women were all around us now, smelling, not unpleasantly, smoked – cured like kippers, I suppose, from sitting over so many camp fires. They looked so hard and brown and Mrs Fenner so soft and red that I suddenly felt frightened, and ventured, in a feeble attempt to defuse the situation, 'At least we know now they speak English.'

Mrs Fenner, heaven be praised, dissolved into one of her great and wonderful laughs.

'And do it so ladylike too! It do your heart good to hear it.'

The plucking shed was a long, low building with windows to which clung feathers and less identifiable debris from chickens that had long since gone to the great roost in the sky. At one end was a brick copper with the wooden cover off, so that one could hear, if not see, the water bubbling within, and watch the steam rising up to the metal beams in the roof and falling back in a continuous dew.

Trestle tables, with benches either side, took up the best part of the space, the gypsies sitting on one side, the village women the other: some forty or fifty in all. It looked as though the foreman, who did the hiring, had hit upon a strict equality of numbers as the best compromise between getting the birds plucked properly and averting the curse of the Romanies.

By mid-morning the shed was hellishly hot. The day was summery, the copper kept well stoked. Each bird was immersed briefly before being passed to one of the pluckers, its time in the boiling water too brief to do much in the way of loosening the feathers, but at least it killed off most of the assorted lice which had called that once brave plumage home. Since the chickens carried their guts still inside them, and would until they were spilled forth on to some kitchen table, a longer and more effective bath would have shortened their shelf-life beyond what even the refrigerator-less housewife of the Twenties was prepared to put up with.

The foreman and his two male helpers tended the copper, removed the sacks filled with feathers, kept the women supplied with birds, and removed the plucked chickens, exchanging each for a metal tag which was to be turned in at the end of the day as evidence of how much pay was owing. Before the morning was half-gone, two of the gypsy women came to blows, one asserting that the other had stolen two of her tags. They clawed at each other like wild things, the men looking on with broad smiles, nobody else taking any notice: such entertainments cost money in precious plucking time lost. Off came the headscarves, revealing bleached-blonde heads that looked comically incongruous above the weatherbeaten faces. The shed resounded with blasphemies.

After a while, during which a fair quantity of the yellow hair was disengaged from its anchorage, the two contestants simmered down, and minutes later were shouting amiably to each other as they settled afresh to their plucking. There was about them a virtuous air, an awareness of having made a contribution to the proceedings.

The air was rancid, full of dust and feather particles that fell in a constant drizzle on the heads and shoulders of the operators. Everyone was coated with grey. When I suggested to Mrs Fenner that the gypsy women were wise to wear headscarves and we should have covered our heads similarly, she brushed feathers from her mouth with the back of her hand, and exclaimed, 'What! An' look like a bloody fortune teller!'

As a child, I did not rate a seat at the table. I sat on a sackful of feathers on the concrete floor, with a chicken between my knees, having a go at the stumps Mrs Fenner hadn't had time to get at. At first the sight of the dead heads, the filmed eyes, floppy combs and sad, naked necks was more than I could stomach, and I was quietly sick under the table, taking care that none of the vomit got on to the chicken I was currently working on.

But then I found a friend.

'You do it this way,' said a voice at my side, and I had my first sight of Nellie Smith.

Nellie Smith was a scrawny child with a thin, pointed face which looked at the same time both young and old. I never knew how old she was – I doubt whether she knew herself – or if she were younger than me or older. She had enormous dark eyes rimmed with flesh which was darker than the rest of her sallow face – eyes which, even when alive with mischief, still regarded the world with a melancholy unredeemed by hope. Her hair, round which she wore a bandeau of rag, was black and curly and hung down below her shoulders.

She had on a woman's dress, fussy with too many frills, and pinned up at the hem with safety pins. Even so, it reached nearly to her feet, its excess width belted in with a piece of string knotted at the waist. Its sleeves flopped over her bony wrists. On her feet, sockless, she wore a pair of boots several sizes too large for her. The little miss from Eldon House thrilled to be speaking to a girl who looked the way Nellie Smith looked.

The girl put her dirty thumbs together, the nails bitten to the quick, and pressed them down on either side of a stump of feather filled with some black secretion, embedded in the pallid corpse of the chicken. The fragment of quill jumped out smartly, the horrible goo with it.

'Don't pull,' said the girl. 'Press. That's the trick of it.'

I tried it myself, and found the method worked beautifully, if that was the right word to apply to such an occupation. I was about to thank the gypsy girl for her help when 'Crikey!' she exclaimed, and dodged under Mrs Fenner's skirt. A tall man with pince-nez had come into the shed and was speaking to the foreman who had his hands spread out in elaborate disclaimer about something or other. The man began to walk along the length of the trestle tables, up one side and down the other. There was something chilling about his passing, and the gypsies and the village women alike fell silent, afraid of they knew not what.

To my dismay, the man stopped and stood looking down at me. He gave a little nod of satisfaction, as if he had found what he was looking for; took a notebook and fountain pen out of his

[97]

jacket pocket. Then he took another look at me, a proper look this time, and his expression soured with disappointment.

'Chickenpox!'

He put the pen and notebook away, ramming them into his pocket with unnecessary force.

I vouchsafed timidly, 'I can't go back to school till the scabs drop off.'

'You don't have to tell *me* that!' The eyes behind the pince-nez became suddenly sharp and suspicious and I thought, he's noticed the glue. But all he said was, 'I've had no notice of any case of chickenpox in the village school.'

'I expect that's because I don't go to the village school. I go to Eldon House in Norwich.'

'Eldon House!' Now the man looked completely floored, not to say disbelieving. 'What on earth are you doing here if you go to Eldon House?'

Mrs Fenner spoke up.

'She's staying with me, Mr Nosy Parker, not that it's any of your business. Still, if you want to sit down an' lend us a hand with these here birds while I'm talkin', I'll be happy to squeeze up an' make room an' tell you how such an amazing thing comes about. If not, mister, bugger off an' try somewhere else. Here in St Awdry's we don't think much of dirty old men who go about making conversations wi' little girls.'

'Madam!' the man roared. 'I am the school attendance officer!'

'Oh ah?' Mrs Fenner sounded as if she did not believe a word of it. 'In that case, go and attend, and let folk as han't got time to dawdle about get on wi' making an honest living!'

When the man had gone, face puckered, Mrs Fenner bent down, lifted her skirt and commanded, 'You c'n come out now, you cheeky mauther.'

'Ta, missus.' Nellie Smith crawled out of her hiding place. 'Thought the old goat had got me to rights that time. Been shitting his britches to do it ever since we come here, I can't think why, when I can read an' write, I bet, well as he can.' Adding ingratiatingly, 'You got lovely legs, missus.'

'Tha's right.' Mrs Fenner nodded in grave acknowledgement

of the compliment. 'Tha's what come o' being a bally dancer, up on me toes all hours.' She let out one of her enormous guffaws. 'Ruddy little liar, like all your kind . . .' She spoke, for a wonder, with something close to affection: I had never heard her use that tone to a gypsy before. 'You two hungry? Sylvie knows where the sangwiches are . . .'

We sat, the two of us, on a bale of straw under the table, eating the onion sandwiches, breathing the smell of them into each other's faces, our eyes watering, the mucus from our noses running into the bread. The straw pricked my legs whilst we ate, and I thought, from now on, whenever I feel straw pricking at my legs, even if it happens when I'm an old, old woman, I'll remember sitting here eating onion sandwiches with Nellie Smith.

She looked admiringly at my scabs and commented, 'Some buggers have all the luck. I had some o' those, that bloke could stuff his snout up his own backside. Two kids at the camp got scarlet fever. It's a secret, or they'll take them away to Isolation, so you won't tell, will you?' I shook my head fervently. I would not have given them away if it had been the Black Death. 'Well, I bin sharing a bed wi' one of 'em for a month, but d'you think I caught it? Not on your nelly!'

That was when she told me Nellie Smith was her name, and no, in answer to my query, she hadn't come plucking with her ma, but with Mavis, the one with that red-haired baby as big as a bus.

'Is Mavis part of your family, then?'

'No!' Nellie Smith's mouth closed like a trap. I wondered what I'd said wrong. In a minute, however, she began to tell me about her ma, who was up in Yorkshire living on a farm, and who was going to send for her once she'd got the feller she'd gone off with used to the idea.

With no apparent perturbation she told me that they'd all been up to Appleby for the Horse Fair like they always did, and the farmer to whom they'd sold the roan colt had fallen head over heels in love with her ma, which was no surprise, seeing she was a Romany princess, not like that Princess Mary who was only a Gorgio, like any other.

Although I knew from reading the *News of the World* to Mrs Fenner that husbands and wives did not always stay together till death did them part, and that marriages could end in several ways, some of them very nasty, I found it impossible to conceive that my own mother might one day elect to run off with a fellow from Yorkshire or anywhere else; or that, if she did the inconceivable, I would be able to talk about it in the matter-of-fact way in which Nellie Smith spoke of her mother's desertion. She laughed aloud to think what the farmer had paid for the roan colt, the besotted fool. Her dad had cleaned up a packet.

'Mind you, he were a lovely bit of horseflesh. Wouldn't be surprised if he won the National. I don't mind telling you, I was right sorry to see that colt go.' She finished, 'Still, what I say is, since ma's living wi' the bloke what bought it, it's still in the family, in a manner of speaking.'

I offered, 'You'll see it again when your ma sends for you.'

'Tha's right,' said Nellie Smith, her eyes bleak.

Meantime, it turned out, the gypsy girl was earning all the money she could, saving all the money she could, stealing all the money she could – she said this last with a hard stare as if daring me to make something of it – so that, when the call came from Yorkshire, she'd have the price of the fare, and a bit over.

'Want to hear somethin' funny? I like school, I actually do. I like all that learning, an' doing tables. On'y you can't get rich sittin' in a school desk, can you? An' then again, I won't be forced. That old pruneface got no business to force me. It's a free country, tha's what my dad says, though he don't say wha's free about it, 'cept his hand always ready with a clout, for nothing. You can't get to Yorkshire free, I know that all right!'

Which brought her back to my scabs, that perfect alibi for non-attendance at school. She asked wistfully, 'Are you dead sure you aren't still catching?'

'Dead sure,' I confirmed. 'But –' a glow spreading through me as the idea took hold – 'I tell you what –'

My chest, invisible to the outside world, was still spattered with several scabs not yet ready to drop off. In their state of near-ripeness, I was pretty sure, it shouldn't be too difficult to prise them from their moorings. And I had brought my glue with me to St Awdry's in case the ones on my face fell off betimes.

'Would you do that?' Nellie Smith cried, when I had unfolded my plan. 'Would you reely do that for me?'

'Yes.' I could hardly speak, so choked was I with the happiness of cementing – or rather, gluing – my friendship with this marvellous girl. 'It's nothing, really.'

By the time the working day was over, the sun still scorching the sky, we were, all of us, grey all over, our throats so coated we could only croak. The bottle of cold tea, the juicy onion rings, had become a tantalizing memory.

I don't know how much they paid Mrs Fenner for her nine hours of unremitting labour, but she seemed satisfied. The gypsies, to the manifest pleasure of the foreman and his assistants, picked up their skirts then and there, and stowed their pay away in their drawers or their petticoats. I was given fourpence and a pat on the head for my pains, which seemed to me such monstrous injustice that I burst out without thinking, 'Is that all?'

Whilst the other workers stared in admiration, I was given an extra tuppence and a chuck under the chin – I have said I was a fetching child. When, on the way back down the loke, I asked Nellie Smith how much she'd got, she opened a tightly closed fist and disclosed three sixpences.

'One they gi' me. Two I took.'

'You didn't!'

'Knocked over one of them little piles on the table accidental, an' then helped stack 'em up again, like the little lady I am. I'd 'a got more if it hadn't bin for that fucking foreman watching me like a cat watching a mousehole.'

'I wish I'd thought of that.'

Nellie Smith paused in mid-stride and looked me over reflectively. 'Nah,' she pronounced at last. 'You don't reely. You ain't the type. Give the game away just looking at you.' She asked conversationally, 'Your ma or pa ever swipe anything?'

'I – I shouldn't think so.'

'There you are then!' Nellie Smith spoke with a touch of patronage; even of pity. 'You can't go agin nature. It's got to be in the blood. Someone like you might as well give up afore you start.'

*

We arranged to meet, after tea, behind the ruined pigsties which were a little along the road from the gypsy encampment. Nellie dismissed my invitation to come to Opposite the Cross Keys as if I were a bloody fool to suggest such a thing. I soon learned that the gypsy girl had an instinctive distrust of any house which was not on wheels; and wondered how she would make out on that Yorkshire farm where the Romany princess awaited the coming of her daughter.

I suggested, carefully casual – I'd have given anything to see the inside of a real gypsy caravan, 'I don't mind coming over to your place, if you'd rather.'

'Don't talk daft!' was her answer which, perhaps because I was tired (for I had, of course, known all along what her reply would be), had me sulking all the long walk back from Stratton Strawless, through Salham Norgate and beyond.

As we neared the encampment a red sports car nosed out of the entrance. A large man with a black felt hat pushed back on his bushy red hair, his collarless shirt unbuttoned and stomach hanging over a wide leather belt worn well down on the hips, stood on the steps of what turned out to be Nellie Smith's caravan. Otherwise there was only an old woman about, sitting on a stool outside a caravan which was painted a dark green and looked like an outsize barrel. Further back, some naked children played with a piece of wood, and a woman bent over something that steamed in a big black pot hung on a tripod over hot ashes.

Before Miss Lee drove her car over the grass verge, she twisted round in the driving seat, looked back at the red-haired man and waved. The man raised a lazy hand in acknowledgement, and in another second the car was out on the road back to Norwich, disappearing pertly round the next bend.

As it vanished from sight my pent-up spleen exploded.

'You let *her* into the camp!' Then I looked at Nellie Smith's face and was sorry I had spoken.

'That bleeding Chink!'

I was really too tired to go out again after tea, but I had promised. Mrs Fenner and Ellie sat outside on the pavement, enjoying the cool of the day. For once, Mrs Fenner had borrowed Ellie's comb and was using it to get the chicken bits out of her own hair. I had never seen her hair down before; not so long as Ellie's, and touched with grey, but soft and springy in texture, the way hair ought to be, not like Ellie's dank spaghetti. For the first time I realized that Mrs Fenner wasn't old at all, younger than her daughters in her warmth and vitality.

I said that it had been a lovely day.

'Lovely!' She stopped combing and burst out laughing. 'Some people have a funny idea of lovely! I reckon your ma'd have the Prevention of Cruelty on to me if she knew where I had you today. An' as fer Maud –'

'I won't tell, I promise.'

'I know that.' She spoke without laughter now; with a purity of trust that made the evening sparkle like a crystal, every outline precise and perfect. 'Otherwise I wouldn't 've done it.' Looking at me critically: 'You could do with a bit of a comb yourself.'

I backed away from the fearsome object which could only, I felt sure, make my hair filthier than it was already. I could feel the jar of gluc which I had concealed in my knickers oozing some of its contents on to my thigh through the slit in its rubber cap.

'I shan't be long.'

'Off to play wi' that little gypsy gal? She's all there, that one. But you mind out. Keep yer eyes peeled. You know what gypsies do wi' little children. Kidnap 'em – take 'em away an' nobody ever hears of them again.' The familiar laugh broke out again, rocked the chair on the uneven ground. 'Good riddance to bad rubbish, eh? No such luck!'

'No such luck,' I assented, smiling.

Nellie Smith was waiting for me. She was sitting on an up-turned pig trough moodily munching on a stalk which she spat out when she saw me coming.

'You took your time.'

'I had to have my tea first.'

'Oh ah? What did you have?' She might have been a zoologist inquiring into the eating habits of some strange animal.

'Sardines.' Going over to the offensive myself: 'What about you?'

'Stew. Hedgehog an' squirrel.'

'You didn't!'

'Want me to go an' fetch you some?'

'No thank you.' We stared at each other in hopeless silence. We might have been Jew and Gentile, divided by the unbridgeable chasm of kashrut. Then, with a sudden change to a quicksilver charm which was irresistible, Nellie Smith demanded, 'Did you bring what you said you would?' and when I fished the leaking glue out of my knicker leg, she exclaimed, eyes dancing, 'You're a ruddy angel!'

I had to take my dress off to get at the scabs which were left on my chest. As I stood there in my vest and knickers, by the decaying sties filled with nettles, I felt very peculiar, almost religious. The sun was going down, orange and slow. The place still smelled of pig manure, but old and dry, not unpleasant: spicy, like incense.

The scabs were not as ripe for picking as I had thought. They clung to my skin like shipwrecked mariners to a floating spar. Each left behind a red oval which I had been warned, I don't know how many times, by both my mother and Maud, meant a scar, a lessening of my beauty for which I would grieve all my days. (They spoke truly, except for the grieving bit. The scars are still there.)

I offered up my scabs willingly, glad to have them in my gift. I stuck them on to Nellie Smith's face with dabs of glue, a mystic union of her flesh and mine. I placed two in the centre of her forehead, one either side of her nose, one in the middle of her little pointed chin. I only had an odd number left, so one cheek had to have four scabs and the other three, which perhaps was as well: too great a symmetry might have aroused suspicions.

When I had done, Nellie Smith looked wonderful. No truant officer would have let so much as her shadow fall across the school door.

She danced about in excitement.

'How do I look? Han't you got a bloody mirror?'

I hadn't, and she was so eager to see what she looked like that she hardly stopped to say ta before running off home to her caravan to look in the glass. Left alone, I scrambled back into my dress, thrust the jar of glue back into my knickers, and went back to the road. The sun was behind the trees, but the sky was still bright – richly purple below, with, higher up, fluffy white clouds gilded at the edges, looking as if they too had been stuck on with glue, only by a more practised hand.

I got home so dazed with tiredness I couldn't stand straight, and Mrs Fenner made up my bed on the sofa even though Mr Fenner was still eating his tea, reading his *Old Moore's Almanac* between mouthfuls. I washed neither my dirty hair nor my dirty body. My chest felt sore, a soreness I treasured, though I was too tired to remember why. I think, that night, the rats in the derelict cottage next door must have gone to bed early too. At any rate, I never heard a peep out of them.

Chapter Nine

IT was during my convalescence at Opposite the Cross Keys that the matter of the AA sign came to a head. In those days and, so far as I can remember, right up to the outbreak of World War II, when they were taken down for security reasons or else requisitioned for scrap, every village in Britain, by courtesy of the Automobile Association, sported, on a conveniently sited building, an outsize metal medallion, black-printed on a background of mustard, giving the name of the village and the names and distances of the next populated places along the road in either direction.

The occupiers of the premises on which these useful objects were displayed received the princely sum of five shillings per annum for allowing them to be so used; and Mrs Fenner was one of the AA's beneficiaries in this respect. The five shillings was her private income, notionally spent and re-spent a dozen times before the actual postal order arrived in the post. It gave her status as a woman of independent means. As to the sign itself, it was nailed to the front wall a little above the living-room window, so much part of the façade that nobody (the notional passing motorist apart) ever gave it a thought.

Until, that is, the day it was taken down and put up on the Leaches' cottage instead.

The reason for this unheralded sideways movement was that, a little before, Mr Leach had left his former occupation, whatever that might have been, to become an AA scout, one of those stalwarts who patrolled the highways and byways of the UK on motor-cycle combinations raising their gauntleted hands in salute to any driver whose vehicle sported the gleaming AA insignia on its radiator.

Apart from this modern equivalent of forelock-pulling, they

also rendered assistance in cases of puncture or minor mechanical breakdown, though – or so one got the impression – not enough to risk dirtying their natty uniforms of mustard and black, which none of the Association's members, even *in extremis*, would have wanted, for the sight of one of those godlike creatures touching his cap was enough to make a driver's day. If, on the other hand, you preferred blue-grey to mustard and black (as my mother did) you joined the Royal Automobile Club instead: but as to the sheer panache of their individual salutes, there was nothing to choose between them.

When the news of Mr Leach's new job filtered through to the neighbours, the Fenners fell about laughing, because there was nothing either stalwart or godlike about Mr Leach. But it was amazing: buttoned tightly into his mustard jacket, the two rows of buttons slanting down from broad-seeming shoulders to slim-seeming waist, his breeches tailored to a T and his black-peaked cap on his head, he looked transformed, whilst his salute alone was worth the annual subscription.

As if they weren't uppish enough already, the Leaches in their new role became insufferable. Mrs Leach stopped going about with her hair in curling pins, and went into Norwich once a week to have it marcelled. She let it be known that they were thinking of taking their annual holiday in Dunkirk sur mer, which was a place in France, very French.

Having got the AA to shift the sign to their wall, they went to the police – specifically to PC Utting, who lived in the Salham St Awdry police house – when, or so they alleged, Charlie Fenner shinned up a ladder one night when they'd gone into Norwich to the pictures, and painted it black all over.

PC Utting didn't think much of the AA scouts, whom he saw as encroachers on his own bailiwick. He didn't think much of the Fenners either, but at least they didn't act as if they were a superior order of police. Before the Fenner–Leach feud blew up, separating the village into two opposing camps, most people in St Awdry's would have been surprised to learn that there ever was an AA sign on Opposite the Cross Keys; but once their attention was directed to the circular discoloration left by its abduction they instantly remembered that of course there was.

[107]

Most of them became angry with the Leaches, not so much because they were for the Fenners, who, to be truthful, were not all that popular in the village – though poor they weren't meek, as God had intended the poor to be – as because, on principle, they did not care to have things altered, even things which they hadn't noticed in the first place. PC Utting, having pondered the facts submitted to him by the Leaches, gave it as his considered opinion, off the record, that the obliteration of the sign was most probably the work of RAC saboteurs, though he doubted if it could be proved.

The AA sent down a new sign.

Mrs Fenner was so upset about the loss of her private income that, without telling her, I wrote to the AA, to their regional headquarters in Norwich.

Dear Sir, I wrote.

I am writing on beharf of Mrs Fenner who has ruhmitisem and cant write herself at the moment. (It was an unwritten convention at Opposite the Cross Keys that Mrs Fenner could read and write as well as anybody, if only she hadn't just broken her glasses, come down with writer's cramp, or was seeing spots in front of her eyes any time those skills were called for.) *I am writing to say it isnt fare to take her sing away just because Mr Leech has gon to work for you. Mrs Fenner has had it for donkies years and needs the 5/- a lot mor than Mr Leech does. My father has a car, a Moris Oxford, only he belongs to the RAC because my mother doesnt like the culler of the AA, but if youll put the sing back on Mrs fenners I am pretty sure they will joyn the AA if I ask, because they do most things I ask them to do.*

Hopeing you are well,

Yours sincerely,

Mrs Fenner (on beharf of)

After I had written the letter and posted it, I asked Miss Lethaby to get St Giles reverse charges because I wanted my father to start in right away getting my mother used to the idea of being saluted by men in mustard and black instead of blue-grey. When I explained my reasons, my father, to my surprise, sounded serious. He said that what I proposed doing was attempted bribery which was a criminal offence, and I wasn't on any account to send the letter. I didn't let on that I had already sent it.

As the post van hadn't yet called, I asked Miss Lethaby to

unlock the box and let me get the letter out, but she went livid and told me that tampering with His Majesty's Mails was something I could go to prison for; to say nothing of where would she be, for aiding and abetting. So I went back to Opposite the Cross Keys and wrote another letter to the Sir at the AA, cancelling the earlier letter because I didn't want to go to prizon either for bryberry or tampring with the males, but I still didn't think it was fare and when I grew up and had a car of my own I would never joyn the AA, never, not if they beged me on bended knee.

Within days a letter came back, addressed to Mrs Fenner (on beharf of), and enclosing a postal order for one pound which they hoped would prove acceptable as some recompense for the loss of the AA sign. They hoped the postal order would not be construed as an attempt to bribe me to join the AA instead of the RAC when I had a car of my own. There was no such intention and they hoped I was well, yours faithfully.

After that, things in Salham St Awdry cooled down, though we no longer spoke to the Leaches and, whenever we went down the garden and saw Mr Leach's feet and ankles showing below his lav door wearing the mustard colour socks which were part of his uniform, Mrs Fenner would make some loud remark about what the colour put her in mind of.

It wasn't until ten days later, when a car stopped alongside one morning as I was out on the pavement, that I realized the Affaire AA had not quite run out of steam.

'I'm looking for Salham St Awdry,' the driver explained; and when I answered, naturally enough, that that was where he was, he looked at me as if I were the original village idiot. Pointing to the sign on the Leaches' wall, he demanded, 'What's that, then?'

For the first time in days, I looked up at the sign which said, as plain as black on mustard, *Salham Norgate*.

The man took some convincing that, appearances notwithstanding, Salham St Awdry was where I said it was. Once I'd got rid of him I walked the mile or so up the road to Salham Norgate to see if their sign – fixed to a house whose front parlour was the village grocery shop – had got it right.

I took a look at the sign, and then went inside, where the woman who ran the shop, a comfortable, grey-haired body, greeted me with the smile due to an important customer for sherbet suckers.

'Please, is this Salham St Awdry or Salham Norgate?'

The smile faded. 'Don't talk daft! You know as well as I do!'

I persuaded her to come outside and look at her sign, which said, beyond denial, *Salham St Awdry*.

'Oh, that!' she said, to my disappointment. 'Someone did mention somethin' a couple of days ago. Funny, in't it? But I can't be bothered. Five bob a year's not worth spending a stamp to let 'em know.' The shop lady was obviously in a different financial bracket from that of Mrs Fenner. 'If they aren't satisfied wi' what it says, let 'em come an' take it away, for all I care. I shan't lose any sleep. I mean, arter all, St Awdry's near enough, in't it? Anyone going there's bound to come to it if they keep on down the road a bit, an' anyone coming the other way, well, they'll have been there already, won't they, so they'll know it couldn't be.' She smoothed her apron and dismissed the matter from her mind. '*We* know where we're at, don't we? Tha's what matters, in't it?'

When I had a chance to speak to him privately, I asked Charlie if it was he who had switched over the signs.

'Switch?' he repeated, blank-faced: but little pinpoints of light danced in his blue eyes, so like his father's, and I came to my own conclusion.

'You goin' to let on to the Leaches?' he demanded.

'Course not!'

After that, though I never felt about Charlie the way I did about Tom, we got to be much better friends. As for the signs themselves, if it weren't for the exigencies of war I bet those switched mustard and black tin plates would be there still, reversed for all eternity. It's a pity they aren't, really, to the confusion of map makers and the pleasurable confabulation of local history pundits. Someone might even write a book about it.

Chapter Ten

WHENEVER, at Opposite the Cross Keys, I fancied a little peace and quiet, I crossed the High Street and followed the churchyard wall until I came to the church gate; let myself in and took possession of my favourite spot, between an elderberry bush and a tombstone so delicately patterned with lichens and moulds as to look, for all its ancient stoniness, like softest suede. Thanks to Maud, I was something of an *aficionado* of cemeteries. Maud was forever being crossed in love, I don't know why, unless it was that she was plain, dowdy and totally lacking in sexual attraction. Even her cornucopian offerings to the current love object of Woodbines and Cadbury Dairy Milk (the half-pound size!) seemed to pall in time when proffered by an unglamorous virgin bent on matrimony and willing to settle for nothing less.

Whenever, then, Maud was jilted, which was roughly three or four times a year, she turned melancholy and addicted to intimations of mortality. At such periods, our walks together tended to take us either to one or other of Norwich's two lunatic asylums, or else to cemeteries and graveyards, of which there was a plentiful selection within the city boundaries.

I did not much care for the lunatic asylums, fancying I heard shrieks and groans coming from behind their high walls; but the cemeteries were lovely and quiet. Nobody there seemed to have any complaints about their situation. No screams from people roasting in hell came seeping up through the grass or the marble chippings which paved their neat little front yards. Plainly, all the dead people in Norwich were good and had gone straight up to heaven.

Whilst Maud paced the paths wearing her longest face – give or take the irrepressible smirk of gratification when, as

[111]

happened every now and again, someone took her for a newly bereaved widow – I ran about the narrow grass aisles visiting my favourite graves (an admiral's, girt about with ropes and anchors; a sepulchre on whose lid sat a perspiring marble angel, pressing down with all its weight to keep it shut against the push of a skeletal hand; a memorial to a young woman, decorated with a closed fan and a furled parasol) and was quite sorry when the end of the current period of mourning was signified by a shy stopping off at the sweetshop or the tobacconist's on the way home.

That part of Salham St Awdry churchyard planted with the younger graves was kept trim and tidy, the tombstones bolt upright, like guests at a cocktail party who hadn't yet drunk enough to feel sociable. In what I was pleased to think of as 'my' corner, the memorials leaned towards each other like elderly friends a little hard of hearing and not wanting to miss a word of the other's conversation. There, the grass was long and peppered with poppies. When I lay on my stomach, as I did the day after Mrs Fenner and I went plucking, the yellowing sprays of fescue and cocks-foot met above my head. Panicles of hairy brome drooped over my book, which was *Holiday House*, an old favourite inherited from my sister, about a family of Scottish children who were always getting up to tricks except for Dick, who was delicate and spent most of his time on a couch by the window until the day God took him to heaven, which, in the circumstances, was the best thing that could have happened to him, especially as he was musical.

I always wept buckets over the chapter about Dick's death, most enjoyable. I knew it by heart, which was why I didn't mind the brome grass getting in the way, or its prickly spikelets catching in my hair.

Every now and again as I lay drowsing, still tired from my efforts of the previous day, three or four ants, working in teams in the best mountaineering tradition, crawled up the spine of the book and hauled themselves into sight at the top of the open page as if they had just conquered Everest. Insects with translucent wings paused there briefly on legs that were threads of spun silk. Bees buzzed and bumbled, rooks cawed in distant trees. From the High Street the sound of passing cars was reduced by distance to merely another insect noise, as much a part of the natural world as all the other hummings and buzzings, clickings and rustlings which encompassed me.

'Hushabye, Baby, on the tree top.
When the wind blows, the cradle will rock –'

The piercing voice of Nellie Smith obliterated my insect world. I sat up, glad that she should choose to seek me out: sorry to call an end to my mindless reverie.

'I wasn't asleep. I was reading.'

'Oh ah.'

Nellie Smith was sitting astride the churchyard wall, one leg out of sight as if she hesitated to commit herself to God's Acre in her entirety. She looked quite ill with her enormous eyes, the scabs on her sallow face rimmed with glue that looked like pus.

'Your chickenpox looks fine,' I said, to remind her of her obligations. I hadn't liked the sound of that 'Oh ah.'

Nellie Smith grinned hugely and at once looked healthy.

'Don't I just! Mavis nearly had a fit. Made me sleep in the old un's caravan, case I give it to the kid.'

'You mean you didn't tell her it was only pretend?'

'I never tell *her* anything.'

'Who's the old un?'

'You seen 'er. Smokes a pipe.' The girl leaned towards me and nearly lost her balance. 'Been talking to your missus. She told me you're goin' over to the White House tomorrow, spud-grubbing.'

'She did mention something.' Unable to hide my curiosity: 'Did you actually go indoors to speak to her?'

'What you think?' – contemptuous that I should even ask. 'That barrel o' lard what's always sitting outside combing her hair, she were there an' I asked her was the missus home. Gives me the creeps,' Nellie Smith asserted cheerfully. 'Anyways, your missus must 've heard me, an' she come out. When she said yes, you two was goin' spudding, I arst could I come with, an' she said I could.'

'Why? Aren't any of the gypsies going?'

'Wednesday. Market Day. They're all off to Norwich.'

'It isn't much of a market Wednesdays. Nothing like Saturdays.'

'They still reckon they'll get more there for less work than grubbin' about on their hands an' knees, spoiling their beautiful white hands.'

'What'll they do in Norwich?'

Nellie Smith made a face and began in a high-pitched monotone: *'Buy a bit o' white heather, dearie! Buy yer luck an' yer love an' yer money!'* The voice deepening, incorporating into its obsequious whine a note of menace, though the words, remained innocuous enough: *'Bit o' silver fer a bit o' white heather! Bit o' silver fer a life o' luck!'* Nellie Smith preened herself as best she could on her precarious perch. 'I could do it as well as any on 'em, *an'* get more, on'y the constabulary'd be on to me like a ton o' bricks. Kids isn't supposed to work –' the words were coated with an ironic humour beyond her years – 'which means I can go an' break me back in them bloody spud fields an' nobody says a word because it's just a dear little kiddy havin' a game picking up them pretty pertatoes.'

'Why don't you come down off that wall? It's lovely down here in the grass. I'll read you some of my book, if you like.'

'I can read my own bloody book, ta,' was the girl's gracious response. 'An' gypsies don't ever go into cemeteries. It's bad luck.'

'They have to go when they're dead.'

Nellie Smith looked down on me, her eyes curiously opaque. 'So you say.'

I persisted: 'They have to be buried like everyone else.'

'What you know about it?' Nellie Smith's gaze swept the churchyard and came to rest on the most imposing monument there, a marble plinth on which an overweight angel cradled a young soldier, dead or sleeping, in one arm, the other raised in an imperious gesture as if to summon a taxicab or, maybe, a chauffeur-driven chariot of fire. 'If I *had* to be buried in some bloody place like this I'd have an angel like that put over me. What you reckon that one cost to buy?'

I had no idea, and said so. The question surprised me, the one that came next even more so.

'I bin meaning to ask. You know St Awdry's. You know where there's a spring somewhere round here?'

'A spring?' I repeated stupidly. 'What kind of spring?'

'Not one to put in me mattress, dummy! Wet, like you!'

Her mockery hurting me, I shut my book, picked it up, and went over to the wall, close enough to her leg, bare beneath the grown-up dress, to see the scratches and scars which decorated it from calf to ankle.

'Yes,' I said. 'I do know where there's a spring, only I can't tell you. It's a secret.'

My secret and Tom's.

One Sunday, earlier in the same year – it must have been late February or early March – as soon as the Morris Oxford with my mother and father and Alfred had disappeared round the bend by the Swan, Tom had taken me by the hand, his other one tapping his lips to stress the importance of secrecy, and whispered that he had something to show me, something that – he had no words to describe it: the glory in his face did it for him.

Hand in hand, though I had been indoctrinated to walk along the main road always in single file for safety's sake, we walked a long way, past Stratton Strawless, almost as far as the turn-off to Hevingham. To be truthful, safety was not the only reason I should have preferred not to walk hand in hand with Tom. His hands were the only thing about him which made me uneasy. They were very large, with a lot of bristly fair hair on the backs of the fingers. They were also soft, almost mushy. When we walked hand in hand my small child's hand disappeared into his large one as into dough that was yielding but astonishingly adhesive. His were hands that not so much held your own as absorbed them; so that, when at last you got them back, it almost seemed necessary to count the fingers to make sure they were still all there.

Once we left the road my discomfort was at an end. The path through the wood was narrow, invaded by outstretching trees. Tom went ahead, chivalrous at no matter what cost in tears to his old army greatcoat, to bend brambles out of my way, lift drooping branches so that I could pass beneath.

I asked no question as to our destination, content to enjoy the entertainment along the way – the woods ready to haze with green, the snowdrops and celandines, the fresh tips to the bottle brushes of pine. Water dripped from every surface, a lively, bejewelled wet; bedewed the cushions of moss which dotted the path like vegetable hedgehogs. All this we passed by until we came out into a clearing, a glade, perfectly circular, where the soft bubble of water was the sound of silence.

An incomparable place.

Tom stopped and demanded, in that thick voice of his which set no boundaries between vowel and consonant: 'What you say to that, then?'

At first I thought the glade itself was what we had come to see, but then I followed the direction of his pointing forefinger and saw it – water gently lifting itself out of a small bank and flowing away along a sunken track between violet leaves.

A spring.

'It never stop!' Tom exclaimed in tones of wonder. 'I bin here watching sunrise to dark an' it never bloody stop!'

He bent over and let the newborn water fill his cupped hands which he raised carefully to my face so that I could partake of the precious libation.

Suddenly, I didn't know why – I still don't know why unless it be that an instinctive knowledge is built into infant ignorance – I felt afraid. I felt afraid of Tom, of that imprecise heaviness of jaw which was not like other people's; of those enormous, mushy hands carefully cradling the water. I drank because there was no choice, but I quivered with fear.

Tom came close, too close.

'Want to see another secret?'

'Not now,' I managed. 'Another secret, another time.'

The big man assented cheerfully enough.

'Another time!' He thrust a boot into the spring, trying to stem the flow. The water welled up all round the mud-caked sole. 'See that! It *will* come! Do what you like, it *will* come!' Hooting as at a great joke: 'Know what they say? They say water like that's what makes a river. Tha's what they say!'

We laughed together at the absurdity of the suggestion that this peerless crystal could bear any relation to the Sal, the drab little stream which grizzled across the suburbs of St Awdry's, or the Wensum, which slithered through Norwich like a dirty old snake. We laughed and I forgot what I had been frightened about.

'You won't tell anyone?' Tom asked anxiously. 'They could come an' take it away if they knew it was here.'

I promised.

When we came out on to the road again on the way back, I took Tom's hand without his asking, and we walked back to the village as we had come. I didn't enjoy holding his hand coming back any more than I had going. But it seemed a small enough price to pay for that hateful, unbidden moment of distrust, a small return for the gift of such a secret.

'It's a secret,' I said again.

Nellie Smith treated this as a statement of no importance. She shifted her position on the churchyard wall as an expression of impatience. 'What if it is? I'm yer friend, ain't I?'

I hoped she was, I desperately wanted her to be: but I nevertheless felt constrained to point out once more that I had promised not to tell.

'Promised!' the girl returned contemptuously. 'Promises are made to be broken.'

Are they, I wondered confusedly; and, fine friend you'd turn out to be, if that's what you think. But I still, more than anything else, wanted her to be my friend, on any terms.

'Tell you what I'll do,' I proferred, happy to have glimpsed a possibility of compromise. 'I'll ask Mrs Fenner for a jam jar and I'll go myself and bring you back a jar. A bucketful, if you want.'

'Huh! Prob'ly go an' fill it up at the pump an' say it's the real thing.'

'I wouldn't do that!' No promises, no trust either, it seemed. 'What d'you want spring water for, anyway?'

'Tha's my business!' Relenting: 'Something the old un said, tha's all.'

'What did she say?'

'Anyone ever tell you you're the world's prize nosy parker?' Nellie Smith leaned forward and gave me a hard look, eye to eye until I felt obliged to look away. 'Ought to know it were bloody daft to hitch up wi' a sodding Gorgio!'

She swung her leg back over the wall, and slid down on the further side, out of sight. One of the frills on her awful dress came off with a rip, caught on a protruding flint. Nellie Smith did not come back for it.

I looked up at the frill for a moment, then reached up and tugged it from its mooring. It split into two longitudinally, one section in my hand, the other still on the wall, where I left it.

I picked up *Holiday House* and started back to the church gate, wondering what I was going to do with the strip of rag. Return it to its owner? Chuck it on the fire at Opposite the Cross Keys?

In the event – with no idea of what triggered my decision – I made a detour to the monument with the angel on it, scrambled up the plinth at some expenditure of skin, clambered over the soldier, and tied the frayed remnant to the angel's summoning arm. Suddenly afraid that the rector might catch me and misunderstand my motives, whatever they might be, I descended with less solicitude for the sleeping hero than I had shown on the ascent, got myself out of the churchyard with all haste, and ran home.

Mrs Fenner was sitting at the living-room table, peeling potatoes on to a sheet of the *News of the World*, and popping them, as done, into the saucepan already steaming on the fire and emitting a smell that might have been meat or fish, or, again, neither. It was proof of my acclimatization to the Fenner *cuisine* that the aroma, of whatever it was, made my mouth water.

The room was doubly dim after the glare outside, cool despite the fire. I went up to Mrs Fenner and kissed her.

'*Now* what you bin up to?' she inquired, eyes twinkling.

'I haven't been up to anything.'

'Oh ah.' Mrs Fenner gave me a keen look. 'Feeling a bit homesick, are you, for yer ma an' pa? On'y natural.'

I was fly enough to know that, flattering as it might be to Mrs Fenner's ego, it was not the done thing to admit the truth, which was that I had not had more than a fleeting thought to spare for the St Giles establishment from the moment Alfred had deposited me at Opposte the Cross Keys' door. For the sake of appearances, then, I produced a piteous sniff, and whimpered, 'A bit.'

'I got somethin' to cheer you up. That Nellie Smith's coming wi' us termorrow, spud-lifting. You'll like that.'

'She told me.'

'Ah! I told her you was over the road, having a quiet read. Did she tell you about what she calls her scheme?'

I shook my head.

'She's a bright one, I give her that. Must've got it from her ma, can't be that bloody Irish tinker of her pa. Had the cheek to charge me fourpence, when they was here last year, to put a bit o' solder on my kettle, an' two days later, what you think, the bloody spout dropped off. He show his mug round here, he'll hear something!'

'Irish tinker? You mean, he isn't a gypsy at all?'

'He's as much a gypsy as I'm the Queen o' Sheba! Her ma, now – her ma were the genuine article, poor sod, for what that's worth.'

'She's a Romany princess,' I said, proud of my vicarious association with royalty.

'You don't say!' Mrs Fenner sounded amused. 'Didn't look much o' one the day she fell down in front of the Post Office an' the ambulance come an' took her to the Norfolk an' Norwich. Blood everywhere – from her nose, her mouth, I don't know where else. You wouldn't think such a bag o' bones could have that much blood in her. Lasted a couple of weeks, so I heard.'

'Oh, that must be another Mrs Smith,' I asserted confidently. 'Nellie Smith's ma's run off with a rich farmer in Yorkshire. She's going to send for Nellie as soon as she gets him used to the idea.'

'That what the poor little chit told you?' Mrs Fenner put her half-peeled potato down on the newspaper. 'Look here,' she said, ''don't you go letting on that I told you anything else –'

'I told you –' anxiety mounting – 'it can't have been Nellie's ma who –'

'You listen to me, young Sylvie.' Mrs Fenner's voice was gentle but firm. 'It don't do no good to let that gal fill your head wi' fairy stories. Poor thing, consumption's what she had, an' that man of hers already carrying on like Sodom an' Gomorrah, judgin' from the number o' redheads they got running about bare-arsed up the road. I were real sorry for that Nellie Smith when I heard her ma'd copped it. You look outside the Post Office, where the post van pulls in. You can still see the stain on the cement. Give me quite a turn to see him back this year, bold as brass.'

As for me, my heart was bursting with sorrow for the friend whom I had just treated in such cavalier fashion. My promise to Tom was not quite forgotten, but now I told myself that telling a secret to a friend was not really telling, because a friend was part of yourself, and telling yourself wasn't telling, was it? Having resolved the moral problem to my satisfaction (though I recognized the unwisdom of trying out such a Jesuitical solution on Tom), I couldn't wait till tomorrow to show Nellie the spring, show her anything it was in my power to show.

I asked, 'Did they bury her in Norwich cemetery?'

'Reckon so. I don't suppose the hospital would 'a let her be buried gypsy way.'

'Which way's that?'

'Blamed if I know, exactly. They never let on. On'y people do say, the on'y gypsies you ever see in a graveyard is when they die in hospital, or prison, or the workhouse, where the government know they're dead an' so they have to be put away proper. The rest? Buried out on the common, most likely, or in the hedge bottoms, or maybe an old quarry. They say there's a whole shoot of 'em put away in them gravel workings other side of Spixworth.'

After tea, I went up the road to the encampment, not daring to hope I might actually see Nellie from the entrance, beckon her over, offer to show her where the spring was that very moment, if that was what she wanted; but day-dreaming in the golden evening that all those things were about to happen in happy sequence. Mrs Fenner, who guessed where I was off to as I made for the front door, left open to let in the last of the day, advised me to wait till morning. Anything I might want to say to Nellie Smith could be said as we took our way to the White House which, near Horsford Point, was more than half-way to Norwich.

I said, 'She might change her mind about coming.'

'Bullshit! We're going to make our fortunes!'

Nellie Smith's scheme for upping our income from spud-grubbing was one of classic simplicity. The potatoes we were going to lift were new ones – small, much more tiring to pick than the later crop; but even though to fill one of the outsize pails provided by the farmer with little spuds took twenty times the effort needed with the later, larger, ones, the pay was the same for both: penny a pail. And that was for grown-ups. Children, however diligent, could consider themselves lucky to come away with a sixpence for eight to ten hours' backbreaking toil.

The injustice which made Nellie Smith mad was that, while the women might be better pickers of maincrop potatoes than the children, the latter, being closer to the ground, their hands smaller, their movements nimbler, were far and away the best pickers of the new varieties.

The gypsy girl's plan, then, was for her and me not to accept pails at all from the checker who, as always, would have set up his table just inside the field gate. We were just a couple of kids brought along by Mrs Fenner because she couldn't trust the little devils out of her sight. All the potatoes the three of us grubbed up would thus go into the same pail, to be credited to Mrs Fenner's account, attracting the adult rate of remuneration. At the end of the day we would share out the total received, half to Mrs Fenner, the other half to be divided between Nellie and me.

After what Mrs Fenner had told me about Nellie Smith's ma, I had already made up my mind that my earnings next day were going to go to Nellie Smith as well, to help towards paying for a stone angel to take up residence on an unmarked mound of earth somewhere in Norwich cemetery.

When I came to the encampment, Nellie Smith was nowhere to be seen. Nobody was, except the old gypsy woman I had seen before – the old un, as I now thought of her – sitting on the steps of her barrel-shaped caravan, smoking her pipe. Somewhere at the rear of the camp, out of sight, there was something going on: wood smoke rising, babies crying. A harsh voice was singing, to the jangle of a banjo: *'Oh, I do like to be beside the seaside . . .'*

I did not dare to put a foot into gypsy territory. Standing on the roadside verge I bent my body as far forward as it would go without losing its balance, looking for my friend.

The old un took her pipe out of her mouth, spat a disc of yellow saliva on to the sooty earth at the side of the steps, and demanded, 'What you want?'

She wore a purple kerchief on her head, tied at the back in a way only the gypsies seemed to know, so that it was more than a scarf – a head-dress, stately and forbidding. The woman's nose was narrow, but large and commanding, parting the ridged cheeks on either side like an Israelite, dry-shod, crossing the Red Sea. The black eyes with which she regarded me – there was something wrong with her black eyes.

Whilst I pondered confusedly what it might be, she raised a bony hand and forearm, dug out her right eye and put it in her pocket, producing in exchange a grubby handkerchief with which she proceeded to wipe out the empty socket.

'Bloody sweat!' she grumbled, more to herself than me; blew her nose on the handkerchief and put it away.

'What you want?' she asked again.

I faltered, hating to look at that empty socket, unable to take my eyes off it. 'I wanted to speak to Nellie Smith.'

'You *wanted*!' The words came back, jeering, spittle at the corners of the mouth. 'Want's a good thing. Have's a better.'

The observation did not sound promising. Still I stammered, 'Do you think – I mean – could you please give her a message from me?'

'Pishy-poshy!' exclaimed the old woman. 'What a little madam we are!' She drew on her pipe, expelling the smoke with a luxurious deliberation. 'What kind o' message?'

'Just that I'm sorry I said no, and I'll tell her about the spring when I see her, even though it is a secret.'

'Ah – the spring!' The woman put the pipe down on the step beside her, fished the false eye and the handkerchief out of her skirt pocket, and began polishing the one with the other, breathing on the brightly curved little object from time to time. In the evening light it shone like a jewel. When the job was done to her satisfaction she slid it back into the empty socket with a practised ease, before fixing me with her two eyes, black and unblinking. I had the unnerving impression that the false eye saw better than the real. 'I'll tell her that.' The head-dress inclined regally. 'I'll tell Nellie Smith you was here.'

I skipped all the way back to Opposite the Cross Keys. Two

separate people, passing in the other direction, called out greetings, confirming that I was part of Salham St Awdry, that I belonged. The second, a woman who lived up Back Lane, shouted across the road, 'You're looking pleased with yourself!'

I was, I was. I skipped home through the waning day, midges dancing, the hedgerows sweet and musky, sports cars speeding past full of beautiful young people, their hair streaming in the wind. I sang at the top of my voice, *'Oh, I do like to be beside the seaside . . .'*

In my state of euphoria I discovered to my surprise that I even loved Ellie, who was sitting outside the cottage as usual, having her last comb of the day. Sneaking up from behind, I flung my arms round her neck and planted a hearty kiss on her cheek. She stared at me agape, speechless.

I kissed her on the other cheek, laughing.

Chapter Eleven

THAT night I woke up burdened with a worry I couldn't put a name to. Asleep, I had known very well what the matter was. Awake, it eluded me.

The room was light for the middle of the night, moonshine coming through the window, stippling the floor with silhouettes of the geraniums on the sill. I swung my legs off the sofa and went to look out at the moon.

It hung calm and cool, lighting up the road, the houses opposite, the Cross Keys, the village store and the long wall of the churchyard. The sight of the churchyard wall brought back an instant recollection of the dream which had frightened me awake. The rector. The rector had seen the torn frill fluttering from the angel's arm. At the sight he had raised both hands in horror, the way Miss Boothby did at Eldon House when we misbehaved, and cried out, 'Blasphemy! Blasphemy!' before climbing up the memorial – with some difficulty, be it said: he was a corpulent man – and fetching it down.

'Aha!' he had exclaimed then, recognizing the pattern of the material. 'This is part of the dress worn by that dratted gypsy girl, Nellie Smith. She shall pay for this! I shall thrash her within an inch of her life – half an inch, a quarter!' He had just set out for the gypsy encampment armed with a whip which he made go *wheeeee* through the air, this way and that, when I woke up.

I was old enough to know a dream when I saw one. Rectors did not go shinning up funerary marbles in real life. If it were considered necessary, they got their vergers to do it. On the other hand, I had it on the best authority – Maud's – that a dream was a warning. Next time the rector took a stroll in his churchyard to make sure all the dead people were sleeping comfortably, he would be sure to see the rag tied to the angel's arm, and give orders for its removal. I doubted if rectors, in real life, noticed what gypsy girls were wearing, one way or another, but Mr Winch, the verger, certainly did, because he looked at little girls a lot, as I could have told anyone who asked; and he would be bound to tell the rector, 'It's that Nellie Smith up to her tricks again!'

My heart missed a beat. Unless I took immediate action my mindless prank could have the most appalling consequences: the gypsies driven from Salham St Awdry like Adam and Eve from the Garden of Eden. I would lose Nellie Smith, my friend, for ever.

Stuffing my feet into my plimsolls, I unbolted the front door and went out into the moonlit world, crossing the empty High Street and running round the churchyard perimeter to the church gate. It was neither hot nor cold. Though it was real, though I knew it was real, it felt more like a dream to be hurrying towards a graveyard in night-clothes, in the moonlight.

Thanks to my countless visits of inspection to churches in the company of my father, I had no stupid fear of the dead. Indeed, I was rather partial to them as people who, unlike their living counterparts, never found fault or made one feel small. Climbing the angel memorial made me soaking wet. Pockets of dew had settled in every fold of the angel's toga; but when I was high up enough to tug at Nellie Smith's frill it came away without difficulty.

I got back to the cottage to find Gyp, the old snorer, awake, for a wonder, standing on all fours just inside the door, shaking his head to and fro in a manner at once concerned and disapproving. He ostentatiously did not favour me with any sign of relief at my safe return, merely waited grumpily for me to bolt the door and get back into bed before settling himself afresh on the hearthrug.

I carefully folded the strip of Nellie Smith's dress and put it under my pillow; pulled the coverlet up to my neck, the way I liked it summer or winter. I slept without a dream.

Next day, working Nellie Smith's system at the White House, we made eighteen shillings – nine shillings for Mrs Fenner, four and sixpence each to Nellie and me: an unheard-of sum. When it came to counting Mrs Fenner's tags at the end of the day, the teller at the gate looked at us suspiciously and counted them three times over before shelling out the money. You could see he thought he'd been made a fool of, in some way he couldn't fathom.

I wanted to give Nellie Smith my share right away, before I weakened, but I didn't know how to – not, that is, without letting on that I knew about her ma and the reason for the stain on the cement outside the Post Office. In the end I held it out gracelessly and mumbled that she could have it if she wanted, towards the fare to Yorkshire. Somewhat to my disappointment, she merely said, 'Ta', and took it without demur.

All day long, side by side, scrabbling in the warm tilth, she had been pleasant, but aloof. I was glad at least that she had another dress on, though it was still one made for a grown-up, printed with ugly flowers and hitched up, like its predecessor, with a length of twine. She did not say whether the old un had passed on my message, and I was too mulish to ask.

It was only when Mrs Fenner and I were about to drop off at Opposite the Cross Keys, Nellie Smith courteously declining an invitation to come in for a cuppa, that the gypsy girl whispered eagerly in my ear, 'What you say, then? Can we go this evening?'

All in after the day's labour and the long walk home, I had already armed myself to return a curt negative should she put forward just such a proposition. As it was, my heart pierced with joy, my fatigue forgotten, I whispered back, 'I'll be by for you soon as I've had a drink of water.'

The wood – for which I was grateful, it made me feel less guilty – was quite different from the one Tom had brought me to, in the morning of the year. Vanished was the cathedral architecture of pillars and fan vaulting, of branches spread against the sky. In its place was a muddle of leaves that shut out the light, and, underfoot, a mess of growth which obscured the footpath and made me uncertain of the way.

I cast about this side and the other, whilst Nellie, clasping her empty jam jar to her bony chest, grew grim and

[126]

unbelieving. When we eventually stumbled upon the glade, it seemed a place so unmagical that I might have crossed it unaware, had not a fugitive murmur of water caught my ear among the brash leaf rustle: the spring, less ebullient in July than in February, a seepage rather than a gurgling, but unmistakably there, tunnelling under a cover of coarse grasses towards that distant river.

Nellie Smith eyed the small upwelling with suspicion.

'You sure that's it? Not some ol' pipe what's sprung a leak?'

'There aren't any pipes out here. 'Course I'm sure!'

Nellie Smith squatted on her haunches and filled the jar at the spring. She still looked unconvinced.

'It don't feel different from any other water to me.'

Tears of anger and remorse filled my eyes and made the spring waver. I had betrayed Tom's confidence for nothing. 'Last time I tell you a secret, I can promise you that!' The water, once captured and still in the jam jar, did indeed look like any other old water. 'Don't know what you want it for, anyway!'

For a moment Nellie Smith's mood softened. She became almost pleading.

'I told you – the old un. She told me, to be any good, it has to be real, virgin water.'

'Any good for what?' I challenged, unappeased. 'And what's virgin water, anyway? There isn't any such thing!'

'There is!' the other disputed hotly. 'Like in the Virgin Mary. You know what the Virgin bit means in the Virgin Mary, don't you?'

'Of course I do!' But I spoke without conviction. I had never thought about it. 'It's her name,' I ventured rashly. 'Like yours is Nellie Smith.'

'Tha's jest where you're wrong, then! You never heard of nobody else 'cept her called that.'

'Because there was only one of her, that's why, silly!'

'That isn't why she's called –' Nellie Smith broke off and cast her eyes up to heaven. 'Gawd gi' me strength! Where was you brought up, fer Christ' sake? A virgin –' she began again, composing herself for the lesson – 'is a special kind of mauther –'

'Special how?'

'Special that she ain't ever bin wi' a bloke.' After a pause: 'You're one yourself, if you want to know.'

I laughed outright.

'But I've been with millions of blokes! There's my father, and my brother Alfred, and Mr Fenner, and Tom and Charlie and –'

Nellie Smith looked at me in silence and my list petered out betimes. I began to feel uncomfortable – as if, though I truly didn't know what she meant by never having been with a bloke, something deep inside me, something that was a me I hadn't even been introduced to, did know, or, at any rate, had an inkling. Or an inkling of an inkling.

'Ferget it,' Nellie Smith said, unexpectedly gentle. 'I must've got it wrong. What the old un said was that if I could get hold of some water from a spring what come straight out of the earth an' never been anywhere else first, an' if I give some to that bloody Chink what keeps coming round, she won't come round no more – not her nor that swanky car o' hers neither. It'll keep them both away like Flit keeps the bloody flies off.' She leaned towards me and gave me a quick peck on the cheek which so surprised me I nearly lost my balance on the muddy ground. I could feel the filled jam jar pressed between us. 'If it works,' Nellie Smith promised, 'it'll be all your doing.'

By the time we got back to the encampment Nellie Smith's dress was dark all down the front from water which had spilled out of the jar. The top was not a good fit.

'It don't matter,' she said. 'There's plenty left.'

It seemed a doubly long way back. I was very tired. Nellie Smith looked as fresh as when she'd started. We didn't have much to say to each other. I found myself thinking about the Virgin Mary, but only in a desultory way. Sadie and Pauline, the children of Mr Hooper the barber, thought about her all the time, they said, because they were Roman Catholics and had to. I made a mental note to ask them about the Virgin bit to her name, when I got back to Norwich.

The sun was low as we came down the last part of the road. It shone straight into our eyes, so that I did not immediately see, as we came abreast of the opening into the encampment, that

Miss Lee was a few yards inside the field, in her little red car, revving up the engine as if she were getting ready to move out into the road.

As usual, I parted from Nellie Smith at the entrance, and, as usual, I hung around for a little, to see what there was to be seen in that maddening land for which I possessed no passport. The old un was sitting on her caravan steps sucking on her pipe like an ancient baby. Nellie Smith's father stood at the further side of the car, as if he had just been saying goodbye to Miss Lee. The Chinese girl's beautiful face was half-turned towards him, so that all I could see from where I stood was a high-boned cheek brushed by long black lashes.

Lit by the setting sun, the bushy red hair of Nellie Smith's father stood out round his head like a halo. He looked as if he were on fire. It was a pity the rest of him was not beautiful like his hair, and that he was not a gentleman either. Salham St Awdry had taught me that you did not – as, back in Norwich, I had been led to believe – have to dress and speak and use your knife and fork in a certain way to qualify as a gentleman. Mr Fenner was one, and so was Tom. About Charlie I had not made up my mind, but about Nellie Smith's father I was quite sure. He was not a gentleman and never would be, not if he lived to be a hundred.

He looked at Nellie Smith as she came through the opening, but he did not say anything. Nellie Smith did not say anything either. Miss Lee, low down in the sports car, looked up at the girl hesitantly, as if unsure what expression to put on her painted face.

Miss Lee said, 'Hello.'

Nellie Smith plucked the lid off the jam jar and flung the contents into Miss Lee's face.

I ran away because I was afraid to stay and witness what I knew was going to happen. Well, perhaps. On reflection, I don't know whether, in fact, I ran away slower than I intended to, and so saw something; or if I ran away with all speed and only imagined what I thought I saw because I expected it to happen.

What I either saw or imagined, then, was the Chinese girl with the water from Tom's spring making channels in her white face powder, water running out of the corners of her mouth, which was the same colour as her car. I saw or imagined her blouse transparent with wet, the nipples on her small breasts visible through the thin fabric. I saw or imagined Nellie Smith, still clutching the jar, looking at her father with a look of challenge and expectation on her face; and her father's hands moving with a horrid slow-motion towards the wide leather belt which supported his paunch. He took the belt off, and ran one hand along it affectionately, testing its potentiality for pain. The ornate silver buckle shone in the sunset. And then he –

But no. I must have imagined it all, I ran away from the gypsy encampment so fast. I ran home to Opposite the Cross Keys, praying in great gulps to the Virgin Mary not to let Nellie Smith get hurt even though I wasn't a Roman Catholic. Sadie and Pauline Hooper would give me a reference, if she wanted one.

Ahead of me, once I had rounded the bend by the Swan, I saw that Ellie's chair, out on the pavement, was empty, so I knew that the Fenners must have sat down to their tea. Tom would be there, his face lifted with love as I came through the door, his hands fishing out of the pockets of his old army coat the particular treasure – acorn, pebble, sensationally striped brandling – which he had set aside for my delectation that day. I snivelled a little to think that I could never go with him to the spring again. I was not worthy.

The living-room was dark, but not so dark as to need the lamp lit, for which I was grateful. I could not tell what might be there to be read in my face.

'You took your time,' Mrs Fenner remarked amiably, as she got up to spoon on to my plate some of the mess remaining in the saucepan.

I ate voraciously, and made no polite demurrals over accepting the one and only second helping. The meal over, I fell asleep on the sofa before my bed was even made up, my last conscious intimation of the day the prickle of horsehair on my bare legs and arms. Mrs Fenner must somehow have inveigled a pillow under my head and wrapped a blanket round me, but I have no recollection of it. When I woke up next morning, still fully dressed, I found that Tom had tucked a couple of cock pheasant's feathers into the carving next to my head, to keep me company.

Chapter Twelve

O<small>N</small> Saturday Mrs Fenner went up to Norwich for the day as usual. She had expected me to accompany her, but I said I would rather not, if she didn't mind. To that she returned, 'Please yourself,' not in a nasty way, but as if pleasing myself was what she wanted me to do most in the world.

When I saw her got up for the journey, in her coat with all the buttons and her go-to-Norwich hat, I almost changed my mind. But in the end I was glad I hadn't, because then I couldn't have seen her off on the bus, for all as if I were the one who belonged to St Awdry's and she the visitor.

Instead of going to Norwich, I went with Mr Fenner to his allotment. He didn't exactly ask me to go with him and I didn't exactly ask to go – we were both too shy with each other for the suggestion to be put into words – but I could tell by the way he brushed his moustache with his forefinger, a brief staccato swish, first to one side, then the other, that he was glad to have me along. I had noticed that it was a gesture he only made when he was pleased about something.

Just the same he asked, 'Sure you wouldn't rather be off playin' wi' that young gyppo gal?'

'Quite sure.'

I hadn't seen Nellie Smith since the incident with the spring water. I hadn't gone to the encampment and she hadn't come looking for me, either, for which I was grateful. I had spent a lot of time and effort since that Wednesday evening trying not to think about her, and even more trying to unthink the thoughts which came regardless.

Mr Fenner normally worked on Saturdays like any other day. He had the day off because his war wounds were troubling him, as they did from time to time. The farmer he worked for was a man who had fought in the war himself and knew what it had been like, and so wouldn't dock his pay for taking time off.

I never knew the exact nature of Mr Fenner's war wounds, only that they had affected his walk, so that, although the only alcohol he ever drank was a single half-pint on Armistice Day, he rolled along as if he had had too much to drink. As a result of this trouble in keeping his balance, he hadn't been able to ride a bicycle since coming back from the war, and so a grateful country had provided him with a tricycle, which, Mr Fenner said, was such a pleasure to ride, it was almost worth getting yourself blown up for.

Apart from anything else, he said, the tricycle seat was so much more comfortable than a bicycle one, and he needed a well-padded place for his bum ever since, plodding along the Somme with a box of ammunition big as a house, he had sat down for a minute to take a load off his feet; and, blow him, if he hadn't sat down square on the spike of a Prussian helmet buried in the mud. The bloody thing had gone straight up his back passage.

Laugh? His mates had nearly bust a gut. But it weren't such a laugh for him, landed with a sore arse for the rest of his natural. Nor, come to think of it, for the helmet's owner, either. When his mates had got a grip on the ruddy thing and pulled, blow him if it didn't come away with the head of the bloody Hun still inside it.

Tricycles were fine for passengers as well as for riders with tender arses. You stood erect on the bar between the back wheels, your hands resting lightly on the driver's shoulders, perfectly secure and with a splendid view of the surrounding landscape. No other conveyance, except perhaps the Royal Coach, with its knee-breeched lackeys clinging on to the back, could give one such a feeling of consequence.

The allotment, along with Mr Fenner's campaign medals and the tricycle, was one more bonus for helping to save the world for democracy, ex-servicemen being excused the yearly rental of half-a-crown demanded of civilians. Mr Fenner's was a model of its kind, astonishing compared with the patch of *maquis* laughingly dubbed garden at Opposite the Cross Keys, where he grew nothing except the noxious weed he insisted on calling tobacco. The exquisite order of the ten square rods in

Back Lane was enough to bring tears to the eyes. Mr Fenner tended them with a loving care tinged with melancholy – the latter, I could only guess, brought on by the knowledge that all his lovely victuals were doomed to end up as the same unidentifiable mush in Mrs Fenner's saucepan.

'Look at that cauli, will yer?' Mr Fenner would invite, giving the creamy curd a congratulatory pat. 'Snow don't come no whiter.' And he would sigh heavily before passing on to the next beauty along the row.

Whenever I went with him to the allotment, Mr Fenner, as if to make sure that some at least of his produce had not lived in vain, would press me to eat as many raw vegetables as I had a mind to, or a stomach for. (They were, I suppose, the only food I ever ate in Salham St Awdry which was good for me.) There was a little shed on the allotment which contained gardening tools and a pile of *Old Moore's Almanacs* falling apart with damp, but was mostly taken up by an outsize wicker armchair in the last stages of dissolution. This shed was Mr Fenner's study, his snuggery, hermitage, to which I felt deeply privileged to be admitted; and there, after the weeding and the watering were done, would we repair, together with a selection of whatever were deemed the choicest of that day's delicacies; he to his chair, which, beneath his weight, creaked and groaned like the rigging of a three-master ploughing a heavy sea; me to one of its residual cushions – chintz chrysanthemums glazed with a delicate mould which rose in the air like talcum powder when I took my place at Mr Fenner's feet.

When he was not entertaining guests, I reckon, Mr Fenner sat enthroned in his chair in quiet content, munching his carrots and peas, and mulling over his vintage *Old Moores*. When he had company – i.e. me – he talked about the Great War. *His* war.

To listen to Mr Fenner, anyone would think the war had been won by horses – Tickler, Bruno, Benjy and Chow, to name but a few, every one of them the recipient of the Victoria Cross, if there were any justice in the world. Mr Fenner would go red in the face with emotion as he recounted the saga of Tickler, who had got supplies to a beleaguered outpost when the entire

Transport Command had declared the mission impossible: or Chow, who, despite a rain of enemy shrapnel, had dug in his hooves alongside a collapsed barn and refused to budge until the men who had come to fetch him away finally cottoned on, and dug his unconscious rider out of the rubble. I heard how Barley Mo, bearing a cavalry officer obviously bent on fighting the wrong war, had tipped the bloody fool into a quickthorn hedge and by his quick thinking saved the lives of a regiment, if not an entire division; and Barnum and Bailey, two Suffolk Punches who, unaided, had charged a Boche tank and accepted the surrender of its animal-loving crew. The tales were endless, the recital interrupted only by expressions of anger at the insufficiency of recognition accorded the four-legged heroes who alone had made victory possible.

Mr Fenner had an indelible crayon which he kept specially for writing on war memorials. Whenever he came upon one with a blank space at the end of the list of the fallen, he would add the names of horses known to him personally who had sacrificed their lives for their country. Once – in Bawdeswell, I think he said – the vicar had caught him in the act, and threatened to call the police. Luckily for Mr Fenner, there had been a lady in the church doing the flowers. She came over to find out what the fuss was about, and when Mr Fenner explained what he had been doing and why, she was so taken with the idea that she had a plaque put up: *In grateful memory of the horses of the British armed forces who gave their lives for their country in the Great War 1914–1918.* Underneath was engraved: *They graze the pastures of Heaven.*

Mr Fenner did not seem to have a lot of luck with the clergy. Maybe because he was Chapel himself, he always seemed to be getting on their wrong side. One Plough Sunday he, along with the other ploughmen of the parish, brought his employer's team to the church to receive the traditional blessing. Being Chapel, he brought the horses strictly on master's orders and against the promptings of his own conscience.

Describing what happened, Mr Fenner said he had no doubt that this theological unease communicated itself to his charges, Charley and Perce, two perfectly matched Shires who, in his own words, were 'sweet as honey, but nobody's fools'. If they had been offered the choice between Church and Chapel he was

[134]

positive they would have said Chapel without a second thought. Decked out with brasses, manes braided with ribbons, their white feathering brushed from hock to heel until it shone like silk, they looked a picture as they lined up in the church-yard with the rest of the horses, waiting for the rector to come out and do his stuff.

The rector, who inclined to High Church, was making rather a meal of the proceedings. 'Got up like the bloody Pope,' was how Mr Fenner phrased it, 'with a kid in front of him swinging one o' them smoking things what let out a fart every five paces.'

Charley and Perce behaved beautifully while the rector blessed them. It was simply unfortunate that they had been placed at the end of the front line of horses. As the rector, preceded by his censer-swinging acolyte, rounded their flanks to get to the second row, Charley, as is the way with animals, feeling a sudden call of nature, answered it.

'Had to go back to the rectory an' change his fancy dress,' Mr Fenner recalled with satisfaction. 'Came back in a plain suit, not even a dog collar. Blew me up, though, afterwards, some-thing sinful. What he expec' me to do, the silly ole fool? Put a cork in it?'

Mr Fenner selected a young turnip, a charming little vegetable, its creamy coat flushed at the base with a delicate rose. He got rid of the clinging earth by rubbing it along his trouser seam, from waist to thigh, and back again: took a bite out of the sweet flesh and settled back comfortably.

'Talkin' of horses,' he remarked, 'you ought to get your pa to get you lessons. Lots o' posh little girls ride.'

'I'm *not* posh!'

The word cut me to the core. After all my delusions of having settled into Opposite the Cross Keys as to the hovel born, it appalled me to hear myself so labelled. Beside, it was untrue. I wasn't: my family wasn't. I knew quite well, as Mr Fenner evidently did not, that I had not been born with a Pony Club rosette in my mouth. Dancing lessons, yes; piano, even elo-cution. But not riding. The likes of my father's child did not go swanking off to gymkhanas got up in velvet caps and jackets, breeches and boots that must have cost the earth.

[135]

Actually, except for an occasional wistful yearning after those fetching accoutrements, I was grateful for my lowly status because I had no desire – indeed, quite the contrary – to get on terms with that other essential item of gear, the one with four legs at the corners, an uncertain disposition and large teeth.

'Know what?' said Mr Fenner. 'You ought to get that gypsy gal to learn you. They got a rare way wi' horses, gyppoes. Born to it, d'yer see? They got a raft of 'em out in that field back o' them caravans. Why don't you arst her learn you how, while you're here?'

This mention of Nellie Smith, about whom, even since Wednesday, I had been unthinking with all my energies, unmanned me. Weeping, I confided to Mr Fenner all about the spring water (all, that is, except for revealing my promise to Tom and my betrayal of his trust: I even made out that the spring in question lay in quite another direction, towards Hautbois) and how Nellie Smith had got a beating from her father because of it.

Haltingly, for I lacked the mental sophistication to arrange my thoughts in manageable order, let alone express them clearly in words, I tried to convey what an unbridgeable gap the man's violence had opened up – not just between Nellie Smith and me, which would have been bad enough, but between me and Salham St Awdry where I had been so happy. If Mr Fenner wanted to know the truth of it, the real reason I had chosen not to go with Mrs Fenner to Norwich that morning was that I was afraid I might have decided not to come back.

'Them gyppoes ain't St Awdry's.' Mr Fenner finished his turnip, threw away the stump. 'Never were, an' never will be.' Taking his time, he reached into his pocket for his pipe. Not until he had got the horrible shag smoking away nicely – at least, out of doors, it had the virtue of keeping gnats and midges at a disgusted distance – did he make any further observation upon what I had said. Then he asked, in a casual way, 'Beat her up bad, did he?'

'I – I don't know. I saw him undoing his belt. I didn't wait to see.'

'Oh ah.' A long puff on the pipe. Then: 'This was when – Wednesday?' I nodded. 'You bin to ask how she is?'

I hung my head as I admitted that I had not. I did not know how to explain my craven need to distance myself from that flashing length of leather which had invaded my dreams, that silver buckle catching the light of the setting sun as it found its target again and again.

'Well . . .' said Mr Fenner, taking his pipe out of his mouth. In that one word he made me aware that things were going to get better from then on. 'Bugger me if I know what the fuss is about. Don't your pa never give you a belting?'

'Of course not! He'd never do anything like that!'

'Oh ah?' Mr Fenner considered, then offered, 'Maybe it's on account of he's a gent. Can't be because you're a little angel, 'cause we know better, don't we? Or maybe it's on account o' being eddicated, he don't need to. He's got the language. We country bors, not being what you would call civilized, we have to make do with our hands. It's all we got.'

'But it's so cruel!'

'Is it now?' Mr Fenner's blue eyes twinkled. 'You ever asked Maud how many times her cruel ole pa clouted her over the lughole when she was a kid getting above herself, which was seven days outer seven, on the average? You ask her – hear what she says.'

I felt confused. Nobody needed to tell me that Maud loved her father with a love devoid of reservations. I believe that even then, young as I was, I sensed that at least part of the reason why her pathetic little attempts at love affairs came to their premature, unconsummated conclusions was that the love object of the moment never came within miles of coming up to her pa.

I felt even more confused when the iron gate to the allotments creaked open and Nellie Smith came in, looking terrible, with one eye shut and empurpled, a bump on her left temple, and the spaces between the chickenpox scabs, which seemed to have held to their places with undisturbed equanimity, filled in with claw marks which looked as if they had been made by a wild beast or the spike of a large buckle – or possibly both. At the sight of that small, damaged face I felt a powerful urge to run to Nellie Smith, my friend; put my arms round her, speak words of comfort. At the same time I wanted to run a mile.

In the event, I was spared a decision between those

incompatible alternatives. The girl approached the shed with quick, purposeful steps, bent over the basin at our feet, and helped herself to a carrot.

As she stood biting into it, showing a gap in her upper jaw where one of her middle teeth was missing, Mr Fenner said in a friendly way, 'Glad to hear you say please,' whereupon Nellie Smith tossed the carrot back into the basin with, 'Keep yer mouldy carrot!'

Mr Fenner observed, 'I begin to see why yer pa give you a belting. Waited longer than he should 've.'

'My dad thinks the world of me!'

'Oh ah? Funny way he's got o' showing it.'

'The world of me!' the other repeated. 'An' I think the world of my dad!'

What I had failed to notice among all the evidences of her hurt was that Nellie Smith was bursting with self-satisfaction. She barely noticed me, save as an audience. Any other audience would have done as well.

'A king o' men!' she insisted, whirling round so that her skirt flared out in a circle. 'What you think? That snotty-nose PC Utting come into the camp an' wanted to fetch him down to the nick. Sauce! I told him I fell out of a tree, not that he believed a word of it, but what could he say? He said people half a mile down the road heard me screeching.' The girl giggled. '"I got a loud voice," I said, "an' it were a high tree."'

She was wearing yet another dress: spotted muslin, full in the skirt but nearer her size this time, which made me realize for the first time how thin she was, a matchstick girl, no thickness to her at all, almost. The dress had short puffed sleeves, the skinny arms they revealed nearly as clawed as her face. She waved them about as if she wanted to draw them to our attention.

'"In that case," the copper says, "I'll get an ambulance out here, take you into casualty, make sure there's no bones broken." I told him what he could do with his sodding ambulance! Did we laugh, when he'd gone off with his tail between his legs! Reckon he could have heard *that* half a mile down the road and all!'

With a sudden movement, like a dancer in a cancan, she flung the back of the muslin skirt up and over her shoulders. To my shocked surprise she was wearing absolutely nothing underneath, unless the still-angry weals which criss-crossed her back and buttocks could be considered something.

She let the dress fall.

'Couldn't 'a gone to the hospital an' let 'em seen that, could I?' she asked cheerfully, not making it clear whether it was the weals or the absence of underwear to which she referred. 'Anyways, the old un plunked some stuff on, took the sting out afore you could say knife.'

'Oh, Nellie!' I got out at last, and burst into tears.

'What the hell's got into her?' demanded Nellie Smith.

Chapter Thirteen

W E sat on the bank in the cowslip meadow dabbling our feet in the Sal. In the field behind us buff-coloured cows lay about in the sun, whisking their tails every now and again. You could never have guessed what apricot-scented treasure the field harboured in its proper season. I wondered if Nellie Smith would be there next spring to pick cowslips with me.

I must have mentioned something of the sort, because she said, 'I dunno,' with no special feeling and as if anywhere was the same as any other where.

Feeling sorry for my rootless friend, I asked, didn't she miss having a home, a real home stuck fast to the ground so it couldn't be moved.

The answer was a laugh that sounded more of a jeer.

'Rather be a bloody tree, you mean, stuck where you grow, 'stead of having legs to go wherever you want to?' Without waiting for a reply, she went on, 'You heard of a place called Ancient Greece an' Rome?'

Taken aback by this sudden turn of the conversation, I nevertheless admitted that I had heard of it.

'Well, then! That were full of houses, weren't it? Big uns – palaces. They had a book in school wi' pictures. Pictures of what's left: bit o' wall here, a couple of pillars there, or a statue of a man wi' no clothes on. Not all of him neither. Tha's what happens to places stuck in the ground. Sooner or later they fall down or get broke up, an' all what's left in the end is a pile of rubbish for the gypsies to pick over.' Nellie Smith regarded me with more disdain than pity. 'You'll see. Except I shouldn't think as you'll be there to see it. It takes time, ruins does. But sooner or later there won't be no St Awdry's any more, nor

Norwich, nor nowhere folk live in houses. But us gypsies'll just get ourselves into our caravans an' drive off whistling!'

I was silent, mulling over what she had just said – or not really mulling, it was too hot: letting the prospect of the downfall of civilization swish over me like the swallows which kept swishing past, up and down the air, hawking for flies. Since the episode of the spring the relationship between Nellie Smith and me had at once deepened and become more fragile. I had enjoyed the delights, now I understood the dangers, of calling someone friend.

Together, children though we were, we had accomplished something powerful: we had actually influenced, not to say decided, the course of events in that adult world, which, closely as it impinged on our own, was normally outside our ordering. *They* pointed us along the way we had to go, like it or not. For once, *we* had pointed *them*.

The old un had been dead right about the efficacy of virgin spring water. The beautiful Miss Lee had not reappeared in St Awdry's since her drenching. Her cheerful little sports car was no longer seen in the gypsy encampment. Nellie Smith's father, once he had finished beating up his daughter, had taken off for Norwich, and returned tipsy and morose. Since then, according to Nellie, he had not been anywhere; spent his days sitting on his caravan steps drinking beer and looking so defeated that, if you didn't know the truth of it, and if it hadn't been for Nellie's weals and bruises, slow to heal, you might have thought it was she who had belted him instead of the other way round.

How I wished, when the occasion called for it, that the spring water might work in reverse – instead of separating lovers, bring them together! Maud had come down to St Awdry's the Sunday before looking very down in the mouth. That is, to the uninitiated eye she looked the same as usual, except for her wart, which I knew to be an infallible barometer of her inmost feelings. When Maud was in her usual humour it sat pat on the ridge of her nose; but when she was melancholy it flopped sideways, limp as a wind sock when there wasn't any wind. The Sunday before, it had flopped all over the place.

I did not have to ask the cause because I knew it already. Just as I had had a hand in the banishment of Miss Lee, so – though in that case not deliberately – was I in part responsible for the collapse of the most recent of Maud's affairs of the heart.

The latest object of her affections was a young man named Eric, who was some kind of distant cousin of the Fenners'; an awful weed, I thought, but glamorous at twenty paces because he was a soldier. Maud and I used to wait for him outside Wellington Barracks, at the end of Riverside Road: and when he came along, stepping smartly out of the gate in his dress uniform of red tunic, blue trousers and hat with a white band and a shiny peak, he looked marvellous – until he was close enough for you to see his stupid face, which bore a marked family resemblance to Ellie's.

Maud, as always, came provided with Woodbines and packets of slab chocolate – gifts which he grabbed with scant grace. Though she coloured prettily at sight of him, even to my partial eye she looked, in her frumpish costume and hat, more like his maiden aunt than his girl friend; and Eric, for his part, always did his best to hurry her away from the Barracks, up the road towards Mousehold Heath, as if he did not want his mates to see whom he was walking out with.

Eric wasn't very nice to me, either, which irked me, for I was comfortable in my role of little charmer. Looking back, though, I realize that the surprising thing was that Maud – as she did with all her beaux – took me along at all. Was I her ultimate insurance against what might otherwise befall up the road, in some secret hollow of the Heath, where the spicy smell of the gorse and the heather, titillating the senses beyond bearing, might seduce even a virtuous young woman with a wart on her nose into forgetting in a moment of madness that marriage or nothing was what she held firmly in mind?

A little before I came down with chickenpox my father had brought home a kite from his weekly lesson with Mr Lee: a Chinese paper kite, shaped like a bird such as had never flown on land or sea, a bird with a scaly neck and a cruel, imperious head crowned with jewels made out of coloured tinfoil which flashed in the sun. My mother had wanted to hang it up on the wall as a decoration, it was so beautiful and so frail, but my father had insisted that if Chinese children could fly such kites, so, surely, could I.

As it happened, I had not, to date, had much success even with the English variety; and for days I waited impatiently for either my father or Alfred to find the time to come Chinese kite-flying with me, both to provide assistance and, if necessary, to be there to take the blame if the fabulous bird, for its own inscrutable, Oriental reasons, refused to take to the air.

In Norwich the place *par excellence* for kite-flying was a knife-edged excrescence called St James's Hill which, as it happened, was just across the road from the Barracks. All the same, and even besotted by love, it was rash of Maud to assert so confidently, 'Eric'll fly it for you.'

Whilst I lacked her trust in the youth, I was seized with desire to see my Chinese kite soaring into the English empyrean. I could not bear to wait a moment longer. After all, I reassured myself, if a soldier trained to guard the British Empire couldn't fly a simple thing like a kite, who could?

'Wha's that, then?' Eric asked in his surly way, when he came out of the Barracks. Even he, stupid as he was, must have seen very well that it couldn't possibly be anything but a kite.

'A kite,' I answered nevertheless, putting on my winsome smile. 'Maud said you'd help me fly it.'

Eric looked more human than I had ever known him.

'A kite!' he echoed, rosy with pleasure. 'A ruddy kite!'

The wedge-shaped end of St James's Hill was sandy and of gentler gradient than its slippery, grass-covered sides. The three of us toiled up it to the top, aglow with anticipation. Though I balked at letting him carry the kite, I decided that Eric was not so mouldy after all.

At the top of the hill a brisk breeze was blowing. It was agreed that Maud, being taller than I, would hold the bird up ready for the take-off whilst Eric, taking charge of the reel, tweaked it into the air. When it was safely up and away he would hand over to me and I could carry on from there, flying my kite.

It was a sensible arrangement, yet I passed over the bird and the reel with foreboding. The two of them, it seemed to me, giggling and nudging each other in the soppy way of lovers, lacked the *gravitas* which marked out the dedicated kite-flyer.

Still, the plan worked. The bird swooped upward as if it couldn't wait to get airborne, and hung there, so magnificent with its spread wings and flashing jewels that we all three cried out, 'Ah!' involuntarily, the way one does when rockets burst into stars at a fireworks display.

Unfortunately for us, there was one other spectator, equally transported. A dog, a pure-bred mongrel the size of a donkey and of roughly the same coat and colour, had come bounding up the slope to see what we were up to. Still a puppy for all its dimensions, it was, I reckon, already old enough to have discovered that its size was a barrier to social acceptance because it did not approach us directly, but lay down a little further along the ridge, nose between paws, following our every movement with absorbed attention.

When the Chinese bird flew, however, it was too much. I cannot, of course, profess to know what the dog had in mind. I can only guess that, colour-blind as dogs are stated to be, this was nevertheless a dog with an aesthetic sense who, sighting an object of such beauty overhead, reached for it as a child might stretch out its tiny hand to grasp a bright bauble, instinctively.

Except that, being a dog, and a donkey-sized dog at that, it was no tiny hand. Suddenly, with a throaty roar, the animal took an almighty leap, all four feet off the ground as it reached for the swaying loveliness intolerably out of reach.

The details of what happened next are entangled in my memory like the kite cord itself. In a matter of moments the dog and Eric, conjoined in yards of cord, the Chinese bird plummeting out of the sky to land on top of them, rolled over twice on the narrow path which ran along the top of the ridge, and disappeared from sight over the edge.

Maud screamed. I think, though I can't be sure, that she screamed, not 'Eric!' but 'The kite!' We ran to the easy way down, and then round the base of the hill to where we found Eric sitting up and furious, and the dog biting pieces out of the remains of the paper bird with the tentative air of a wine taster trying out an unknown vintage. Both man and dog, though now separate entities once more, were bound about by odds and ends of kite cord, long strands of which festooned the hillside in a most untidy way.

'Look at that, will yer!' Eric shouted at sight of us, pointing to the grass stains on his red tunic and white webbing belt. I went and retrieved his cap from some distance off. It was a sorry sight.

'Look at that!' Eric sounded beside himself. I no longer thought he wasn't so mouldy. He was mouldy in the extreme. 'They'll dock me for that! Christ knows what they'll dock me! You an' yer fucking kite!'

Had he cracked his skull or broken a leg I am sure Maud would have fallen upon his breast with loving lamentations. As it was, she said coldly, 'None of your bad language in front of the child, *if* you please!'

Eric rounded on her.

'You! You stupid old fart!'

Maud reddened, but said nothing. She fumbled in her handbag, bringing out an envelope which I recognized as one of those into which, with a delicacy appreciated by both, my mother always put her weekly ten shilling note. Maud handed it to Eric with a sniff.

'Tha's for paying back the Army to get you clean. Tell 'em to wash your mouth out while they're about it.' She snapped the bag shut and took me by the hand. 'Come on, Sylvie. Nex' time we got a kite to fly, we'll make sure to pick a gentleman.'

We walked back to the tram terminus, both of us, I think, more exhilarated than sad. *This was life!* The dog followed a little behind and tried to get on the tram with us. I wouldn't have minded taking it home if the conductor had allowed it on, but Maud snapped, 'Don't be daft!' and the world, like the tram presently, began to run on its accustomed rails again.

When Maud turned up at St Awdry's looking out of sorts, I knew she must be grieving, not that mouldy Eric was out of her life, but that, weeks after, she still had not found anybody to replace him.

'Never mind,' I whispered, when I got the chance. None of the Fenners seemed to have noticed that anything was the matter; or if they had, hadn't said. 'When I get back to St Giles we'll take a nice walk to the cemetery, like we always do. That will make you feel better.'

She made no reply, but gave me a hug that, even though I couldn't see anything morally against killing two birds with one stone, made me feel a bit guilty. I hadn't mentioned anything about wanting to go to the cemetery on my own account – to wit, to see for myself the grave of Mrs Smith, the gypsy princess.

After a while we took our feet out of the stream and let them dry in the sun. Nellie Smith's legs were longer than mine, but her feet were smaller, high-arched: the right kind for a princess's daughter. Her face, still bruised, still scabbed with my chicken-pox, looked less patrician, her black curls positively nihilistic. But her feet were beautiful. The sight of them made me feel emotional. I hated to see them vanish into the boots, several sizes too large, into which she usually poked them.

We were having a day off, well earned. Day after day, accompanying Mrs Fenner to the dusty fields, we had lifted potatoes, and more potatoes and more potatoes, until we none of us wanted to see a potato again. Working the Nellie Smith system we had done well for ourselves financially. Mrs Fenner was quite beside herself: she had never brought home so much money in her life. Most of my share was passed on to Nellie – no act of charity but a pleasurable self-indulgence.

That's for the angel's toes, I would say to myself, handing over the silver, keeping only the coppers back for myself. *That's for his insteps and his heels. Now I'm up to his ankles . . .* and so on.

Drugged with the heat, we slouched along Swan Lane, came out on to the main road by the pub. Across the way, the reeds round the pond had begun to set up a clatter, a warning tattoo drummed by a nasty little wind which brought no refreshment of the heavy air. A bank of cloud had appeared from nowhere, shutting off the sun. The rooks in the beeches had fallen silent.

The first drops of rain began to fall as we neared the smithy. By the time we reached Opposite the Cross Keys the skies were teeming. We were soaked.

'Mrs Fenner's gone to Horsford with Ellie, to the dentist.' I panted out the implicit invitation: but Nellie Smith still refused to enter. She stayed outside the front door, inadequately shel-tered by its apology for a porch, her muslin dress moulded against her body, the curls on her forehead channelling rivulets to her nose and cheeks.

'Come inside!' I coaxed, safely under cover myself. 'I won't tell anybody.'

[146]

Nellie Smith shook her head; only at that moment the world rocked with thunder. Almost simultaneously, lightning cleft the sky and the girl came rushing in, stumbling over the door sill, angry with the elements and with her own fear of them.

Angry with me as well, for having witnessed her weakness, an anger which she took out in spiteful denigration of the room which, she well knew, had become the sweet, still centre of my universe.

'Cripes!' she exclaimed. 'What a ruddy dump!'

The fact that I could see Opposite the Cross Keys through her eyes as, at the beginning of my stay, I had seen it through Alfred's – the shabbiness, the dirt, the chest of drawers one foot short, the sooty swag above a fire banked up with coal dust: the smell of sulphur, of Gyp, of absent, unwashed Fenners – in no way lessened my resentment. It was not polite, it was not friendly, to run down other people's heavens.

Nellie Smith circled the room warily, as if afraid of contagion. I sat on the horsehair sofa watching her: thinking how much easier it was to hate a friend than an enemy.

I burst out bitterly, 'I wouldn't go on like that about your caravan, whatever I thought.'

My depth of feeling did not touch her in the slightest. 'Our caravan, lemme tell you, 's a blooming Buckingham Palace compared to this hole.' She made a face at the baskets of roses and lilacs on the wallpaper, the trellis and songbirds clinging perilously to the walls, then concentrated her attention on the door at the side of the fireplace. 'Wha's that, then? A cupboard?'

'It's the way upstairs.' At the sight of her fingering the latch: 'You can't go up there! It's private!'

'Private?' As a caravan dweller, Nellie Smith seemed genuinely puzzled by the word. '*You* sleep up there, don't you?'

'Private to the Fenners. I sleep down here on the couch.'

'So what if you do? It don't mean you can't go up. Or did they tell you not to?'

I hesitated.

'Not exactly. I just know I mustn't.'

'Cracked!' pronounced Nellie Smith. 'Anyway, tha's you. Nobody said nothin' to me.'

She swung the door open, more open than I had ever seen the

Fenners open it. I ran across the room and tried to wrest the latch from her, shut the door up again.

'You're not to go up there! You mustn't!'

Nellie Smith grinned at me without letting go.

'Bet you're dying to know what it's like yourself.' The degree of truth in this made it all the more important that the Fenners' privacy remain inviolate. 'What you think they keep up there, then? Dead bodies?' She went up a stair or two, me hanging on to her skirt. 'Stinks enough.'

Voice, body, trembling, I got out, 'If you got up there, I'll never speak to you again!'

'What a bloody take-on about nothing!' Nellie Smith remarked brightly; twitched her dress out of my hand and ran up the stairs.

Was it? – a bloody take-on about nothing, I mean. At the time it didn't seem so. It doesn't seem so now, sometimes. At other times, dependent on my mood, I wonder if it wasn't a poor excuse for breaking up a friendship.

Because I kept my word. I did. I never spoke to the gypsy girl again. When she came back downstairs, black eyes sparkling, and insisted on telling me what it was like on the upper floor of Opposite the Cross Keys, I stuck my fingers into my ears and refused to listen. At this she got so annoyed that she tried to prise my fingers away, and because she was stronger than I, succeeded.

She held my hands in her own, rough and brown, and began afresh. I could no longer close my ears, so I closed my mind. I shut myself off from Salham St Awdry and from everything to do with it. I thought myself back in St Giles, with my father and mother and Alfred, and Maud and Mrs Hewitt and May Bowden and Pillow the toad: even with mouldy Eric. With my patchwork quilt and the beautiful little jar in which my father kept his brushes for doing Chinese writing. With playing 'Oh will you wash my father's shirt' on the black notes of the piano, crossing over hands for the second part, like a proper virtuoso. Anything to keep out the hateful things Nellie Smith was saying.

The storm was over, the sun was out again. Nellie Smith

[148]

must have become suddenly afraid Mrs Fenner might return and find us in a posture which required explanation. Or perhaps what she had seen upstairs had confirmed her in her fear of houses. At any rate, she stopped speaking, and let me go.

I said nothing, not even when she smacked me on the side of the head, making my eyes spurt tears.

I said nothing, not even when she smacked me on the other side, before running out of the door. When Mrs Fenner came back with Ellie, who was whimpering like a puppy because she'd had a tooth filled, I reminded her that the new school term would soon be beginning, and in a couple of weeks' time it would be my birthday.

Time to go home.

Chapter Fourteen

Alfred made a special journey to collect me and my belongings. He couldn't bring out the piled-up sheets and towels fast enough. I could just see Mrs Hewitt's face when she found them in the wash next Monday, the sheets grey, the towels scratchy as emery paper. I could see Alfred, every time he returned for a fresh load, taking a deep breath before he stepped inside Opposite the Cross Keys and then holding it until he was safely back in the air again.

Of the Fenners only Ellie was at home, combing her hair as usual. She simpered at my handsome brother and informed him with unusual animation, 'Went to the dentist Tuesday.' Opening her mouth wide, a forefinger poked inside by way of pointer: 'Filling.'

I could see that Alfred was embarrassed. Protected by a pile of blankets, he mumbled over the top of it, 'Hope it didn't hurt,' and made for the car.

I said no formal goodbyes. I *felt* goodbyes, though. As we sat round the table that last night I could have howled with the feeling of goodbye which pierced me like a sword. They had only to beg, 'Don't go! Don't go!' and I would have stayed for ever.

Instead, all that happened was that Charlie, idly turning the pages of an *Eastern Evening News* he had picked up somewhere, observed, 'They got Charlie Chaplin on at the Haymarket, Sylvie. You ought to get your ma to take you.'

Tom was upset because he had brought me a toad to keep Pillow company, and I had turned down the offer. His soft, red lips quivered with unhappiness. I couldn't very well explain that, after Nellie Smith, I felt that Pillow was safer without friends, so I pretended that May Bowden had proclaimed that there was only room enough for one toad in her rockery.

'She's barmy!' he protested. 'If there's room for one, there's room for two.'

'That's what I told her. But she still says only one.'

'Barmy!' he repeated with unaccustomed moroseness. I gave him the whipped cream walnut I'd been saving for the journey and he cheered up. He bit the pointed top off, then leaned across the table smelling of the milk chocolate, and whispered, 'You won't ferget, back in Norwich, to keep that secret I told you?'

'What secret's that, then?' Mrs Fenner intervened, smiling.

Tom, taking elaborate precautions not to be overheard, whispered, 'I shown her the spring.'

'Oh, *that* secret!' exclaimed Mrs Fenner in her normal strength of voice. 'Sylvie wouldn't go telling anybody about that – would you, Sylvie?'

'What an idea!' I said.

Bathed and in clean pyjamas, tucked in and kissed with due regard to protocol by my mother, father, Alfred and Maud successively, I lay in my fresh, sweet bed, above my head the greedy guts who, grabbing at too much, held nothing fast. Every now and again a tram went past in the street with a swish like silk, humming the homely little tune trams hum. Very occasionally there was the crisp sizzle of sound which, translated, meant that the long pole with grooved head which stuck up from the tram roof had momentarily come off the wires, spilling sparks like a sparkler.

I lay in my bed and felt homesick for the prickle of horse-hair and the whang of ancient sofa springs; for the benediction of Mrs Fenner's grandpas, the guardian angels of Salham St Awdry.

I was slow to fall asleep in the bed to which my body had become a stranger. Next morning, at breakfast, I answered my parents' questions as to what it had been like at Salham St Awdry with vapid generalizations which seemed to satisfy them well enough. When I launched into a rapturous description of the old-world charm of Mrs Fenner's living-room, Alfred wiped his lips on his napkin and left the table without finishing his toast.

After breakfast I announced that I was going next door to see May Bowden. By then my parents were out of the dining-room and Maud, who had come in to clear away, felt free to observe nastily, 'Tha's right! Mustn't lose any time sucking up if you don't want her to change her will.'

Just the same, I saw by the gleam in her eye, the one with the cast in it, that she wasn't sorry to have me resume relations with her ancient enemy. I had the impresion that, with me away in St Awdry's, the war between the two of them had lost its savour. Without me, they had been like two opposing hockey players, bullying off with grim intent, only to discover at the last moment that there was no ball.

As it turned out, my reunion with May Bowden would have rejoiced Maud's heart. I had opened and shut her gate as quietly as possible, hoping to tiptoe unnoticed over the cobbles to say hello to Pillow before knocking on the house door.

Engaging as ever, the toad came to my whistle as if I had never been away. Squatting on my haunches, toadlike myself, I had just lifted him on to my palms, his eyes already rolling upward in anticipation of ecstasy, when May Bowden's voice, high and unfriendly at my back, caused the poor little thing to leap for the safety of the rockery, to disappear among the ferns.

'Well! You're a sight, I must say!'

I scrambled to my feet and stood, head hanging, whilst she circled me, making an inspection.

'You look like a gypsy! Brown and scratched, hair like a bramble bush. Ladies', she added complacently, touching her own powdered cheeks, 'have complexions like rose petals, not skins you could make shoes out of. If I'd known you were going to get yourself into that state, I'd have lent you a parasol to take with you.'

I had a momentary vision of myself grubbing for spuds with one hand whilst, with the other, I held aloft one of May Bowden's French parasols, all flounces and tassels. I concentrated on 'parasol' thankfully. It enabled me to put 'gypsy' out of mind. I was trying not to think about Nellie Smith.

Something of the devil which informed the gypsy girl's

skinny frame took possession of my own, and I said, 'I don't think I want to be a lady. It's too much of a bother.'

'When you are rich,' May Bowden answered, 'you have to do a lot of bothersome things. Ladies have obligations. You'll find out for yourself when I die and leave you all my money.'

Still prompted by Nellie Smith's demon, I asked with minimal politeness that, in that case, would she please leave her money elsewhere, because I didn't want it.

May Bowden's face became plum-coloured under the powder, not ladylike at all.

'I'll leave my money where I like, Miss Impertinence! If you don't like it, you can lump it!'

I would have run home crying to my mother to come and stop May Bowden from leaving me her money, if the old spinster hadn't gone on to mention something about my impending birthday. As it happened, I desperately wanted for my birthday something that cost a lot of money – a bike – and my mother had said I couldn't have one. Maisie's bicycle, good as new, had been standing in the shed doing nothing ever since my sister had gone to live in London, and there was absolutely no sense in spending money on another which, at the rate I was growing, would be outgrown before the year was out. When I wailed that Maisie's bike was miles too big for me, my mother smiled that seldom smile which, sweet as it was, meant a 'no' not to be changed by wheedling or whining, or both. 'You're shooting up like a weed, darling. All you need is a little patience.'

I did not possess a little patience. I did not possess any patience at all. Could I possibly get a new bike out of May Bowden? Not necessarily as a present, but as an advance on those riches which – she had said it, not I – she was going to leave me anyway? Venal as only a child can be in pursuit of its heart's desire, I smiled up into May Bowden's powdery face and coyly admitted that yes, it *was* going to be my birthday and I was praying night and morning – May Bowden was very churchy – for a new bicycle, which was what I wanted most. My mother and father had already said no, I couldn't have one, but I kept on praying, because I knew about the power of prayer and God might see a way to my getting one after all, just as He had seen that the Israelites had got manna falling down from heaven.

[153]

My religiosity fell on stony ground.

'If the bicycle has to fall all that way,' was May Bowden's dry comment, 'there won't be much left of it by the time it plunks down in your backyard.'

What she herself had got for my birthday present, she promised me, was something that knocked bicycles into a cocked hat. Something precious. Something I would still be treasuring when I was old and grey. She so excited us both with her rhapsodies of description of the unnamed object that the slightest hint from me was enough for her to adopt as her own idea the decision that I should receive it forthwith instead of having to wait until the great day.

'It will take a little while to wrap up,' she warned me, as she went into the house.

I sat down on one of the rockery stones, happily expectant. Pillow, over his fright, came out from under the ferns and sat on my lap, sunning himself. I stroked his head and he went into his eye-rolling act. I could almost have done the same myself, without the head-stroking, because it had occurred to me that a precious something could well be exchangeable for a bike, one with turned-down handlebars even, to give me joy while I was still young enough to enjoy it.

The package with which May Bowden returned was disappointingly small, but then, you never knew. Rubies and diamonds took up little space and could be worth a king's ransom. I undid the tissue paper with trembling hands, May Bowden looking on, her hands crossed in front of her, the picture of self-satisfaction.

Pillow took one look at my birthday present and hopped off my lap, back to the refuge of the greenery. I became aware that May Bowden was bending over me, presenting her cheek for a kiss.

Nellie Smith, I reflected fleetingly, wishing I possessed even a little of the spirit of my lost friend, would have chucked May Bowden's present straight back in her kisser. I, the little lady of St Giles, dusted my lips among the white powder and said, 'It's lovely. Thank you very much.'

What May Bowden had given me was a hairbrush, silver-backed and therefore arguably precious, but with most of the bristles worn away and a kind of compacted fluff caking such stumps as remained. Some red hairs, caught in the few bristles which survived intact, moved their tentacles in the warm air.

'Promise you won't use it till your birthday,' May Bowden admonished.

I promised, and took my leave, repeating the grateful phrases which I knew were expected of me. I dawdled homeward until, risking a quick look backward, I saw May Bowden go into her house; then stopped, looking down at the revolting object in my hands, wondering what on earth to do with it.

My prime thought – oddly enough, for I was not an unselfish child – was not for myself and my disappointed hopes, but for May Bowden herself. I couldn't bear to face Maud with that hairbrush, see the expression of glee spreading over her face as she took in its awfulness, watch the wart on her nose shaking in the gale of her derisive laughter. My mother and father and Alfred, whilst less cruel, would not be exactly kind. They would be sure to repeat that May Bowden wasn't all there. The fact that I knew this as well as anybody didn't give them the right to say it.

Perhaps, too, there was a substratum of feeling that, having lost Nellie Smith, I needed all the friends I had, even the not-all-there ones.

What was I to do with the ghastly thing? In the end, I went round to the dustbins, in their niche by the bicycle shed. Not to throw the hairbrush away. You didn't throw away silver: it was unthinkable. After agonized excogitation I climbed up on to a dustbin lid, reached up and hid the hairbrush in the gutter of the bicycle shed.

When the day of my birthday came round Maud gave a sniff at May Bowden's birthday card – padded silk scented with Parma violets, expensive as cards go, but her sole apparent acknowledgement of the occasion. That was only to be expected, and I felt that both I and May Bowden had got off lightly. What I had not expected was the latter's continuing interest in the welfare of her birthday present.

'Have you brushed your hair today with your lovely brush?' she would waylay me in the street to ask. Or, accusingly, if she came upon me in my normal state of dishevelment, 'You didn't brush your hair today with your lovely brush!' Until one day, strained beyond endurance by the guilty knowledge of what I had actually done with it, and the necessity of fending off Maud's puzzled 'Wha's the old geezer on about?', I flung out, 'It isn't a lovely hairbrush! It's a rotten old mouldy one!'

Having listened impassively to my tearful admission as to what I had done with her gift, May Bowden sent me to retrieve the evidence. The brush was not improved by its three weeks' sojourn in the gutter. I brought it back, already mourning the imminent loss of the little cloth bags with their inimitable contents. And not only the cloth bags. As if nine were a water-shed which, surmounted, revealed a totally different landscape on the further side, I suddenly understood what it meant to be rich. I mourned my lost inheritance.

May Bowden took the hairbrush from me. She turned it over in her hands as if she had never seen it until that moment; as if the monogrammed M and B on the silver back meant nothing to her. At last, looking up, she demanded, 'And who had the cheek to give you this bit of rubbish?'

'You did,' I faltered.

'Poor old May Bowden,' said May Bowden. 'She must be soft in the head.'

Next day a dressing-table set of silver and tortoiseshell arrived for me from the best jewellers in the city – brush, comb, hand-mirror, a covered cut-glass bowl with a swansdown powder puff inside it, and a little silver stand with branches for hanging rings on. When I went over to May Bowden's house to say thank you, she gave me a little gold ring set with three emeralds to hang on my new ring-stand.

That night I brushed my hair with my new brush, looked at myself in the new mirror, and went to bed with my emerald ring on my finger. I lay against the pillow thinking luxurious thoughts until Maud poked her nose through the door and inquired sardonically, 'Her Ladyship got everything she wants for the night?'

'Oh Maud!' I jumped out of bed, ran to the bedroom door and threw my arms round her unluxurious figure. 'I'd much rather be poor like you, honestly I would!'

[156]

'Oh ah? And I thought May Bowden was the only one round here with a screw loose!'

I hadn't been to the cemetery with Maud after all, when I got back from St Awdry's. That was because she had found a new recipient for her Woodbines and slabs of Dairy Milk. His name was Curly and he drove the pirate bus which, operating out of the carters' depot in Duke Street, was trying to undercut the fares of the official buses based in Recorder Road. Curly's fare was three ha'pence less each way, which more than made up for seats without upholstery and the general dilapidation of the equipage.

Besides, Curly was a lovely man, always laughing and joking, and a great one for the ladies who formed the majority of his customers. Once when the engine gave up altogether, outside St Awdry's, they piled out of the bus and pushed it bodily into the village, Curly at the wheel shouting encouragement, all the way to the smithy, where Mr Ames, the smith, patched it up fit for the road again. With such a bright new peg to hang her dreams on, Maud – for the time being, at any rate – had cast off melancholy.

So I went to the cemetery alone.

The day after my birthday I took some of my birthday money and went to the Market Place to buy a bunch of flowers.

The Market flowers, packed tight into their metal vases, seemed not at all the right kind for a gypsy's grave. I finally settled for some tiger lilies, not because they were any more suitable than the rest, but because of their name, wild-sounding and dangerous. They were expensive – fivepence each – so I could only buy three.

I took the tram to the Earlham Road terminus. The tram-lines finished exactly at the cemetery gates, which always disturbed me a little, as if the terminus really was the end. The way in was by a broad avenue, quite imposing. The graves nearest the entrance gates were those of people who had died a long time ago. The more recent burials stretched further and further into the distance, making the dead seem very far away, which, after all, was what they were – further than you could ever see, no matter how big the cemetery grew: until, as

[157]

was bound to happen in time, it was the size of the whole world.

I once asked Maud who would bury the last person left alive, since, obviously, he would be in no position to do it himself. It seemed a reasonable enough question, but Maud snapped, 'Don't be daft!' Adding – rather as an afterthought, it seemed to me, 'God, o' course!'

A short distance into the cemetery was a little house where I intended to ask the way to the grave of Mrs Smith, the gypsy princess who had died the year before in the Norfolk and Norwich Hospital. Only, somehow, as I drew near the sign which said 'Inquiries', I grew reluctant to ask, reluctant to be told. The truth was, I was not all that keen on naked graves: too little separated you from their occupants. I preferred them dressed up with urns and angels and broken columns, with names on them and dates that were past, so that you could be reasonably sure the people inside were decently dead.

A man in uniform came out of the little house, took a look at my flowers and asked, 'Need any help, girlie?'

'No thank you,' I answered, deciding then and there to give Nellie Smith time to earn enough to pay for an angel before I paid my respects.

I left my flowers instead on the admiral's grave, the one with the ropes and the anchors. As it said he had died in 1897 I didn't suppose he had had many flowers recently. I pictured him looking out of heaven and exclaiming with surprised pleasure, 'Well, shiver my timbers! If there isn't a dear little girl down there putting some tiger lilies on my grave!' I put on my holiest expression, just in case; strained my ears and thought I almost heard a faint 'Ahoy, there!' sliding down the wind, though I couldn't be dead certain.

Chapter Fifteen

ONE evening my father returned home looking puzzled. It was the third time running he had gone round to Mr Lee's for his handwriting lesson and found the shop locked, with a sign saying 'Closed' hanging on the inside of the glass door. When he had pressed the bell which rang in the flat above the shop, nobody had answered.

'I don't understand it,' my father complained. 'It's not like Mr Lee to go off without letting me know.'

My father was upset. He loved his Chinese writing. In China, he was fond of saying, handwriting was regarded as the noblest form of art, surpassing even painting which, in the classic Chinese view, was only a debased form of calligraphy anyway. Watching him as with seriousness and concentration he used the brushes he took out of the jar with the pattern of butterflies, first touching their tapered tips to the lovely little blocks of ink, I sometimes felt, in my inchoate, childish way, that he was not really writing at all but performing a kind of music whose rhythms and harmonies I was not equipped to hear.

'He's usually so punctilious.'

My father sighed and tenderly put away his rolls of paper. In those days there was not so much as a Chinese takeaway in the city. Copying out classical Chinese texts must have been a lonely pursuit in that easterly bump of England which was the only thing oriental about it.

A week or so after that third unsuccessful visit to Mr Lee, I came home to find my mother and father looking distressed, conversing together in low tones which they cut off altogether immediately they became aware of my presence in the room.

'What's the matter?' I asked.

[159]

'Nothing,' they said, both together, and would doubtless have gone on saying it if Maud hadn't come into the room.

'Tin't no good covering it up,' she advised tartly. 'It's bound to be in the *News of the World*.'

It appeared that, the night before, some hooligan had chucked a brick through the window of Mr Lee's shop, breaking not only the glass, but some of the Chinese vases on display; and naturally enough, the police, once called in, needed to get in touch with the owner of the premises. They spoke to the neighbours who said they hadn't set eyes on either Mr Lee or his daughter for – how long was it? – two weeks at least, going on three. What with one thing and another, the police got hold of the fire brigade who fetched a long ladder which stretched from the street to one of the upper windows. A fireman climbed up the ladder.

As a result of what he saw, the police broke the lock of the side door and went upstairs to the flat, where they found Mr Lee hanging from the electric light fitting. Of his daughter, Miss Lee, there was no sign.

As the story unfolded, my parents watched me anxiously. I can't honestly remember feeling anything but a kind of shame-faced pride at actually knowing somebody who was going to get into the papers. That, and my mother's tremulous observation that only a frail little man like Mr Lee could have hanged himself from an electric light fitting without bringing it down.

'What on earth could have happened to the girl?' she wondered aloud.

'I can guess,' my father replied grimly.

I, on the other hand, knew.

Next morning I awoke to an understanding of the meaning of delayed shock. *What mischief had we wrought with that spring water?* A waking dream, as vivid as the night had been sweet and dreamless, projected Mr Lee slowly revolving underneath his chandelier, his little feet pointing to the floor, the hairs of his wispy beard moving in the draught. I saw the beautiful Miss Lee, her blue-black hair streaming behind her, hurtling her red sports car round blind corners, oblivious of the oncoming traffic, driving hell-for-leather to the end of the world.

I knew myself to be doubly damned for having given away Tom's secret, after I had promised. If I hadn't said anything, nothing would have happened, and my father would still be going happily to his handwriting lessons. As it was, others, innocent of offence, had been punished for my sin. Mr Lee revolved first one way, until the cord by which he hung was all twisted, then the other, as it slowly unravelled itself. *I* was the murderess who ought to be in the *News of the World*.

I was filled with an overwhelming desire for the company of Nellie Smith, my companion in crime. I longed to speak to her. I wanted to see her black curls bobbing, see myself reflected in the enormous eyes which took up so much of her face. I needed to check up on which of her appalling dresses she had on that day, and if she were still wearing my scabs.

Breakfast was an uncomfortable meal, my father and mother preoccupied. I noticed that the little jar with the butterflies was no longer on the sideboard.

The two of them looked on with pleasure as I ate with unimpaired appetite. Differing as they often did over the right way to bring me up, on one point they were in accord. Nothing fundamental could be amiss with a child who finished up its porridge.

My mother said, 'We really must go to Green's this morning and order your new school coat. If we leave it any longer and it needs altering, there won't be time before school begins.'

'It's much too warm for trying on!' I protested. I had other plans for the day. 'If we get it now I may have grown again by the time I need it, and then you'll be sorry you didn't get a bigger size.'

My good sense was recognized and applauded, and I left the table a free agent. Only Maud remarked suspiciously, as she wielded the crumb tray, 'You're up to something. I can see it in your face. What you up to, then? Don't deny it!'

I dithered between wide-eyed innocence and hurt reproach, and plumped for the latter. For all the good it did me.

'I only have to breathe and you suspect me.'

'Not without cause.'

*

I took the bus as far as Salham Norgate, an extra penny each way, but worth it. I didn't want to risk the Fenners knowing I was in St Awdry's. As the bus drew up to the Cross Keys stop I kept my head down, pretending there was something the matter with the buckle on one of my sandals. The Salham Norgate stop was a fair way past the encampment, but I wasn't sorry for the walk back. Now that I was on the point of reaching my destination I became less and less certain of what I had come for. The blackberries in the hedge were large and luscious and for a moment I thought of retracing my steps to the Norgate grocery shop, begging the loan of a basin, and filling it with the berries as if that alone were the purpose of my outing.

'*That's* what I was up to!' I saw myself crowing triumphantly, as I presented the brimming bowl to Maud, for turning into blackberry pie or blackberry fool or blackberry and apple pudding. '*That's* what I was up to, so there!'

I kept on towards the encampment, but slowly, my lips purpling with blackberry juice. I found a whippy length of privet and marched along, flailing the wilting greenstuff which edged the road. Almost, so preoccupied was I, I passed the gypsy camp without so much as noticing it.

Almost.

The Smiths' caravan was gone. In the middle of the maltreated oblong where it had stood, somebody had been burning rubbish. Half-consumed nastinesses and some things which had resisted destruction were humped in a slatternly mess – bits of Turkey carpet, a frying pan without a handle, a breadboard blackened with smoke. The old un, sitting in her usual place on her caravan steps, took her pipe out of her mouth and inquired, 'Lookin' fer someone, dearie?'

'Please –' I called across, still not daring to put a foot inside that foreign country, the unexpected endearment putting me even further out of countenance – 'could you tell me if Miss Lee has gone away with Mr Smith in his caravan?'

'Chu-Chin-Chinaman!' The old woman put the middle finger of each hand to the corner of her eyes, pushing the flesh up to turn herself into a parody of the stage Oriental. 'Wha's Miss Lee to you?'

'She's . . .' I hesitated. 'My father knows her.' It seemed a

[162]

shorter way than having to explain about his hobby, and the lessons in the flat over the curio shop.

'I bet he does!' The old un cackled, as if she had said something funny. 'Well, you can go home an' tell your pa the bird has flown!'

Confused, I stammered that actually it was not my father who wanted to know, it was me because – I broke off in the middle of the sentence, the old woman puffing away at her pipe as if whether I spoke or stayed mum were a matter of profound indifference. Instead of her turban, which had given her a certain dignity, she wore, probably in acknowledgement of the damps of the turning year, an ancient deerstalker whose ear-flaps, hanging down on either side of her long face, gave her the look of a decayed spaniel. For the first time it occurred to me that she was as much to blame as anybody that poor little Mr Lee had hanged himself from his chandelier. More. Whose idea was it to get the spring water in the first place?

I pointed out, with a satisfaction which I am sure she understood perfectly, 'She came back after all. The water didn't work.'

'No good putting it on to me!' The other brushed my words aside. 'If I told that Nellie once I told her a hundred times – get on with it, yer silly chai! Not my fault she didn't get round to doin' something till that Chinky bitch were three months gone.'

'Gone where?' I asked stupidly.

'Up the spout – down the drain – in and out the keyhole!' Again the cackle. 'Oh you ladies of high degree!' She drew deeply on her pipe, let the smoke out with an air of voluptuous enjoyment. 'An' I suppose you don't want to know, neither, if Nellie went along o' them, or if she didn't? Not on talkin' terms any more, are we? Not good enough for the likes of you, hey?'

'She is! She is!' I cried. 'And I *am* on talking terms! Did she go with them? Did she?'

The old gypsy heaved herself to her feet. She poked an exploratory finger under an ear-flap and scratched. I had never seen her standing up before, never realized how tall she was, not bent with age at all. She mounted the steps sure-footed and turned at the top, her back to her caravan door, commanding, contemptuous.

'Please tell me,' I begged. 'Please!'

[163]

The old woman took her pipe out of her mouth. I waited, breathless. For a moment I dared to hope that Nellie was inside the barrel-shaped abode, from which the old un was about to produce her like a magician producing a rabbit out of his hat. Instead, she opened her mouth wide enough for me to glimpse the few brown stumps embedded in her shrunken gums. Slowly, with the deliberation of an adder uncoiling itself in the sun, she stuck out her purple tongue. Long, longer, longest it emerged, flowing over her lower lip, the crescent-shaped hollow beneath, all the way down to her chin. She let the incredible object hang there for a moment, then whipped it back quick as a flash, and disappeared indoors.

'Nellie!' I called, pouring my love like spring water into the name. 'Are you there, Nellie Smith?'

No answer.

PART II

The way back

Chapter Sixteen

S o. Now that I have put you into the picture and you know all about the Fenners of Opposite the Cross Keys, I can return to that summer afternoon when I first rode – if you could call it riding – my sister Maisie's bike to Salham St Awdry, a day on the surface indistinguishable from all the days of my life up to then, but one after which my life was never the same again. I can return to the dread board at Horsford Point – *Ma gerto o ca!* – the angry man in the pony and trap who lashed out with his whip and flicked off my bicycle lamp, the men piling their telegraph poles by the roadside. I can smell again the creosote, or whatever it was, and put the smell of it into your nostrils: the stuff that stuck to the backs of my legs and, according to Mrs Hewitt the washerwoman, put paid to a perfectly good pair of socks.

I can go back to Chicken.

The Saturday after that momentous afternoon, Mrs Fenner came up to Norwich positively quivering with news of the lovely bor who had moved into the cottage next door. Not even Maud's natural scepticism, which made her instantly retaliate that nobody who could bring himself to set up home in that rat hole could be up to much, could moderate her mother's enthusiasm.

'Jest you wait till you see him!' she prophesied. 'You'll be same as the rest of us – wondering how we ever got along without him.'

His name, she told us, was Chicken.

'Chicken!' Maud echoed derisively. 'What kind of name is that?'

'In't it a laugh?' Mrs Fenner's face shone with an innocent love. 'But arter you've known him a day or two it seem to fit, somehow, an' you couldn't think of a better if you tried.'

'Wha's so special about him, then?' Maud, who was still getting over the defection of Curly, the pirate bus driver, who had just been run in for bigamy, spoke out of disillusion with all male mankind. 'Got two wings an' crows every time he lays an egg?'

'You'll see,' Mrs Fenner returned comfortably.

Next day, squashed in the back of the car between my mother and Maud like a sandwich filling between two slices of bread, one fresh and yielding, the other hard as a brick, I mouthed, '*Ma gerto o ca*' with silent fervour as Alfred veered right at Horsford Point. It was, as I saw it, only this which, every time, prevented him from forking left to Horsford and Holt – and Timbuctoo, for all I knew to the contrary.

'It won't be long now,' said my mother, 'before you'll have grown into Maisie's bicycle, and then you'll be able to ride to St Awdry's yourself.'

'With Maud on the back,' added Alfred.

'Don't talk daft!' said Maud, who could never take a joke against herself.

I had been out to St Awdry's lots of Sundays during the months that had passed since Nellie Smith had disappeared from my life. Twice – during the Christmas, and again, during the Easter holidays, I had stayed a week there – good times, but different, lacking the excitement with which the gypsy girl had infused every single day of our acquaintance.

For that was all it had been, I was forced to acknowledge, sorrowfully. An acquaintanceship, if that. I felt I knew the gypsy princess lying buried somewhere in Norwich cemetery, trapped like a wild bird and imprisoned in a cage of earth, better than I knew her daughter. As it was, I had actually got myself another friend, sort of: Dora Chapman, a large, cheerful girl whose unfailing readiness to go everywhere I wanted to go, do everything I wanted to do, bored me to tears more often than pleased me. What drove me round the bend was her placid acceptance that, coming as I did from the city and speaking posh, I was different from the rest of the village, and superior.

I had spent enough time at Opposite the Cross Keys to know that I was not superior, and I hated to be told I was. To compensate, I suppose, the moment I arrived at the Fenners' I got myself into a state of scruffiness the most intractable native would have considered overdoing it. It was a happy day for me when Mrs Fenner, taking a good look at me one morning – my matted hair, my dress with the hem hanging, plimsolls with the lace missing from one and a toe poking out of its fellow – remarked, 'Know somethin', Sylvie. You're getting me a bad name in the village. Know what Her Majesty (she meant the ex-kitchen-maid at Sandringham) said to me? "Don't she ever wash?" she said. Cheek!'

'What did you say to her?'

'What you think I said? I said, "Not if I can bloody help it!" '

Looking the way I did it was no surprise that Patricia Livermore, coming upon me in the Post Office, had hesitated before coming over to speak. If I'd seen her first she wouldn't have seen me for dust. Patricia Livermore was a new girl at Eldon House, who had moved to Norfolk with her parents from Birmingham. She was plain, uninteresting, and none of us at Eldon House cared for the funny way she spoke. There was nothing about her to induce us – little horrors that we were – to open our closed circles of friendship and let her in. Her father was something at the Midland Bank in Norwich, which made me glad my father banked with the National Provincial. When I heard that the family had moved into a house with mock-Tudor beams called Old Saffrons just outside St Awdry's on the Spixworth road, I was furious. I didn't want my Norwich life and my Salham St Awdry life to touch at any point.

Unfortunately, Patricia took my presence in St Awdry's during school holidays as a heaven-sent opportunity to get herself a friend at last. I tried to put her off by letting her see the interior of Opposite the Cross Keys, but still she stuck like a burr. The Fenners aroused her horrified but titillated curiosity. 'Sylvia, they're so *common!*' she breathed to me in wonder. She said the same about Dora Chapman. Girls who didn't wear school uniform were common by definition. That was the kind of girl she was.

Still, there was a limit to the number of times you could say no. When I said I couldn't come to play tennis – there was a tennis court at Old Saffrons – pleading in excuse that my racquet was back in St Giles, she assured me there was a spare I could use, just the right weight and a Slazenger, to boot. And when I said I couldn't come to tea on Monday, she would ask me for Tuesday, Wednesday, Thursday, Friday, Saturday, Sunday – any day I fancied, so long as I came.

As it happened, Mrs Livermore was a very good cook, and I wouldn't have minded going to tea at Old Saffrons so much if it hadn't been for the fuss. I was too young, too wrapped up in my own selfish concerns, to see the pathos in her laying on of those cakes and jellies and sandwiches cut into fancy shapes, all to snare a friend for her unattractive daughter. God knows the poor woman must have felt she was scraping the bottom of the barrel to be encouraging such a ragamuffin as I.

The Sunday I arrived with Maud for our formal introduction to the new tenant of the cottage next door, Patricia Livermore was hanging about outside the Cross Keys, waiting to ask me to tea.

'I can't possibly come.' I dismissed the invitation with scant courtesy and secret mirth. 'We're having Chicken!'

Chicken was sitting at the table with the rest of the Fenners, already so much part of the family that it seemed inconceivable he had not always been there, in his black clothes which were not at all mournful, his black cap on his head, his white teeth shining in his dark face. When we came in through the door he got up from his seat, came across and took Maud's hand with a mock gallantry, a little bow from the waist which made us all laugh yet contained an essence of genuine courtliness which had Maud colouring to the eyebrows. To me he said, one eyelid drooping in a wink imperceptible to the others, 'So this is the famous Sylvie! I'll have to mind my fuckin' p's an' q's, won't I?'

I can't hope to pin down the man's raffish charm: only that we all – and not only the Fenner ménage, the whole village, with one or two exceptions – succumbed to it. He kept us all laughing: but then, round that table at Opposite the Cross Keys, we had laughed a lot before he came. Simply, I think, when we were in his company we all felt more alive, full of

[170]

potentialities previously unsuspected. The fact that, on the face of it, he was as poor as, if not poorer even than the Fenners, carried no weight at all. Had he a mind for it, we did not doubt, he could conquer the world.

Chicken was very foul-mouthed. Next to him the Fenners sounded like a Sunday School class. Yet that is to do him an injustice. 'Foul' betokens a predetermination, *mens rea*, and Chicken, I could swear, had no such evil intent. My guess is that – as with the Fenners, except that, having travelled further afield, he had garnered an expression or two out of their ken – the obscenities which peppered every other sentence were the only way he knew of breaking out of that narrow cage of language in which circumstances and lack of educational opportunity had imprisoned him.

Before we ate tea, he took Maud and me next door to see what he had done to his new home; myself, of course, pretending that I had never before seen the place. The derelict cottage was in any event transformed even since my earlier sight of it; the loose plaster cleared away, the walls whitewashed. There was still no furniture, unless you could call a rolled-up mattress, a couple of crates, and an old-fashioned cobblers' last set up by the window, furniture. Where the divider between front and back rooms had been taken away, the ceiling was no longer sagging. On either side, it was supported by what – despite some shortening since our last acquaintance – I had no difficulty whatever in recognizing as four of the telegraph poles I had sat on by the roadside.

'Careful not to brush up against them bloody uprights,' Chicken warned, contriving another wink in my direction. 'You might get black all down yer sodding socks.'

Maud observed innocently, 'They look like telegraph poles.'

'They do, don't they?' Chicken agreed, smiling widely in compliment to her sharpness of eye. Maud glowed: a different kind of glow from the glows she summoned up for an Eric or a Curly. I knew instinctively that she would never try to woo Chicken with Woodbines and slabs of chocolate, the way she had tried to woo *them*.

'Pines, tha's what they are,' Chicken said. 'Special kind, what put out cones as look like china eggcups.' Maud said she didn't remember seeing any like that. 'Common as dirt,' said

Chicken. 'On'y temp'rary this lot, though. Aim to put up marble pillars once I get me curtains up.'

At my suggestion, my mother had sent a fruit cake as a gift to Mrs Fenner. It was, in fact – but this I kept to myself – a gift to Chicken, a celebratory cake in honour of his coming. I only wished it might have been covered in white icing, with the words WELCOME CHICKEN picked out on the top in hundreds-and-thousands.

At tea, thinking of the cobblers' last I had seen next door, I asked the guest of honour, 'Are you a shoe mender?'

'Me, gal?' Chicken took a deep sup of his tea, put down the cup, and wiped the back of his hand across his natty little moustache. I had yet to discover that he almost never answered a question directly. It was, I think, not so much that he was afraid of the truth as that he did not believe in it on principle; or, if he did believe in it, it was something not to be mentioned in polite circles, something to be sidled up to, spoken out of the side of the mouth like an offering of dirty postcards. 'Shoe mender?' Chicken repeated with a note of interrogation in his tone, as if he were asking the question of himself. 'Tinker, tailor, soldier, sailor – Jack of all trades, tha's me.'

Mrs Fenner said, 'You oughter see the way he patched Tom's boot. King George don't get his boots patched better 'n that.'

The conversation veered elsewhere: but a moment or two later Tom, who, bent over, had been struggling with something under the table, straightened up with one of his boots in his hand. Red-faced and triumphant, he planted the unlovely object, its sole caked with mud, straw and worse, square in the middle of the tea table.

Nobody took umbrage. Mrs Fenner exclaimed, 'Tom, you are a one!' Maud moved the cake a safe distance away, otherwise she laughed with the rest of us. In turn we examined the patch Chicken had put on the side of the boot and agreed it was indeed a patch fit for a king. Chicken took the praise as no more than his due, Tom was radiant. Maud remarked to me across the table, 'We'll have to get him to have a go at your ankle straps, Sylvie.'

At that I made a face, which I am sure Chicken noted. My

[172]

mother, let me say, subscribed to what – having exchanged notes with my contemporaries – I now believe to be a commonly held fallacy of the time: to wit, that a child's new shoes, by definition, could not – nay, should not – be comfortable; they had to be 'grown into'. If, by chance, the pair you tried on in the shoe shop felt just right, they were, *ipso facto*, too long, too short, too narrow, too wide, too something, to be acceptable. If they didn't need 'growing into' there had to be something wrong with them.

In no instance were the practical results of this dire creed more evident than with one's Sunday best or party shoes, because, being worn less often than one's day-to-day footwear, they had less chance of ever becoming 'grown into'. What made it worse, in my own case, was that my best shoes – my ankle straps – were invariably made of black patent leather, sweet and girlish according to my mother, but, according to me, unvarnished hell to wear.

If anyone in the world could do anything about patent leather ankle straps, it had to be Chicken.

'Yes,' I answered Maud. 'We must.'

For me the sight of Tom's boot cheek by jowl with the bread and the marge and the condensed milk tin underlined anew my marvellous luck at being *persona grata* at Opposite the Cross Keys. Imagine! If I had been so soft-headed as to have accepted Patricia Livermore's invitation that morning, I should at that moment be sitting round a table draped with an embroidered cloth without a single stain to make it interesting, a cloth without a history; fussy little napkins, fussy doilies, fussy china, fussy silver teapot, sugar basin, milk jug, fussy, fussy. The thought of Tom's boot with its mucky sole set down in the centre of Mrs Livermore's tea table struck me as so amusing that I shared my thought with the others.

Chicken had us all in stitches. Little finger crooked in exaggerated refinement he picked up the condensed milk tin and in a mincing voice inquired of me, 'Can I pour you a little of this sodding condensed milk, ma'am, out of this sodding silver condensed milk tin?'

After tea was cleared away we went for a walk, Mrs Fenner, Maud and I. It was Mrs Fenner's idea to take the Spixworth road. I imagine my description of tea *chez* the Livermores had

[173]

aroused in her a desire to take a look at Old Saffrons, if only from the outside.

We hadn't gone far along the High Street before Chicken, whom we had left out on the pavement sprawled on a kitchen chair watching Ellie with an air of mesmerized disbelief as she sat combing her hair, caught us up.

'Felt lonely without you,' he explained, launching the compliment into the air for each of us to catch individually as addressed to herself alone. We turned merrily into the Spixworth road, falling silent as we neared the Livermores' home; quickly crossing the entrance to the drive with its wrought-iron gate, with 'Old Saffrons' woven into its black curlicues; and stopping only in the shelter of the hedge, having first satisfied ourselves that none of the family was out on the front lawn.

My father's tuition had made me snobbish about houses which aped the architectural language of former times, and I said what an awful house Old Saffrons was. Mrs Fenner, who judged by different standards, asked what was so bad about it: she wouldn't mind finding one like it in her Christmas stocking.

'It's because it only pretends to be a Tudor house,' I explained, 'and it isn't. It was only built five or six years ago.'

'Oh ah?' Mrs Fenner considered. 'How long ago do it have to be built, then, to be real?'

'Four hundred – three hundred and fifty years at least. And it would have been built with great big oak beams, and lovely old bricks that would just get mellower and mellower. In four hundred years' time,' I ended with contempt, 'Old Saffrons will be a crumbling old ruin, with the roof fallen in, and the woodwork all rotted away –'

'An' a family of Fenners living in it, I'll be bound!' Mrs Fenner's wonderful laugh rang out and, in the house, I saw an upstairs window open and someone, I couldn't be sure who, look out. The hedge hid us, and after a moment the window was shut and whoever it was went away.

For a moment I felt quite sorry for the Livermores, shut up in their fake Tudor with only themselves for company. But only for a moment. After that, with the hatefulness of childhood, I was even glad of their sadness: that nobody could ever be as happy as I.

[174]

Mrs Fenner declared, 'All the same, I wouldn't say no to being asked there to tea.'

'You'd hate it,' I promised. 'You'd find it horribly uncomfortable.'

'Not half so uncomfortable as Mrs Whatsername, I reckon, having the likes of me drinking out of one of her fancy cups.' As we fell into our stride again, the four of us strung companionably across the width of the road: 'Tell you what, Sylvie. You're bound to get asked again when you're down here Wednesday. You can ask young Whatsername if you can bring me along.'

'I won't – be asked, I mean,' I added quickly, anxious not to be misunderstood. Mrs Fenner could not really mean what she had just said. It was a joke. Or was it? Whilst I loved life with the Fenners I was no social revolutionary. On the contrary: I wanted things to stay the way they were for ever and ever. If there were no establishment where was the fun of escaping from it, and the reassurance of knowing it was always there to go back to? Trying to disguise the relief in my voice I explained that, when Patricia had spoken to me that morning, she had mentioned that she probably wouldn't be able to see me during my week at Opposite the Cross Keys: they were all going up to Birmingham for a few days.

'She can stay there for good, for all I care!'

Chapter Seventeen

When, on Wednesday, transported with my luggage by Alfred, who experienced his usual respiratory difficulties whilst unloading it on to the horsehair sofa in Mrs Fenner's living-room, I arrived in St Awdry's, only Ellie was at home, sitting on her hair in the sunshine. Her ma, she said, speaking to me but looking at Alfred, was off berrying at Caxton's, and had left a message for me to join her if I felt like it. Otherwise she'd see me at tea, please myself.

'Berrying,' said Alfred, when I went out to the car to say goodbye. He was taking in deep gulps of air like a diver surfacing from a considerable depth. 'That sounds jolly.' I could see that he thought anything jolly which would keep me out of Opposite the Cross Keys. 'Strawberries, are they?'

'I expect so.'

'Yum!'

I smiled kindly at my brother. Alfred had lovely hands with beautiful nails. They were never broken and you could see all the half-moons. He had no idea what it was like to pick strawberries hour after hour in the hot sun; had never seen the stain that settled, browning and gritty, into every pore of your hands, the crevices between your fingers and the lines on your palm where gypsies read your fortune. He knew nothing of the straw laid down on the ground beneath the berries which pierced the soft skin under your fingernails like red-hot needles, the slugs that stuck to the ripe fruit and had to be pulled off, little and black or large and grey like gobbets of phlegm, the agony of long squatting and the greater agony, at the end of the day, of sraightening up again.

He asked, 'Are you allowed to eat any of them yourself?'

'All you like,' I said, remembering how, the last time we went

[176]

berrying, Mrs Fenner, Dora Chapman and I, Dora had been turned off without a penny after working hard the best part of the day, all because one of the farm men saw her eating a strawberry that a slug had already had the best part of. I couldn't tell that to my beautiful brother. He had to be protected from the facts of life.

'Makes me wish I had the time to go myself,' Alfred declared. 'This Caxton's – is it far? I can drive you over before I go back.'

'Not far,' I said, though it was a good mile and a quarter. Once I was in St Awdry's I couldn't get rid fast enough of everything to do with St Giles, even Alfred. Actually, though I didn't say so, I'd already made up my mind to give berrying a miss. True, it was easier work than lifting spuds, and certainly better than plucking; but there was something about it I didn't care for. It wasn't so bad when there were only village women picking the fruit. The trouble arose when not enough of them showed up and the growers had to take on some of the gypsies.

If that sounds what today people call racist, it wasn't so at all. The trouble with the gypsy women wasn't their fault. It was to do with their nature, which was to think of today and bugger all tomorrow.

The correct way to pick strawberries was this (for all I know it's the same today): you took your punnet – actually you took four at a time, set out at one side of you – and first you picked some small strawberries to go in the bottom. Then you picked some medium-size ones to go on top of the little ones, and finally you picked some of the best ones to go on top and give the appearance that they were all like that, large and red and juicy, all the way down.

Then again, strawberries don't all ripen at once. On every plant, at any one time in the season, there are ripe berries, and others that are only partly ripe, as well as some that are still completely green and hard. Sometimes, when there hasn't been much sun to turn them red, or you're getting to the end of the crop, you are forced, to make up a punnet, to pick a few of the half-ripe berries, hiding them at the very bottom, underneath even the little ones; but the totally green ones, never. Apart from getting the grower a bad name with his retailers, which might not ordinarily worry you, it's a stupid thing for a picker to

[177]

do. The green berries are your insurance that there will be more work picking them when they, in turn, come to maturity.

Strangely, however many times they were told, the gypsies could never see this, or chose not to see it. Once they began to pick over a strawberry plant, they never stopped until it was bare: green, half-green or ripe made no difference to them, they picked the lot. You could hear the grower's voice half-way down the road, shouting at them when they brought their punnets to the collecting point. He would pick out a few punnets at random and turn them upside down on to the trestle table, uncovering all the unripe berries hidden out of sight. Sometimes he grew so angry that his voice grew too hoarse to bring out words, only an animal anger, and he would throw the green berries on the ground and grind them into the earth with his boots.

When that happened, the gypsy women would act very meek. They hadn't understood, they would do better next time. But they had understood all right, you could tell by the devil in their eyes; and next time they did the same again, and the time after that. I couldn't understand why they were never turned off, like poor Dora. Perhaps the grower was afraid of a gypsy curse. I can't say.

At other times, when the grower wasn't about, only the foreman and some men who worked on the farm, things went very differently. Then, the gypsy women stole shamelessly. Their mouths, red with strawberry juice, dared the men to make something of it, but they never did. They wore petticoats with big pockets sewn into them, and these they filled with the ripe fruit to take home with them. As the day wore on, the juice gradually soaked out of the pockets into their skirts and then through their aprons, until they looked like menstruating women who had forgotten to put on sanitary towels. When they came to the collecting point a kind of horseplay would begin which made me uneasy, I didn't know why. The women, despite the evidence of the stains, would flatly deny they had any of the strawberries concealed about their persons, and the men would grab at their skirts, raising them if they got the chance, in order to see whether they spoke the truth. Everybody was laughing and screaming and jumping about. It should have been great fun for a child, only somehow it wasn't. I was old enough to know there was more to the game than appeared, but too young to know what.

So I decided not to go to the strawberry field that day. It wasn't as if, by not going, I deprived Mrs Fenner of increased earnings. Since Nellie Smith went away we had, by tacit agreement, stopped working her system, as if it were her patent, of which, by her withdrawal, she had cancelled our licence. The most I ever made for toiling all day picking strawberries was ninepence, and Mrs Fenner, I knew, counted herself lucky if she came home with as much as half-a-crown in her pocket.

What to do, then, until the family came back, to that glorious gathering round the table? Chicken must be out because, had he been at home, he would surely have put in an appearance at the sound of our car drawing up, if only to see Alfred.

It was a meeting I had both hoped for and feared. Hoped for, because I was curious to test the limits of Chicken's power. Was it only countryfolk who found him irresistible, or would my sophisticated brother equally fall for him like a ton of bricks? Feared, because Alfred might instantly recognize him for the rascal he undoubtedly was, and, impervious to his charms, decide that it was his duty to warn our parents I was keeping bad company.

Unable to decide whether to be sorry or relieved at the reprieve, I asked Ellie if she knew where Chicken was. She merely tittered; so I went down the back garden to the privy, not because I needed to use it, but because, in the ruined one next door – Chicken being forced to avail himself of the Fenners' facilities – the house martins were raising a second brood.

When the pleasure of watching the birds palled I pushed open the door of the Fenners' convenience, and was put out to discover that only one hole was available for use, the other two being covered over with a board. Whenever I stayed at Opposite the Cross Keys I always looked forward to my evening visit there with Mrs Fenner, a restful, gossipy way to end the day. A strong odour of kerosene overlaid the normal smell of ripening excrement and I remembered Mrs Fenner saying something about having one of these days to get at those woodworms down at the bottom of the garden, or the bloody bog would be all hole and no seat.

Any slight ennui I might be feeling, any discontent with the quality of my welcome, was rapidly dispelled upon Mrs Fenner's return. She bore great news. Old Saffrons had been burgled! Old Mr Hayes, who did the Livermores' odd jobs, had gone in there Monday evening to water the runner beans, found the kitchen window open, and gone for PC Utting.

'Detectives were down from Norwich like we was Chicago gangsters.' Mrs Fenner sounded proud that Salham St Awdry had joined the great world of crime.

'Was anything taken?'

'They say so. That gal o' theirs 'll be telling you all about it, I dare say. They got 'em back from wherever they gone to. Mr Hayes were there when they got home an' he says the missus took on like she'd lost the Crown Jewels. She told him her gold watch were gone, an' her silver candlesticks, an' I don't know what else.' Mrs Fenner broke off with a laugh. 'One thing, Sylvie. I reckon you won't be complaining so much of fuss next time you visit there. You'll get your tea out of a brown pot like everyone else.'

'You mean, the burglar stole the silver tea set?'

'So old Mr Hayes say.'

Mrs Fenner put the kettle on the hob. Cutting the bread into her usual doorsteps, she dropped casually, 'The cheeky buggers, they come an' had a word wi' Chicken.'

'Who?' My heart suddenly banged against my chest at the recollection that it was I who had spread the word about the silver teapot and its appurtenances. 'The Livermores?'

'The detectives. It were PC Utting's doing.' PC Utting, a lay reader at the Chapel, was one of the few people in St Awdry's to be unimpressed by Chicken's talents. 'Seems they arst him were there anyone new in the village,' Mrs Fenner went on, with no sign of anxiety. 'So o' course he had to say as there were.'

'Chicken's not a thief!' I cried, hardly giving a thought to the telegraph poles.

'Who said he were? All they wanted to know was if he wasn't someone they knew. Someone already on their books.'

'And was he?'

'You'll have to ask him. Shouldn't think so, from what I

heard through the wall. They was jokin' away like they'd been chums from the cradle.'

The rest of us were already seated and eating our tea before Chicken came through the front door in that trim, balletic way of his, making an entrance. You almost expected an orchestra somewhere off in the wings to sound an introductory 'Ta *ra!*'

'Brought you all a present,' he announced, bringing out two small bunches of purple grapes, one from each trouser pocket. He put the fruit down in the middle of the table.

'Better watch out,' Mrs Fenner warned. 'Sylvie here'll think you knocked 'em off, and run for PC Utting.'

Chicken sat down in what had already become his place, sacred to him alone.

'Parson gi' me them, if you want to know, for cutting down some bunches in his conservatory too high up for his holiness to get at. Said heights made him dizzy. Fine thing! His job to lead the way up to heaven an' he can't go three steps up a stepladder without the blood rushing to his head!'

Over tea we discussed the burglary at Old Saffrons some more. Tom didn't like the sound of the word 'burglar'. His face clouded over and he had to be reassured that those who lived at Opposite the Cross Keys were lucky. There was nothing worth stealing.

Tom was only partly convinced.

'There's my snail. I put it back on the geranium.'

We had to admit that the snail on the geranium was indeed a prize worth breaking and entering for, one that had slipped our minds.

Tom, his beautiful, unfinished features screwed up in concentration, thought hard and solved the problem. 'I'll put it in my pocket, tha's what I'll do!' he declared; got up from the table, went over to the plant on the window sill and was as good as his word. Smiling beatifically, he returned to his place. 'He'll be safe now, along o' me.'

'Tha's right.' Charlie, who did not usually have much time for his brother, put his arm round the other's neck, and repeated, smiling, 'Safe now!'

I slept deeply that night, on the horsehair sofa, deeply happy.

[181]

Instead of rats thirsting for my blood on the other side of the wall there was Chicken, asleep on his mattress, not even snoring: able, I was quite certain, to defend me against all comers if the need arose. I slept deeply, yet awoke when it was still deep night, thinking at first that it was the very silence which had roused me. Then I heard the clank of the pump – at two o'clock in the morning? – the splash of water into the pail, and realized it was not the quiet but the sound of something intrusive, out of context, which had brought me back to consciousness.

I swung my legs out of bed, feeling with my feet for my slippers, and then making my way to the door into the scullery which, pushed open, disclosed moonlight pouring in through the window on to the tiled floor. I moved stealthily, skirting the piercing illumination. Cautiously, I raised my head above the window sill and saw Chicken, fully dressed, with his shirt-sleeves rolled up, washing his arms under the pump.

Oddly enough, the thing which I found most surprising about the picture thus revealed was the khaki-coloured slab of soap, the kind that used to be purchasable by the pound for heavy domestic chores, with which the man performed his ablutions. Never had I seen anyone at Opposite the Cross Keys wash himself with such dedication. Certainly, unless it were some trick of moonlight, Chicken's hands and arms looked even dirtier than usual; an adhesive dirt he seemed to be finding difficult to remove. From time to time he raised his hands to his face or lowered his head into the bend of his elbow and sniffed.

When at last he appeared satisfied, he emptied out the bucket and refilled it with fresh water, which he proceeded to slosh over what I now saw was a package of some kind on the ground beside the pump. It was large and bumpy, with a sheen to the wrapping, as if it might have been oilskin or something similar. As I watched, Chicken, using the toe of his boot – he seemed unwilling actually to touch it with his freshly washed hands – turned the parcel over to get at the underside. It made a tinkling sound.

Up to that moment I had watched, making no sense of what I saw. With that tinkle came enlightenment. I opened the back door without care for quiet. The bolts were stiff, the hinges grumbled as usual. The man at the pump looked up at the sound, saw it was only me, lifted a hand in greeting and went back to his labours.

Without haste, he sluiced the oilskin clean and moved the package to a fresh patch of ground before strolling over to me in a leisurely way, unrolling his shirt-sleeves as he came.

'*You* put that woodworm stuff on the seat!' I burst out as soon as he was near enough. '*You* covered up those holes with the board! You had Mrs Livermore's silver hidden there all the time!'

'You aimin' to wake up the whole sodding village?' Chicken sounded amused rather than angry. He came nearer, and held out his arms towards me; not pleading for mercy, as, for a moment, I had romantically imagined, but for inspection. 'Smell anything?'

'Only the soap,' I answered unwillingly, aware that my righteous wrath was being bypassed: but I answered.

'Tha's a relief. Thought I were going' to stink till Christmas. You lot,' Chicken observed without animus, 'when you lot shit you certainly let yourselves go. Anyone 'd think you bin weaned on Syrup o' Figs.'

'We never even used the ones with the board on –'

''Course you didn't! Why you s'pose I covered 'em up? I'm not stupid. Wanted a good depth of coverage, if you unnerstan' me.'

He stood there, smiling. Suddenly, against my conscious will, I had a great desire to smile back. More, to hoot with laughter, an owl shattering the night with its manic mirth.

'You never – !'

'On'y thing to do,' Chicken assured me. 'Knew them Norwich gents, even if they got nosy, 'd draw the line at poking about in the jakes.' Looking at me with concern: 'You can't go on standing out here in your pyjamas, gal. You'll catch yer death o' cold.'

He pushed me gently back into the scullery, and followed after. Safely out of earshot of the neighbours, and with my hands over my mouth in case the Fenners should hear me up above, I shook with laughter until I thought I should dissolve in it, like sherbet in water. By the time I was able to gasp out, 'It's very, very wrong of you,' my moral stance had lost a good deal of its force.

[183]

'You didn't have to burgle a friend of mine! You could have gone and burgled somebody else. You wouldn't even have known about the Livermores' teapot if I hadn't said –'

Chicken said, 'Do me a favour! How many silver teapots you reckon goin' begging in St Awdry's? It don't give a bugger a lot of choice.'

He went outside again. I heard the swag clunk as he picked it up from the ground. I bolted the door and went back to bed feeling – I didn't know what I was feeling, my life to date not having equipped me with a set of responses appropriate to the situation. I knew of course that crime was wrong and the thing to do was call a policeman; but I also knew that to call in PC Utting was unthinkable, even though I should never again be able to pass him in the High Street without blushing from head to toe. At least Chicken had not insulted me by begging me not to give him away. As if I ever could!

Burrowing deep under the bedclothes, I discovered that I had after all grown cold in the moonlight, and slid down to sleep shivering with the pain of love.

Mrs Fenner peered out between the geraniums into the freshness of the morning.

'That Livery gal o' yours is over the road,' she announced, 'jumpin' up an' down like she needs to go somewhere. Whyn't she come across if she want something? The bugger afraid we're catching?'

I didn't know what Patricia Livermore was afraid of, either; only that, after her one and only glimpse of the interior of Opposite the Cross Keys, she had never come to the Fenners' door again: she and Nellie Smith both the same, though not for the same reasons. She stayed safely outside the Cross Keys, staring hard at the cottage as if willing me to appear. Every now and again, out of boredom perhaps, or in solicitation of some private god, she went into a little dance, a soft-shoe shuffle diversified with hops and skips that set her pigtails flapping. Spying between the flowerpots I asked myself what on earth I was doing with such a friend.

I laced my tea with an extra lashing of condensed milk

and opined gloomily, 'I expect she wants to talk about the burglary.'

'Wha's wrong wi' that? Should 've thought you couldn't wait to hear it from the horse's mouth.'

'I'm fed up with it. You'd think there wasn't anything else to talk about.'

I took my time finishing my tea, and then began to clear away the breakfast things. Mrs Fenner looked at me curiously.

'I'll see to those. You go on over an' put the mauther out of her misery. She'll wet her pants if you keep her standing there any longer.'

Patricia seemed in extraordinarily good spirits for somebody who had been so recently deprived of treasure. In stilted tones which, to my own ears, sounded like an instant giveaway, I began my prepared speech of commiseration. The girl brushed it aside, her normally dull face alight.

'You'll never guess what's happened! You'll never guess in a million years!'

'What?' The possibilities, for good or evil, were so momentous that breath failed me.

'I found the silver tea service! In that big flowering currant at the side of the garage, you know the one I mean? They must have dropped it there by accident on their way out – or perhaps they heard someone coming, or they meant to come back for it later, I don't know!' The words tumbled over each other in her haste to get them out. 'How we didn't notice it before I can't imagine – except the sun came out this morning and the light shone on the silver and I was out practising hitting tennis balls against the garage wall and I suddenly saw this light, as if someone had switched on a torch in the middle of the bush. You *will* come to tea this afternoon, won't you, and I can show you exactly where they were – the teapot, the sugar basin, the jug, even the sugar tongs, not a scratch on them.'

Tea at the Livermores, with the salvaged tea set in the place of honour, was more of a fuss than ever: chocolate éclairs which must have come from Marchesi's in London Street as well as the usual home-made stuff. Mrs Livermore was so radiant that it annoyed me a little, as the unknown contriver of her joy, to have to forego the thanks and commendations which were my just due.

With a certain spite I inquired, what about the other things? Had they been found as well?

No, they had not, she replied; adding, on the crest of her good humour, 'And a good thing too.'

I can only put down her frankness to the fact that she must have been dying for somebody to crow to – and a child didn't count, did it? You could say anything to a child and it was in one ear and out of the other.

'I can only hope they won't be,' she went on merrily. 'Those awful candlesticks! An aunt of Mr Livermore's gave them to us, so we had to leave them out on display, but every time they caught my eye I'd go "Grr!" inside, thinking how awful they were.'

All I could think to say was, 'Mr Livermore's aunt will be sorry.'

'She'll have to get used to it. And *I* shall have the insurance money!' Seeing my look of incomprehension: 'Surely you know about insurance? If you're insured and something gets stolen, the insurance company pays you money to make up for it.'

At that I perked up wonderfully. So Mrs Livermore wouldn't, after all, be any worse off for Chicken's crime. Indeed, from the sound of it, she would be better off. He had done her a favour. Instead of being lumbered with candlesticks she couldn't stand the sight of, she would have money to do what she liked with. Remembering what Mr Hayes had reported about the way she had carried on about her jewellery, I asked if the insurance company would give her money to buy some more jewellery as well; and she said yes, but going rather red and immediately changing the subject to the chocolate éclairs and what marvellous pastrycooks the Marchesis were.

I knew nothing about insurance companies and little more about human nature, but I felt instinctively that there was something fishy about Mrs Livermore and her jewellery. On the way to Old Saffrons Patricia had told me that the burglar had taken her mother's gold watch and her engagement ring set with diamonds, and the antique chain with its pendant of amethyst and pearls which had belonged to her great-grandmother. Now, prompted by some inner devil more knowing than my conscious self, I said with that transparent innocence which is the mask of juvenile guile, 'Even with the

[186]

insurance money, you must be frightfully upset about your great-grandmother's antique chain and pendant –'

'Oh, frightfully!' Mrs Livermore agreed, with such a caricatured concern that I was suddenly sure as sure it hadn't been stolen at all. She was only pretending so as to get more insurance money. I had absolutely no grounds for coming to such a conclusion, except that she had made insurance money sound so much more desirable than ordinary money. Perhaps it was made out of gold, like the old sovereigns. I suppose it was my passionate desire to exonerate Chicken from blame that had conjured up the bizarre possibility: unless love had given me a sixth sense to pierce through Mrs Livermore's pretence of respectability. I don't know, I didn't know: only that I wanted to shout out, 'You're as much a criminal as Chicken is! You're both as bad as each other!'

Of course I said nothing, and accepted a second éclair with Eldon House grace. When, that evening, I asked Chicken if silver candlesticks, a gold watch, an engagement ring set with diamonds, and an antique chain and pendant had been included in the haul, his eyes and mouth widened in surprise.

'Candlesticks? Watch? Engagement ring? There weren't nothing that didn't come out of Woolworth's!'

But, of course, I didn't know whether I could believe him any more than I could Mrs Livermore.

'Another cup, Sylvia?' she inquired, the silver teapot poised for action. Suddenly I saw, in all its awfulness, where the teapot had been, down that hole at the bottom of the Fenners' garden, buried under a load of shit. All the perfumes of Arabia could not sweeten that silver teapot. I opened my mouth to say 'No, thank you,' which was a mistake. Once open, disaster struck, copious and unavoidable.

When the mess was cleared up, the embroidered cloth put in to soak, the carpet washed, and the french doors to the garden flung open to get rid of the smell, Mrs Livermore commented through lips arranged in a thin line, 'You should never have eaten that second éclair, Sylvia,' as if it were my fault.

Chapter Eighteen

T HE day before I was due back in St Giles, I went next
door and saw something wonderful pinned up on the
wall. I know now that it was a blueprint, but at the time
I had no idea it was other than a picture, one I was not as yet
equipped to understand, other then to have a sharp and instant
conviction of its tremendous significance. Chicken was sitting
on one of his orange boxes in rapt contemplation of this
masterpiece.

'What you think of that, then, gal?' he demanded, not taking
his eyes off it.

'It's beautiful.'

The blueprint was full of lines, some straight, some curving.
The way these lines were drawn in, with strength and at the
same time the greatest delicacy, reminded me, more than
anything else, of my father's exercises in Chinese calligraphy. I
no more expected to make sense of them than I did of those
ideograms, put on to paper with the lovely tapered brushes
which came out of the little jar patterned with butterflies.

That being so, Chicken's next words confused me.

'What you think she'll look like, then, on the water?'

'The water?'

The man twisted round on the box and stared at me. 'Don't
tell me yer don't even know what you're gawpin' at, up there?'
And when I shook my head to signify that, alas, I did not know:
'Can't you reckernize a bleedin' boat when you see one?'

I looked again at the blueprint on the wall, straining to
extract from it what to Chicken was so obvious; and whether it
was truth or the product of my passionate longing, it seemed to
me, after moments of agonized contemplation, that I did indeed
see: a boat, a boat with a cabin presented three ways – in profile,

the hull, and the body. The longer I looked at those lines, the more real they became, their flatness acquiring dimension until I could see, not only the boat, but its upside-down reflection in the water, under a blue sky studded with small white clouds. I looked until I saw not merely the outward semblance of a boat, but its soul. *In the beginning God created lines, and the lines were a boat, and he saw that it was good.*

Chicken said, 'You'll get yerself cross-eyed if you look much longer. What you say, then? What you say to a boat like that?'

Foolishly, I thought that he meant to build me a model, comparable to the model yacht Alfred had given me for my last birthday and which occasionally, so as not to hurt his feelings – it was the most boring pursuit imaginable – I sailed on the pond in Eaton Park.

Now I said politely, 'That would be lovely.'

'That all you got to say?' He tugged at his cap, brought his black eyebrows together, mock-ferocious. 'Maybe I ought ter ferget the whole fuckin' idea.'

I explained that I didn't want to take up his valuable time, that was all, as I already possessed a model boat.

'Who said anything about a model?'

That was the beginning of Chicken's boat, a boat that was the best part of two years a-building, and, during that time, the corner-stone of my life, filling my mind with dreams and hopes I scarcely dared formulate. A refuge. In passages of boredom, disappointment, melancholia, think about Chicken's boat and escape into another world.

By the time of my next visit to Salham St Awdry the downstairs room of his cottage had been transformed. Black-boards chalked with enlarged portions of the blueprint on the wall had been laid over part of the old floor tiles, to be stepped on at your peril. Tools of unfamiliar configuration were laid out ready for use on the workbench which had replaced the shelf and the cobblers' last by the window.

My ankle straps, which Maud, good as her word, had handed over for treatment, had been Chicken's final task in his incarnation as shoe repairer.

'There!' producing them from a dark corner and thrusting

them into my arms as if glad to be rid of shoes once and for all. 'I fixed 'em for you.'

He had indeed fixed them. The next time I wore the ankle straps was to a party where, as was the custom, I changed into dancing pumps for the duration of the festivities. For once, changing back into my outdoor shoes for the walk home was no purgatory. Chicken was a genius. The ankle straps, though to outward appearance unchanged, were now blissfully comfortable.

Three-quarters of the way home they fell to pieces. The uppers lifted off the soles, the seams down the backs of the heels parted like dehiscing seedpods. That, heaven be praised, was the end of ankle straps in my life. My mother – by unspoken agreement between Maud and myself kept in ignorance of Chicken's ministrations – was so bemused by the sight of this utter disintegration that she never bought me a pair again.

When I reported to Chicken what had happened, he winked and pulled down the points of his waistcoat.

'Said I'd fix 'em for you, didn't I?'

I was never actually in St Awdry's when the raw materials for Chicken's boat arrived, so that I knew nothing of who delivered the piles of timber which presently stood about the back garden, resting on sawn-off railway sleepers and covered with tarpaulins; the blocks, the trestles, the sawhorse; the oil drum, rubber hose and plywood shuttering which Chicken, with what seemed to me incomparable ingenuity, converted into an apparatus for steaming wood until it could be bent without splintering. I gathered from Mrs Fenner that the deliveries were frequently made at unsocial hours, which could have meant something or nothing. All that Mrs Fenner contributed was that them bloody Leaches next door were forever sounding off about their lettuces getting trampled underfoot in the dark.

'That pore ole bor –' Mrs Fenner meant Chicken – 'he can't so much as knock in a tintack afore they're hammering on the wall like lunatics. They were glad enough when he moved in and sent them rats packing. They live in the middle o' the desert, they'd be screaming blue murder every time one o' them A-rabs spit out a date stone!'

Surveying the land at the back of Opposite the Cross Keys, which had taken on the look of a mini-Jewson's (the timber merchants down by the Wensum in Norwich), I could understand that, for the Leaches, Chicken's spell must be wearing a bit thin. PC Utting, it went without saying, regarded the accumulation with deepest suspicion.

Until, that is, the day he dropped in on Chicken for a spot of pointed questioning; saw the blueprint and the chalked full-size plans I was beginning to refer to knowledgeably as the loftings; heard what Chicken had to say; and went away thoughtful and uplifted.

'What you tell the ole bugger, then?' Mrs Fenner wanted to know at tea that evening. 'He went away like he jest seen Christ walkin' on the water.'

'On'y that I were building a boat.'

'He could 'a told *you* that. Everyone in the village know that.'

Chicken tipped his chair back on two legs until it rested against the chest of drawers. He thrust his thumbs into the armholes of his waistcoat.

'He didn't know what *kind* o' boat, though.'

'What diff'rence that make?'

'All the diff'rence in the world.' Contemplating his audience round the table with an innocence which set us all agog to hear what lovely mischief he was up to now, he added off-handedly, 'Told him I were building another ark, tha's all.'

'You never!'

'You know wha' the bugger's like. Sin and fornication everywhere, an' the on'y reason God lets us get away with it He's waiting for a fresh delivery of coals to get the fires of hell stoked up real good. When they're hot enough to burn yer balls He'll be sending a flood what'll make the las' one look like a gob o' spit.'

Mr Fenner, in his rocking chair by the fire, took his pipe out of his mouth and emerged from his private fog.

'Don't say nothing about another flood in *Old Moore*.'

'Course it don't!' said Mrs Fenner. 'Chicken were havin' the geezer on. Weren't you, Chicken – havin' him on?'

Taking heed of the anxiety, imperfectly concealed, the man laughed, stroked his natty little moustache.

'No need fer you to worry, missus! We got a flood coming, no

[191]

one gets a seat in my boat ahead o' you. Tha's a promise!' Expanding his regard to include the rest of us at table: 'An' that goes for the lot o' you, even young Sylvie!'

I burst out laughing and said, 'I bet you promised PC Utting a seat too, so long as he didn't ask too many questions.'

'You're so sharp you'll cut yourself! Wanted to know where I got my timber, how much I paid, had I got receipts – I ask you!'

'Did you have any to show him?'

'Did the Lord God, I arst him, ask fer a receipt for the quails an' the manna He rained down on the fuckin' Israelites? Took him back a bit, I can tell you, me quotin' Scripture. Then he wanted t' know how I were goin' to get the boat down to a river. "What river?" I arst. "I'm not goin' out lookin' for a flood, any more'n Noah did. I aim to wait an' let it bloody well come t' me."'

In retrospect, the most extraordinary thing about Chicken's boat, with the exception of its actual building, was the way the village took it in its stride. Nobody questioned the undertaking, nor commented on the oddity of choosing to construct a sizeable vessel indoors. There may have been speculation in the Swan or the Cross Keys, I was in no position to say, but I never heard anyone wondering aloud how, when it was finished, it was to be got through that narrow door.

Perhaps, for PC Utting was not the only fundamentalist Christian in the neighbourhood, the story of the coming flood had taken root and conviction, and the ark was expected to be borne forth on the bosom of the waters as the windows of heaven opened and Opposite the Cross Keys gave way under the strain. Perhaps – since the work progressed very slowly, as was inevitable single-handed – people thought it would never be finished, did not even want it to be finished. It was enough that its presence enlarged their lives, broadened their horizons. Further east in the county, in Broadland, that ambiguous area of rivers and lakes and marsh, which was like the world as it might have been at the beginning of Creation, land, sky and water not yet quite separated, a boat was nothing special. In St Awdry's it was, like the rainbow it presaged, a promise of possibilities.

*

Back in St Giles Maud and I discussed the boat endlessly. I had never said anything about Chicken to my parents, not because I was ashamed of him – Mrs Fenner had taught me that lesson – but because I knew, disadvantaged as they were, lacking a Maud or a family of Fenners in their own childhoods, they could never be expected to understand about the name, and would only be affronted, if not terrified, by the laughing lawlessness I found so powerful an attraction.

My father, a man of honour and innocence, tended to think of all countrymen as nature's gentlemen, practising their rural crafts in landscapes of the Norwich School. He knew nothing of the dirt, the smell of poverty, the grinding labour which made up the life of the agricultural labourer of the time – or, if he knew something, it was only something he had read, deodorized on the printed page, paying as much attention to its literary merit as to the facts presented there. Nevertheless, so full was I of the boat and its building that I could not resist mentioning something about it – 'a man in St Awdry's was making one, all by himself' – knowing he would be pleased to hear that rural crafts were flourishing in the outback exactly as he had supposed.

'A boat, eh? I must see what I can do in that line.'

My father, let me say, among his other accomplishments, was a whiz at cutting out. He could take a pack of playing cards and, using only scissors and a dab of glue, turn it into enchanting three-dimensional models of merry-go-rounds, castles complete with jousting knights, troikas pulled by slavering horses – whatever you asked for would be provided, so long as the cards, which my mother, who was fond of playing whist in the afternoon with selected ladies, secreted in various nooks about the house, could be unearthed over her protests and put to better use than foolish games.

Out of a blue pack and a red pack patterned with tiny fleurs-de-lis, my father fashioned a galley twelve inches long, which looked like something out of an illuminated manuscript with its castles at either end, its pennons caught in frozen flutter, and its great sail – the only part showing the face of a card – emblazoned with the ace of hearts. A tiny figure in the crow's nest had its hand to its eyes, scanning the horizon.

I was so pleased with my father's cleverness that I took the galley next door for May Bowden to admire.

She looked it over without comment, then said, 'I suppose you want to sail it on the lily pond.'

'Oh no!' I cried. The pond, not much bigger than a bath tub, was covered with a green slime in the spaces between lily pads blotched with brown freckles like the hands of very old people. 'I mean –' belatedly: May Bowden was so touchy about her possessions – 'it's not meant to go sailing. It's just for looking at.'

'Rubbish!' May Bowden snapped. 'What's the good of a boat only for looking at? Tell you what –' with sudden animation – 'if the river Yare is clean enough for your Royal Highness, we might take a little ride out to Bawburgh and try it out there.'

Bawburgh, a few miles out of Norwich, off the Earlham road, was the village where May Bowden had been born, and where her father had begun his long climb to riches as the village cobbler. I had accompanied her there once before, in a hired Daimler limousine, to be shown the ancestral cottage, the little hump-backed bridge, the river and the village green where she claimed, improbably, to have been crowned Queen of the May.

I had also been taken to an orchard which lay in a hollow close by the church, where there was what looked like a large black box lying open on the ground, filled to the brim with greenish water. It was not my idea of a well, but that was what May Bowden had called it – St Walstan's Well, after a prince and holy man of God who had died at nearby Taverham working in the fields like a common labourer, so meek he was, so compassionate. His workmates had loaded his body on to an ox-wagon to bring it back to Bawburgh, his own village, for burial. Where the oxen had halted, in the hollow below the churchyard, a spring of purest water had gushed from the ground; a spring which, since that May day a thousand years ago, had never failed, and never would, to the world's end.

That was the story May Bowden told me, long before Nellie Smith and the old un between them had taught me better than to meddle with the power of water. When she had finished she opened her handbag and took out an empty medicine bottle which she bent over and filled at the black box.

'There!' recorking it, full, and returning it to her bag. 'That's to keep by.'

I said that it looked like any other water.

[194]

May Bowden looked disgusted with me. Water from St Walstan's Well like any other water! Water to cure measles and melancholy and keep your winter woollies from going yellow. Water to make you what you wanted to be.

'Did you drink some when you were a child here?'

'Of course.'

'And did it make you what you wanted to be?'

'Of course.'

'Then why do you need to drink some more? Does it wear off?'

'It doesn't wear off. Only it's a long time to be the same person.'

I had not cared for that black box of water down in the orchard; but Bawburgh was a pretty place and I was always game for a ride in a limousine. About risking my dear little boat in the river I was less sure, but I didn't say anything.

My mother having given me permission to go, the limousine called for us next morning, May Bowden dressed up to the eyes, in frills and flounces that made her look like a tester bed with all the trimmings. I suppose she wanted to impress the people in Bawburgh who had known her before her father made his money, though there couldn't have been many of those left, she was so old.

When we drove into the village over the bridge and I saw the grass dotted with daisies and the shiny river flowing with no particular haste towards Yarmouth, I was glad I had come to sail my galley there. I felt that somehow its launching was a prefiguring, a rehearsal, of the day when Chicken's boat would take to its proper element, the two of us on board waving to the people waving back from the bank as we set out together on our journey round the world.

'Take your shoes and socks off,' May Bowden commanded. 'That's what I used to do at this very spot when I was your age. It's quite shallow, so you needn't worry.'

I took off my shoes and socks, stepped off the bank and gently lowered the playing card boat into the water. It sailed beautifully, and I shouted with joy – a short-lived rejoicing before a mute swan, one of that breed with a lump on its beak which makes it look as if it had recently been in a fight, came barging along regardless. With the flick of a scaly toe it tossed the galley into the middle of the stream before carrying on at the apex of its V-shaped wake as if nothing had happened. Through a film of tears I watched my father's masterwork bobbing into the distance.

'If there's one thing I can't stomach,' declared May Bowden, 'it's carrying on. You ought to be glad it's on its way, doing what it's made for.'

'It was made for me.' I was sobbing outright now. How stupid she looked, the old woman, with her white face, her hat perched on her dyed hair. 'I only brought it round for you to look at, and you had to go and say, come here to Bawburgh. I hate Bawburgh, and I hate you!'

For a moment we stared at one another hard-eyed. Then May Bowden clapped her hands together and said, in a completely different voice, 'I know what we'll do! Get your shoes and socks back on and we'll drive to Yarmouth. The car can go faster than any boat. We'll drive to Southtown Bridge and we'll wait there for it to pass under. And then we'll take out our hankies and wave *bon voyage* to it as it sails out to sea and off to the Spanish Main!'

I knew it was ridiculous. I knew the playing card boat could never survive the weir at Cringleford. Or, if it did successfully shoot that mini-Niagara, then the paddle steamers which plied between Norwich and Yarmouth during the summer months would surely chew it into confetti. I knew that if, against all the odds, my boat came through these dangers in one piece, it would unfailingly meet its doom just behind Yarmouth, sucked down into the mud of the tidal flats of Breydon Water.

I knew it was ridiculous. Daft. I also knew that, certain of its coming, I would stand on Southtown Bridge, peering down past the herring drifters and the cargo ships parked alongside Hall Quay, straining for the first glimpse of that bellying sail which sported the ace of hearts, shading my eyes against the glare just as the look-out in the crow's nest would be doing, spying me. Willing it to come, willing it to go, as one day I would come, and go, with Chicken.

Chapter Nineteen

S OUTHTOWN BRIDGE was a noisy place, busy with the traffic of the port. There was nowhere a limousine could park, so May Bowden had the chauffeur stay only so long as it took her to cross the quay to the Star Inn and order our luncheon. While she was gone the man went to the trunk which was bolted to the running board and took out a couple of camp stools and the small table which the hiring company provided for picnickers.

Following May Bowden's instructions he unfolded stools and table and set them up on the narrow pavement, confiding to me as he did so that the old gal was nutty as a fruit cake. 'They don't come no nuttier.' I explained that we were waiting for my boat to come along and couldn't leave the bridge, even to eat, in case we missed it.

The chauffeur stared.

'You mean that bit o' pasteboard you were fooling about with, over in Bawburgh?'

I nodded coldly, not caring for his description.

'Crikey! That makes the pair of you! Hope it ain't catching!'

May Bowden came back and told the chauffeur to take the limousine and park it on the forecourt of the Star, where, she informed him, she had arranged for him to be provided, at her expense, with two rounds of beef sandwiches and half a pint of beer. The man took this intelligence with small thanks, being better pleased, probably, with those clients who gave him cash, enabling him to decide for himself the proportion of solid to liquid refreshment. Soon after he departed, a waiter from the Star wearing a black frock coat and a bulging white shirt front crossed the road from the inn carrying a loaded silver tray balanced on one arm and using his free hand to wave a white damask napkin at the surge of lorries and carts as a sign they were to let him through.

He came on to the bridge with measured tread, lowered the tray on to our little table, and arranged our meal – fresh salmon mayonnaise with a glass of milk for me and a pint of stout for May Bowden – with as much aplomb as if we were seated in state in the Star dining-room. There was even a little silver vase with a single rose, in bud. The sun glinted on his pince-nez. May Bowden explained that we were obliged to stay in sight of the river as we were expecting our boat to come through.

'I quite understand, modom,' the waiter answered, pocketing the shilling she took out of her beaded handbag.

We sat on Southtown Bridge eating our luncheon, keeping an eye on the water below. It being Norfolk, whose official motto is 'Do Different', our alfresco meal attracted only the most delicate attention. If a couple of nutters had a mind to sit down to their food in public where was the harm of it? One apple-cheeked woman, innocently glad to see people enjoying good fare, peered over my shoulder at the salmon mayonnaise and commented admiringly, 'Tha's nice!'

'Would you like some?' I asked, and before May Bowden could object – the dish was too rich for my taste, tinned salmon with vinegar and sliced cucumber being nearer my mark – scooped most of it into the starched white napkin spread open on my lap and handed it over. 'Please take the napkin back to the Star, though, when you've finished, if you don't mind.'

'I'll give it a good wash out first, you don't have to worry 'bout that,' the woman said, taking the gift in the spirit in which it was offered. She glanced at May Bowden, though. 'You sure your ma don't mind?'

May Bowden put down her glass of stout, wiped the froth off her lips with a corner of her lace-trimmed handkerchief, and announced angrily, 'I'm not her ma! I am a maiden lady!'

'Oh ah?' the woman said kindly. 'Never mind, m' dear. You know what they say – where there's life, there's hope.' She settled the napkin-wrapped mayonnaise into her shopping basket and went on her way with a pleasant 'Cheerio, then!'

It was boiling on the bridge. No shade: the changing patterns of light on the ever-moving surface of the river made me feel disorientated. Also, I needed to go to the lavatory.

I held out as long as I could before I told May Bowden.

'Always something!' she returned sourly. And then, as I awaited her permission, 'Off you go, then! I can't go and do it for you!'

She instructed me to go into the Star and inquire at the reception desk for the ladies' cloakroom; but when it came to the point and I stood on Hall Quay peering through the open door into the sumptuous gloom of the Turkey-carpeted entrance hall, my courage failed me. Instead, I went up the shopping street at the side of the Town Hall until I came to the turn-off for the Market Place where I remembered from previous visits to Yarmouth that there was a public convenience. Fortunately, I had a penny in my pocket, Maud never allowing me to leave the house without that essential standby.

'What kept you so long?' May Bowden wanted to know, when at last I got back to our bivouac on the bridge. And, before I could answer: 'Well, late arrivals must take the consequences! Time and tide wait for no man.'

'You don't mean –'

'I most certainly do! While you were busy attending to your animal urges your boat has come and gone. Passed under the bridge like a royal procession. Oh, it was a sight to see! It'll be past the jetty now, and the lighthouse –'

'Please,' I begged, 'couldn't we drive to Gorleston and go to the end of the jetty, just in case we can see it from there?'

'Certainly not! I'm not dressed to go scrambling about on jetties. You've had your chance and you muffed it.'

Nobody in the world could put my back up like May Bowden.

I shouted, 'I couldn't help having to go to the lavatory!'

'*I* didn't have to go,' she responded smugly.

We had a bumpy ride home from Yarmouth. At the humpbacked bridge in the middle of the marshes, half-way to Acle, we were going at such speed that May Bowden's hat and hairdo were banged even flatter against the roof of the Daimler, and we came down to earth again with such a bang that one of the panes of glass between the rear seats and the driver cracked clean across. I think that despite May Bowden's instructions the chauffeur must have contrived to trade in his beef sand-wiches for beer after all.

He was very disrespectful too, telling her to stop nagging for Christ's sake whenever she called out to him to slow down. He also called her an old cow for making the kiddie cry. As it happened, I wasn't crying, but he was – thick, soapy tears that seemed to have a head on them. I leaned over and informed him through the cracked window that it wasn't May Bowden's fault I'd missed seeing my boat. I had had to go somewhere at the very moment it was passing under the bridge, and so I had missed it.

'You tellin' me it actually made it to Yarmouth? I don't believe it!'

'May Bowden saw it.'

'May Bowden couldn't see her arse if it was staring her in the face,' the chauffeur returned coarsely, over his shoulder. 'The old bag's having you on!'

This new scenario, that May Bowden hadn't seen the boat at all, was only pretending, was so much worse than missing it by chance that my own eyes spilled over in earnest. Had my darling *Ace of Hearts*, then, drowned at Cringleford after all, been shredded by a paddle steamer, sunk to a lonely grave in the mud of Breydon?

'Take no notice of him!' May Bowden cut in sharply. 'He's drunk, can't you see that? He's not fit to drive!'

At that, the chauffeur· pulled the limousine up with a jerk which threw us against the sides. He opened his door, clambered out of the driving seat, and stood swaying in the road.

'All right, then!' he declared thickly. 'Le's see if you can do any better.' With which he saluted – smartly, if with some little difficulty in finding the peak of his chauffeur's cap – turned away, and began walking unsteadily along the grass verge.

'Did you *honestly* see my boat?' I demanded. First things first.

May Bowden, who had opened the door on her side of the car, drew herself up. 'Of course, if you prefer the word of a drunken oaf to mine –'

'I didn't mean –' Intimidated, I began again. 'I didn't think –'

'Something I've noticed on more than one occasion! Now

[200]

then . . .' She was out of the Daimler now, and then in again, into the driving seat. 'Do you want to stay in the back or come in front with me?'

My fright was such that I forgot my galley had ever existed. 'You don't mean *you're* going to drive!'

May Bowden fiddled about with the gear lever and the self-starter. She adjusted the mirror fixed outside the door.

'Have you any better idea for getting us back to Norwich?'

'But you have to have a licence to drive!'

'What makes you think I haven't got one?' May Bowden said. 'I'm tired of this conversation.' She pulled strongly on the starting button. It came out on a kind of string, further than I had ever seen a starter pulled before. But the car started. 'There, you see! Nothing to it.'

'But you have to know *how* to drive!' I wailed. 'Alfred had a man from Mann Egerton come I don't know how many times.'

'Whilst your brother is not a bad young man as young men go, he is not exactly a genius, is he? Not everyone who drives needs a man from Mann Egerton to show them how.'

She put the gear lever into first, released the handbrake and we were off with surprising smoothness, the shifts accomplished without jar or hesitation. As we passed the chauffeur standing at the roadside with his mouth open, she squeezed a resounding *toot-de-de-toot-toot* out of the bulb horn.

Of course she had known how to drive all along, but she never said, the old devil, she let me go on worrying. However she had come by her expertise I was too young to recognize it: lay face down on the rear seat with my fingers in my ears so as not to hear, not to see, the inevitably approaching crash. My fear so exhausted me that, incredibly, I fell asleep until awakened by a jubilant May Bowden, her hair and hat canted at a rakish angle, but looking immensely pleased with herself. The car was at a standstill, aligned perfectly with the St Giles kerb.

'Wake up, lazybones!' May Bowden exclaimed, prodding me with her parasol. '*Hasn't* it been a lovely day?'

Chapter Twenty

BEFORE that summer holiday ended, I had one further day out connected with a boat.

A wonderful thing happened in that second week of September. Between one day and the next – for I measured myself against it every single day when I was at home – I grew tall enough to ride my sister's bicycle: *my* bicycle from that moment on. Suddenly I could sit as comfortably on its saddle as on a chair, even slouch there and still reach the pedals without strain. I could take a hand off the handlebars to signal a left or right turn without, as heretofore, the bike wobbling all over the road. I could ride with such sang-froid as, for the first time, to be able to take proper note of where I was going instead of being so taken up with a fierce concentration on keeping the damn thing upright that I had once, for instance, ridden smack into the back of a parked van.

Distance took on a new meaning, Salham St Awdry now no more than a hop, skip and jump away. I took to riding over there even when I could only stay an hour, if that.

However pressed for time, I knew better than to forego that moment of ritual before the great diamond at Horsford Point. It was no time for getting above oneself. *I* wasn't to be like poor old Moses who, after all he had done to get the Israelites out of Egypt, wasn't, at the end of it all, allowed to enter the Promised Land because, when they had murmured against him because they were thirsty – and they were always murmuring about something or other, it was enough to try the patience of a saint – he struck a rock and when water came out he said, 'Here's this water I give you, you murmuring so-and-so's' when he ought by rights to have given the credit to God, who, when all was said and done, was the One who had made them thirsty in the first place.

Ma gerto o ca!

I came to St Awdry's by appointment, in the afternoon, with permission to stay the night. Waiting outside Chicken's cottage was a Ford truck, open at the back, a real old tin lizzy. One side of the bonnet was folded back and Chicken was bending over the engine fiddling with something inside. When he saw me prop my bike against the wall under Mrs Fenner's front window he came over to me, wiping his hands on an oily rag and moving with that balletic grace which always lifted my spirits. He put one of his hands on my shoulder, leaving an oily mark, of which I was glad. It was the equivalent of going through Customs and getting a stamp on one's luggage.

I lifted my pyjamas and my toothbrush and toothpaste out of the bicycle basket and took them into the Fenners' cottage, together with some jam and biscuits my mother had sent as a present. Only Ellie was in, her mother, she said, being off to cut osiers over Horsford way.

Poor Mrs Fenner! This intimation of her hard labour tempered my joyous anticipation of the afternoon ahead. Only once had I gone with her to cut osiers because there was little a child could do in the osier plantations other than bundle the whippy willow shoots up in twenty-fives, tied round with a strand of raffia, as the trade required. The osiers were cut with very sharp knives which invariably, however practised the cutters were, cut more than willow. The time I accompanied Mrs Fenner a woman had cut off the entire top joint of her thumb. The foreman had poured iodine over the stump, told the woman to wrap it round with her handkerchief, and sent her off, unaccompanied, to walk the two miles to the bus stop, to catch the bus into Norwich and the Norfolk and Norwich Casualty.

My joy was further tempered by the sight of Ellie who was, for once, dressed up, which could only mean she was coming with us. She wore a straw hat trimmed with poppies and a clean cotton dress of which little was visible below her long brown cardigan that, buttoned from neck to hem, made explicit without mercy her large breasts and the rolls of flesh which padded her stomach and thighs. She had on white ankle socks under white sandals that had actually been gone over with Blanco, and she so obviously thought she was the cat's whiskers that, almost, she was. For the first time I understood how her family could think her beautiful.

If I was sorry to have Ellie along, it was obviously as nothing to the way she felt about being lumbered with my company. It was her idea that I ride outside in the back of the truck, not the cab, and when Chicken tossed the suggestion aside as daft, she went into one of her sulks, hunching herself up on the lorry bench as close to the door as possible, so as to get away from me, the pig in the middle.

Chicken appeared to notice nothing of this lack of goodwill between his passengers. He drove out of Salham St Awdry singing 'All Things Bright and Beautiful' as lustily as even PC Utting could have wished, even if his catalogue of things made by the good Lord differed in several particulars from the list provided in the English Hymnal. His good humour was irresistible. Ellie began to giggle, which was of itself so remarkable that I even began to like her, for the time being at least.

The day had arranged itself to complement our mood. The sun shone, mellow September. Most of the corn was reaped and standing in stooks. In some fields the ploughmen and their horses were already hard at it, their shadows lengthening in the westering light. Sheep had been turned on to some of the stubbles, to tread the straw and their dung into the ground, readying it for another harvest. The hedges were bright with rose hips and shiny with blackberries, the horse chestnuts yellowing; their fingered leaves, the first to come and the first to go, hung up like bananas that in another day or so would be ripe for eating.

We drove east, our backs to the sun, out of the safe country of St Awdry's into the marshlands, north of those I had crossed with May Bowden on our trip to Yarmouth. We turned off the main road into an area of dykes and rivers and roads that grew steadily narrower, petering out at last in an unmetalled track with a rib of green along its centre. The flatness of the land was astonishing – not because it was flat, but because it was not flatter, not caved in altogether beneath the weight of the enormous sky. The drainage mills which stood about the vast green expanse looked heroic but doomed for daring to be vertical in such a landscape. By the time we reached our destination and got down from the truck on to a small concrete standing heaped with poke nets and sacks, it seemed an impertinence not to go on all fours.

We had come to visit Grig, an eel-catcher who, as Chicken told us, was an old friend from back when. Years later I learned that Grig was no more a real name than was Chicken. It was the name of a young eel.

Grig was not young: short, with bandy legs and great breadth of shoulder, so that at first sight he looked frighteningly simian, until you took in the weatherbeaten face, severe but benign, lit by eyes the colour of moleskin and topped by a thatch of yellow-white hair.

He lived in a tar-papered shack adjacent to a drainage mill which had fallen into ruin but still retained its skeletal sails, its air of defying the fates. When Chicken introduced Ellie and me he nodded pleasantly enough, but said nothing. Even to his old friend Chicken he spoke only a sentence or two: and Chicken, respecting his silence, or perhaps the silence of the place, himself became, for once, a man of few words.

We were clearly expected. The table in the one room of the shack was set with crockery for four. Besides bread and jam there was a fruit cake on a white paper doily and a basin filled with jellied eels. Except for the bed in one corner, the room, so far as furnishings were concerned, had a lot in common with Opposite the Cross Keys save that it smelled of fish instead of the Fenner pot-pourri, and was shining clean.

We sat down to tea at once, and ate our meal in amicable quiet broken only by the sound of chewing and supping and by an explosion of outraged surprise from Grig when I refused a helping of eels. I had never been offered them before, and nothing then – or since, for that matter – could convince me they were edible.

'Wha's up wi' the bloody gal?' Grig demanded of Chicken.

'Barmy,' was the soothing explanation. 'Lives on love an' moonshine. Don't mind *her*!'

Grig, unappeased, eyed me sternly.

'Eighty-seven year,' he declared, striking his chest. 'Eighty-seven last Whit Monday. You want to live eight-seven year, gal?'

It seemed a long time to which to commit oneself offhand. I faltered that I hadn't actually thought about it.

'Then think about it now, an' sup your eels! What else you think's kept me goin' all that time?'

I took another look at the grey chunks suspended in mucus and made up my mind.

'I don't think I really want to live as long as that, thank you.'

The eel catcher turned away in disgust.

'Barmy's right,' he agreed with Chicken, before reassuming his mantle of silence. 'Barmy as a barn door.'

After that inauspicious episode it seemed strange to find myself in a boat with Grig, just the two of us, moving in perfect companionship along the dyke, *en route* to a rendezvous with some tench who – the eel catcher had it on the authority of his long experience – would, at that very moment, between dusk and dark, be spawning. Our quarry was not that dreary fish itself, but the eels who also had their sources of information and would be forgathering to feed on the spawn.

'Watch out fer bubbles,' Grig commanded.

Anxious not to disturb our new accord, I strained my eyes to pierce the skim of mist which hung over the water like dust on old mahogany. The reason I was back in the eel catcher's good graces was the ball of wool which, upon Chicken's mysterious insistence, I had brought with me from Norwich in my blazer pocket.

When, thus prompted, I had asked Maud for some wool, she had countered with the sniff which was her usual response to all such requests.

'I know you! Knit two, purl two, drop two, an' then you can't be bothered.'

'Not for me,' I came back with guile. 'For Chicken.'

That, naturally, was different; and upon my assurance that Chicken had said any old wool would do provided it was strong enough, I was handed a pair of my father's old socks to unravel. Maud, in her so-called idle moments, was never without a tube of worsted divided between four thin steel needles upon which she knitted sturdy if inelegant socks for my father and her own, for Tom and Charlie and her latest love, who did not always last out until the heel was turned, in which case the socks went elsewhere. Only Alfred, who liked silk socks with fancy designs, refused Maud's knitted offerings. It gave me a funny feeling to undo those old socks, the crinkled yarn unwinding round by round, so many hours of Maud's life, the needles clicking. It was as if I were unravelling time itself.

Grig had been delighted with his gift. He had tossed the ball gently from one calloused hand to the other.

'That'll make a good old number o' bobs,' he said. I was too shy to ask what he meant.

The reason there were only two of us in the narrow, flat-bottomed boat which Grig, using a quant – a kind of punt pole, only shorter and with a thick cap at the end to stop it getting stuck in the mud – propelled along the dyke with the secrecy of a Red Indian paddling his canoe through the Everglades, was that Ellie had flatly refused to take part in the expedition and Chicken, obviously against his inclination, had volunteered to stay behind and keep her company. Ellie, in an unaccustomed burst of eloquence, had let it be known that she didn't hold with water (something I had long suspected). Water drowned you dead. If God had meant people to go on water he'd have made them so's they could walk on it, like Jesus.

Chicken winked at me and said, 'Hear that, gal Sylvie? Tha's one less we won't have to make room for, when my boat's launched.'

My heart leapt at his words, and I went off happily with Grig, a prospect I might otherwise have found daunting; eager to demonstrate that, so far as I was concerned, water was my natural element.

The mist had thickened. We sat, in the boat, up to our waists in it. When it reaches the top of our heads, I thought, we shan't be here at all: only the mist and the water, the tench spawning, the eels eating.

I summoned up courage to ask Grig if he had known Chicken long.

'A fair old time.'

Pressing on: 'Then you must know his real name.'

The astonished look on the eel catcher's face was without artifice.

'His name's Chicken!' Then he held up a thick finger for silence. We had come to the bubbles.

Grig fished under the seat and brought out a rust-pocked tin which had once contained Pat-a-Cake biscuits. Enough of the label – an obese infant having its hands clapped together by a besotted mum – was left for me to recognize it. The tin's contents, however, were not what I might have expected.

The eel catcher prised off the lid and took out a couple of eel-bobs: worms by the dozen, pink and orange and brown, pierced through and threaded on to thick wool, crinkly like my ball, except that this was grey and mine a heather mixture. Working deftly despite his misshapen hands, Grig weighted the ghoulish contraptions and attached them to short lines. Then he offered one to me. When I flinched away from the hideous object he pressed it gently nearer, until I had to take it for fear of the worms touching my face.

'It won't bite, gal!' he urged in a hoarse whisper, so as not to alert the fish. 'Do as I do an' you'll see something! Jest don't let go, now, no matter what.'

Taking a firm hold on the line, the worms wriggling fruitlessly among the coiled wool, he dropped his bob over the side. It was barely in the water before the eels, who could not have thought all that much of tench spawn, began biting. They threshed the surface in a convulsion of greed.

Catching their excitement, I too let down my line. Almost instantly it became heavy with the weight of eels. As they bit into the worms their hateful, hacksaw teeth became tangled up in the wool. No wonder Chicken had stipulated it had to be strong! What an end for my father's socks!

'Pull the line in quick,' came Grig's calm injunction. 'They'll saw themselves free afore you can get 'em.' Following his own advice he jerked his line out of the water, the bob a tangle of coils, grey and dirty yellow.

In the middle of the boat was a sturdy box with a hinged lid, propped open, half-full of water. Grig lowered his bob over this container and, with a strong twist of the line, dislodged several of the eels so that they fell into the receptacle provided for them, some going to their doom with the ends of worms hanging down from the sides of their mouths. He produced a pair of nail scissors, something out of a ladies' manicure set, and with meticulous care, avoiding the questing teeth, cut free the eels that wouldn't let go of the bob. They slithered down into the box looking even more revolting than the ones which had preceded them, with strands of grey wool hanging down on either side mandarin-fashion, and slitty, evil eyes like something out of Victorian melodrama.

'What yer waitin' for, gal?'

I raised the bob out of the water, full of wriggling serpents. I felt at once nauseated, frightened and excited: powerful beyond measure. There was no sport in the pastime. The eels positively struggled to be caught. One might have fancied them eager to make an end of the slime of life if it hadn't been for their equal frenzy, once they were in the boat, to get back to it.

We kept at our deadly game until we had used up all the bobs in the Pat-a-Cake tin, and until the wooden chest was full to overflowing. Suddenly I felt a sharp pain just above my sandal strap. One of the overflow, writhing on the floorboards, had taken a piece out of my ankle.

Grig broke into the loudest noise I had ever heard from him, and slapped his thigh. 'Now you're a real eel catcher, gal!'

When we got back to the little staithe, Grig bolted down the lid of the wooden chest, hauled it out of the boat and fastened it with ropes to two poles driven into the dyke bank. He adjusted the ropes until the chest hung just below the surface. I saw that it had holes in the sides, too small for the eels to escape through, large enough to let the water flow in and out again. Once a week, the eel catcher told me, a bloke from Yarmouth came along with his boat to collect the catch.

'We didn't do too bad. Reckon I'll owe you a bit, gal.'

I protested that he owed me nothing, that it had been great fun. At my choice of noun his friendliness drained away.

'Fun!' he snorted.

Chicken and Ellie were sitting at the table exactly as we had left them. They had lit the lamp, a lantern really, the kind used to warn of road-works ahead. It possessed none of the lovely glow

of the lamp at Opposite the Cross Keys. The two looked fed up,
I thought. Probably bored stiff with waiting for us. I was
ashamed for them to see that none of the tea things had been
cleared away. Ellie with her hat on, all ready to go, looked
sloppy. The buttons on her cardigan were buttoned up
wrongly.

Grig got out some ointment and smeared it on my eel bite.
The ointment smelled of fish but was wonderfully soothing.
Then he picked up a bulging sack out of a corner, handed
Chicken an empty bucket, and the two of them went outside,
the contents of the sack clanking. They returned presently,
empty-handed.

Chicken said to Grig in his mocking way, 'You better tell this
bloody mauther what's in the sack or she'll be dropping off at
the first police station to report we bin thieving.'

Grig was kinder. 'She'd never do that – would you now?' And
when I shook my head dumbly: 'There, then! Tin't nothin',
anyways, but some ole brass bits an' pieces I picked up here an'
there, nobody wanted, an' Chicken reckoned 'd do fer his boat.
Bin glad to find somebody take it off my hands.'

Chicken supplemented, 'That and some o' them eels you
caught. Ma Fenner 'll make a lovely stew. You can tell her you
bin in the Garden of Eden today and brought her back the
ruddy serpent.'

'*Mrs* Fenner!' I corrected him, automatically: but a smile
followed immediately after, because what he said was true. I
had been in the Garden of Eden that day. If that meant you had
to bring Satan back home with you, it was a small price to pay.

Chapter Twenty-one

IT was a sweet, long-drawn-out autumn that year. Nothing in a hurry, not even winter. The leaves fell off the trees slowly, one by one. As the days shortened, I was less and less in St Awdry's. Although my bike now possessed a fine battery lamp in place of the old carbide one, I wasn't allowed to ride out after dark, not along unlit roads anyway. I would sit in St Giles, doing my homework in the kitchen where it was warm and fortifying snacks were at hand, wondering how Chicken was managing in the poor light.

So far as the boat's progress was concerned, my absence or presence at Opposite the Cross Keys made not the slightest difference. My delight in its building was purely aesthetic: I was not allowed to have anything to do with its making. I didn't feel angry over this, because the Fenners weren't allowed either. It was as if Chicken, who in every other field of endeavour manipulated us all like puppets made to dance to his tune, in this, the supreme effort of his life, had made a vow that the boat was to be the exclusive product of his own labour, his own cleverness, his own dream.

I sat in the kitchen, my exercise books spread out in front of me, whilst, across the table, Maud knitted socks for her latest love – a widower who handed out tracts on the Market Place telling you to repent while there was still time – and pondered aloud the pros and cons of a winter or a spring wedding. Of all her so-called suitors, the widower alarmed me, both because he seemed to have a say in who went to heaven and who to hell, and because, as he was so religious, I was afraid he couldn't be wooing Maud just for the Woodbines and the Dairy Milk, like all the others.

Raising my head from my long division, I asked, 'Would you

really rather live with Mr Roberts than go on living here with us?'

'What you mean?' Maud demanded, as if one thing had nothing to do with the other.

'Well, you couldn't live here *with* him, could you?'

'Don't be daft!'

'Well, you couldn't, could you?'

'Get on wi' your homework!' Maud ordered. 'Now look what you done – you've made me drop a stitch!' And she bent over her knitting, her face red and confused.

Whenever I did get to St Awdry's that autumn – on Sundays usually, Maud catching the bus now that my parents' jaunts to Cromer were over for the season – it was to find, in some way not easy to define, a changed Opposite the Cross Keys. The mood was softer, harmonious. If the world was still a great laugh, there was less irony about the laughter. Even the two grandparents on the wall seemed to have mellowed with the declining sun, the one with the high collar losing his starchy look, the other his air of derisive unbelief. The boat next door, growing in its whitewashed habitation like a foetus in the womb, filled us with the wonder of creation. While Chicken toiled unremittingly from dawn to dusk, as God must have done during those gruelling first days, snatching (as God could not have, mugs, tea and bread and cheese being not yet created) a mug of tea or a bite of bread and cheese as occasion offered, we crept in from time to time and sat without speaking, watching: and presently, still without a word spoken, crept out again.

It is possible, in the prevailing climate, that I too, young and thoughtless as I was, mellowed a little: noticing for the first time, for instance, that Mrs Fenner's contributions to the family exchequer had fallen off with the end of summer, and that life at Opposite the Cross Keys was harder in consequence. The late peas were picked, the last potatoes lifted. There was not all that much call for pluckers. People, even the better-off ones, were saving up for the Christmas goose or turkey and going easy on poultry in the meantime. Some Sunday afternoons Mrs Fenner and I would walk over to one or other of the poultry farms, hang over the gate and run a practised eye over the fattening flock, our future clients. Good times were coming, we willed them to come quickly. No goose or turkey for the Fenners, of course, but money for plucking, plucking, plucking till the feathers came out of your belly button. In the meantime, to bridge the gap in my small way, I took to laying out my pocket money for the oranges or the jam tarts Mrs Fenner could no longer afford on her Saturday forays into the Market Place.

The gatherings round the table at Opposite the Cross Keys became more subdued in character, Mr Fenner puffing away in his private cloud, his old trilby pulled well down over his ears, *Old Moore* unopened on his lap; Tom sitting quietly smiling at private thoughts, Charlie frowning at his; Ellie, now that it was too cold to sit outdoors, busy with her comb within, Chicken occasionally rousing himself to hold up a hair which he swore he had just that moment fished out of the marge. Most of the time, obsessed with the next step to be taken in the building of the boat, the next problem, he seemed hardly to notice we were there.

One problem, just the same, he took time out to solve with characteristic energy and ingenuity. One Sunday, when we were at table, Mrs Lord called round with her daughter. They refused tea. It was not a social call. Mrs Lord also refused a seat, but Maud got up and offered hers to the daughter, Doreen, who accepted thankfully. Doreen was a short young woman so far gone in pregnancy as to look like a great big ball on which was balanced another, smaller – her head. Not to beat about the bush, Mrs Lord said, what she had called round to ask was, what was Charlie going to do about it?

No sooner had she stated her purpose than Charlie, red-faced, stood up and said that what he was going to do about it, he personally, whatever *it* might be, was go out. Doreen knew very well that all they'd had together was a bit of fun that didn't amount to a row of pins, and if she was thinking to lumber him with another bloke's bastard, she had another think coming. With heavy sarcasm he supposed that she and her ma must have worked their way through the list if they'd got to him at last, scraping the bottom of the barrel.

'Evenin' all!' he finished, ramming his cap down over his eyes as he went out into the deepening dark.

Doreen Lord began to whimper, and Mrs Fenner poured out a cup of tea for her, very strong as it had been brewing I don't know how long. Personally, I found Doreen Lord very interesting because up to that moment I had not actually known for a fact that an unmarried girl could have a baby unless she was the Virgin Mary who did not count, being a special case. When I later mentioned to my friend Dora Chapman how astonishing it was, this further exception to the rule, she burst out laughing.

'Don't they teach you nothing at that posh school of yours?'

Chicken now took a hand, debonair and disarming. You could see Mrs Lord was mesmerized by his Ronald Colman moustache.

'Cup o' tea 'll give you strength, missus' – insisting that she take his place on the sofa. 'Nothin' like a cup o' tea for softening the shock.'

'What shock's that, then?' Mrs Fenner inquired tartly, bringing the tea nevertheless. 'Tin't mumps that gal's come down with. She didn't swell up like that overnight.'

Chicken looked reproachful.

'A sensitive lady don't get over a shock to her nerves that easy – in't that right, missus?' Mrs Lord glowed. 'What we got t' do is stop tradin' insults an' see what can be done tha's best for all concerned, including the babby.'

At that we all stared at Doreen Lord's stomach as if we expected the baby to stick its head out and make its own contribution to the discussion. Instead, the mother-to-be spoke up on his, or her, behalf. 'I dunno,' she reflected, more wondering than bitter, 'you'd think, wouldn't you, out of thirteen on 'em, one at least 'd take his rightful responsibilities.'

'Men!' Chicken exclaimed, in the accents of one who himself belonged to a superior species. 'Not one in thirteen, you say? Always say thirteen's an unlucky number. You got a note of their names?'

Mrs Lord took a piece of paper out of her coat pocket and passed it over. Chicken smoothed it out and took it to the lamp.

'You can call this thirteen eleven to start off with,' he announced at the end of his scrutiny. 'That could change your

[214]

luck. Two o' these here blokes are spliced. You don't want to break up the happy home now, do you?'

Mrs Lord's face set stony and unforgiving. 'They should 'a thought of that afore they took avantage of a poor young gal. How's *she* ever goin' to get herself a husband if the father of that child don't make an honest woman out of her?'

'Tha's jest the problem, in't it, missus?' said Chicken in that lovely, beguiling voice he could put on when it suited him (how cynical I could be about that voice, so long as it wasn't directed at *me*!). 'Which one o' them *is* the pa, tha's the question. One or two – even three – they could 've sorted it out between theirselves. But eleven! A ruddy cricket team! You see the difficulty, missus.'

Now both visitors began to cry. My own eyes watered in sympathy, less for the wronged Doreen than for the poor little baby, doomed to be an orphan before it was even born.

'Charlie, now . . .' Chicken addressed himself to Mrs Fenner. 'You reckon he could run to a tanner a week?'

'Why should he run to anything?' Mrs Fenner began heatedly. 'He never –'

'Never mind what he never.' Chicken held up his hand magisterially. 'We got a little babby to think of. We don' want it to have to go on the parish, do we? Get the village a bad name. What you say, missus? All right if I put Charlie down fer a tanner?'

Mrs Fenner conceded with reluctance. 'On'y if all the others do the same.'

'Leave it t' me,' Chicken assured her. 'They will.' And, to Mrs Lord, 'Eleven at sixpence a week – five shilling an' sixpence! You can bring a babby up like a prince on five an' six a week. Five an' six to do what you bloody like with, no lovin' hubby to give you a clout, take it out of your purse, an' go off with it to the pub. You'll be quids in! What you say?'

Mother and daughter looked at each other. Then Mrs Lord said, 'Suppose they don't pay.'

'Leave it t' me,' said Chicken again. 'They will.'

And they did. Next morning, as soon as the village shop was open, Chicken crossed the High Street and, with his own money, bought Doreen a notebook with a soft red cover. He ruled the pages into columns, each with a name at its head, and a space for the date; and then – it showed how kind he was under the mocking exterior, taking all that time away from his boat – he got hold of all Doreen Lord's lovers, one after the other, and showed each the column with his name at the top.

'Easy as winking,' he replied when Mrs Fenner asked him how he had got on.

Two weeks later the baby was born, a boy. When his mother began to push him out everybody in the village came to peep into his pram; but they were disappointed – or, perhaps, relieved. The little fellow, who was called Rudolph, after Valentino, was the spitting image of his ma.

Every Saturday she went round collecting her dues, licking her pencil point as she entered them up in her book. It became an accepted part of village life. In fact, I think the men on her list became quite proud of stumping up their tanners. It showed they were somebody. And when, fourteen months later, she was brought to bed of another child, a girl this time, they cheerfully upped it to ninepence, Charlie included.

Chapter Twenty-two

ONE afternoon when I got back from school late on account of my music lesson, Maud greeted me with triumph writ large and ugly on her face. She must have been listening for the sound of my bicycle tyres over the paving stones, for, despite the dank mist already rising, she came out to the shed, the quicker to get the ball rolling.

As I shut the shed door and clicked the padlock to, she began in her teasing way, 'Well, she finally went and did for herself, didn't she?'

It was a tone of voice she reserved exclusively for May Bowden, a tone that invariably, if only for the moment, made me like May Bowden more than I usually liked her. I hefted my schoolbag and my music case and went towards the open kitchen door, knowing I had only to stay silent to be told all.

What May Bowden had done, it turned out, didn't sound as final as all that; but it was enough to tip the balance between my parents allowing me to go on visiting her, and their laying down a general prohibition upon any further intercourse between us. May Bowden was a good three inches taller than my mother. That morning, coming up St Giles behind her, she had suddenly, for no conceivable reason, stretched out one of her long, bony hands and tipped my mother's hat – the one with the kingfisher feather on it – forward over her eyes.

That wouldn't have so bad, if only people passing by hadn't laughed. But they had, and May Bowden herself had guffawed in a most unladylike way. My mother, understandably, was less amused. More to the point, more serious issues were involved. It was a case of the straw hat that broke the camel's back. Today a hat, tomorrow, who knew what the dotty old maid might get up to? Henceforth her home was out of bounds to me.

It was typical of my mother to leave to Maud the imparting of what she felt would be distressing news. In this, to be truthful, she was partly mistaken. For some time I had gone into May Bowden's house with increasing hesitation – chiefly, I think, because it had become so dark. In the past, the creeper which covered the outside walls had always been kept meticulously clipped round the windows, but for months now the jobbing gardener who came in once a week had been told to leave it alone. The result, after the summer, was that the windows were covered with long trails that, from within, looked pitch black, not crimson. By autumn, the house had become a cave, dim and mysterious.

I went to my mother and promised that I wouldn't go into May Bowden's house ever again. I was most specific about my form of words. The house. I said nothing about the garden.

I could not, after all, desert Pillow, who would soon be shutting up shop for the winter, descending to some secret hiding place in the depths of the rockery from which even my whistles could not summon him. How long did toads live? I had no idea. Would Pillow ever awaken again to the call of spring? The little creature became dearer to me day by day as the year advanced, and I faced the imminent loss of him, for months if not for ever.

That Saturday morning I got up early, too early for May Bowden to be about, and went into her garden. I moved quietly over to the rockery and whistled softly, hoping it was loud enough for Pillow to hear. After a while I whistled again, Louder. Again no toad appeared.

He's waiting for his blood to warm up, I told myself, parting a browning clump of hart's tongue fern on the chance I might get a glimpse of him in that interesting condition.

The toad lay splayed out, dead; dreadfully dead. Something viscous and horrible had oozed from the smashed skull on to the large, flat stone on which he lay. There was more of the stuff on a smaller stone nearby, a stone which could well have been the instrument of the poor creature's undoing.

Unable or unwilling to take in what I saw, I called him softly: 'Pillow! Pillow!'

'Somebody's up with the lark,' said a voice behind me.

I hadn't heard May Bowden's door open. The woman wore a

burgundy velvet dressing gown, very grand, and on her head a pale blue crêpe de Chine nightcap, trimmed with ribbons and lace. From my crouching position I stared up at her.

Anything better than looking at the dead toad.

'What have you done to him?' I whispered. I can't tell how I knew May Bowden was the murderer. I just knew it.

'Done to him?' May Bowden echoed. She sounded offended. 'I haven't done anything.' She regarded the violated little body without pity. 'Tell him to get up at once, the lazy thing, and pull himself together.'

Suddenly I was standing up, tugging at the fine dressing gown. 'He can't get up!' I screamed. 'He can't pull himself together! You've killed him!'

'Let go my dressing gown this minute, miss!' May Bowden pushed my hands away and smoothed down the velvet pile with tender hands. 'Such manners!'

'Why – why?'

'I whistled and whistled,' said May Bowden, looking at me with childish spite. 'I whistled till I was blue in the face. I gave him every opportunity, but he would not come. Open defiance! To me, the one who provides him with all his necessities, who does everything to make his life one of comfort and ease! *You* only have to whistle once and he comes running. What's so special about *your* whistles that he comes to *them* and not to mine?' Resuming her customary air of self-congratulation: 'That toad had to be taught a lesson, and a lesson is what he has been taught.'

I howled. I was deadly frightened, I wanted to run away, but grief possessed me, glued me to the spot.

'Don't be so dramatic, child.' May Bowden went back into her house. Before she shut the door she poked her nightcapped head out into the air again. 'All this fuss about a stupid frog!'

I stayed on in the garden for a little, crouched over the rockery, my eyes tight shut. I didn't know what to do. I couldn't think.

As usual, when I couldn't think, there was only one thing to do. I ran back home to Maud. She was setting the table for breakfast. I flung myself at her, buried my head in her morning apron, smelling the stiff white cleanness of it.

[219]

When she had heard my story, Maud went and got an old *Telegraph* from the cupboard, told me to go upstairs and wash my face whilst she went round the corner to see what was what. She wasn't away long, although to me, waiting at the back door for her return, it seemed an age. At last I heard her footsteps, heard them stop at the dustbins; heard a dustbin lid being lifted up, and a galvanized clank as it was replaced.

This time, it was at Maud I flew, her crime appearing to me at least as great as May Bowden's. I pummelled her with clenched fists, I tore her apron from its waistband.

'You can't put Pillow in the dustbin! You can't throw him away as if he was rubbish! How would *you* like to be put in the dustbin when you're dead?'

'If I was dead I don't suppose it'd bother me one way or the other. The dustman might have something to say.'

Her calm, her familiar derision, brought me to my senses in a way no loving commiserations could have done. She made no reference to her torn apron other than to remark: 'That one's gone for a burton.'

Still, I whimpered. 'We could take him back to St Awdry's, give him a proper burial –'

'With wreaths, I suppose, the organ playing an' the rector spouting? To say nothing of upsetting Tom something dreadful. You wouldn't want to do that, would you?'

I shook my head dumbly. I wouldn't want to do that.

'Well then –'

Leaning close against her for comfort, I whispered: 'What about May Bowden?'

'Don't you worry yourself about her. She'll be taken care of.'

The following Wednesday, while I was at school, they came and took May Bowden away – which, incidentally, is why I never became rich after all. She was taken away, not in a Machiavellian machination like Eliza, nor yet a van. An ambulance from a private asylum, Maud reported, with attendants in uniforms that fitted them like a second skin. From the way Maud talked, I think she could easily have fallen in love with one of those attendants, if she had been in the mood. As it was, her eyes were red and swollen; she seemed very depressed.

[220]

When I asked, incredulously, if she had been crying because of May Bowden, she took out her handkerchief, took a long blow, and admitted, 'It's always upsetting to see the last of an old friend.'

She said that May had departed without protest, all dolled up as if she were going for a run out in the country in the hired limousine. Her lawyer had been there and had put a padlock on the garden gate. But that evening, as it was getting dark, I climbed over and went and stood by the rockery with my eyes closed, willing God to do everything for Pillow it was possible for Him to do, which was everything.

When I opened my eyes I saw, half-hidden behind the big conch shell, two of the little bags filled with the trinkets I used to sit playing with at May Bowden's dining table. One of the bags had a piece of card pinned to it. On it, in handwriting all thicks and thins, were the words, *For Miss Impertinence, with Love.*

I loosened the drawstring of one of the bags and tipped its contents out on to the cobbles, recognizing as old friends the paste shoe buckles, the pen holder with the Eiffel Tower inside, the beads, the buttons, the hat-pins.

I piled everything back into the bag again, picked up its fellow unopened, and dropped the two into the lily pond. The slime between the lily pads parted to let them through, and soon closed over again. I climbed back over the gate and went home.

Chapter Twenty-three

I N winter it became very cold in Chicken's cottage. The flue had collapsed, the hearth was unusable. Chicken kept a little paraffin stove going, one that gave out more smell than heat, moving it about so that he could direct its warmth on to his hands wherever he happened to be working. Maud had knitted him some mittens, but still his fingers were raw with chilblains. Sometimes, when I sat in the room silently watching, I stopped watching because I couldn't stand the sight of those hands any longer.

The boat grew. Growing, it seemed to consume its builder's energies, even the man himself. He seemed smaller, though that may only have been his shoulders, hunched with fatigue. He could still move in that saucy, challenging way of his, like a ballet dancer, but only after one of his rare days off, before the cold and the heaviness of the work stiffened his bones again.

The boat grew a hull and a deck and the beginnings of a cabin. There were disappointments. At some point I became aware that not only was there no engine, but no provision for one. No mast, nor sails either. Instead of being the galleon in which the two of us were to be free to roam the seven seas, the boat, it seemed, was a mere floating bungalow, such as were to be seen moored one behind the other, as it might be a suburban street, along half the rivers of Norfolk. Eyesores, my father called them, as near to anger as I ever heard him.

Not surprisingly, Chicken looked at houseboats in a different light.

'You ever slep' in a bed tha's like a cradle, Sylvie?' he demanded one morning when I had brought him in a steaming mug of Oxo. 'To an' fro, to an' fro, the water movin' past, always on the go. You ever woke up to the reeds whispering along the bank when there in't a breath of air stirring, yet still they're whisperin' secrets like they was plotting to blow up the Houses of Parliament?' Chicken set the mug down on his workbench. 'What you see,' he asked, 'back there in Norwich, when you get up of a mornin' an' take a look out o' the window?'

'Well . . .' I thought. 'The houses opposite, and the street, and the trams going past –'

'Houses an' street an' trams going past – bloody shit! Wouldn't you rather sit up in yer bunk – yer don't even have to set foot on the floor – an' see a cow an' enough space to make you dizzy?'

Privately, I enjoyed looking at the houses opposite my bedroom window – knew their individual bricks like old friends – and I loved the trams that came clanking up the hill like happy dragons. Given the choice of a cow or a tram to look at, I'd have chosen the tram any day.

Chicken finished his Oxo, and handed back the empty mug.

'Ta,' he said. 'You're a good gal, Sylvie. Better 'n some I known.' As I reddened with pleasure, he added, 'Glad you come by. There *was* one little thing I bin meaning to ask you.' He fished in his pocket and brought out a nail about three inches long, with a big head and a blunt end, which he handed to me. 'You up in the city. Think you could pick me up a bag of those, off the nail stall?'

The nail stall, in the Rag and Bone Market next to St Peter Mancroft, at the top end of the Market Place proper, wasn't a stall at all, properly speaking. It consisted of a long trestle table set out with hundreds of little canvas bags, all containing nails. An overflow was piled up higgle-piggledy underneath the trestle, on the ground. Norwich people said there wasn't a nail made anywhere in the world you couldn't get at the nail stall, and the fact that some of the little canvas bags were printed in Chinese or other foreign characters seemed to bear out the claim. Every bag had a sample nail sewn on to the outside. That was all the help you got from the stallholder, a cadaverous Indian man who professed to speak no English and who my brother Alfred said he knew for a fact slept on a bed of nails when he went to bed every night: it was how he had got into the business in the first place. The man wore a red turban that was

[223]

always half undone, with long black hair spilling out, and he had bloodshot eyes, possibly due to insomnia.

'Hatch nails,' Chicken said. 'Don't ferget the name. An' use your eyes, gal. See the galvanizing's thick an' bright – I don't want no rubbish, mind. Sixteen penny's the right one, but if he haven't got 'em, I'll make do wi' twelveses.'

Until he explained that 'penny' in relation to nails was an expression of length, I thought that the sixteen and the twelve pennies were Chicken's quaint way of acquainting me with the cost.

I asked, beginning to feel bad, 'How much will they be?'

'*I* don't know.' Chicken sounded annoyed. 'You'll see the price on the bag, dummy. Half a crown to three bob, I reckon. That heathen's got 'em all marked up, won't take a penny less.'

Beginning to feel very bad, I stumbled into my apology.

'I'm sorry, Chicken, I've bought all my Christmas presents. I'm sorry, but I've only got threepence left. There'll be my pocket money next Saturday, but that's only sixpence. If I don't spend anything all week, that's still only ninepence.' I stood with my head drooping, puffing out my cold white breath. I felt terrible.

Chicken came close and looked at me. His eyes were dangerous. He put out a hand to touch the side of the boat, stroked a timber of the hull.

'Tell me, gal,' he said. 'You ever thought what I'm goin' to name this here contraption?'

I shook my head dumbly. I had never thought about it. To me it was the boat. Enough. To question further was to seek to know the secret name of God.

'Well, I'll tell you, so long as you don't tell nobody else. They say as it's bad luck to let on beforehand. On'y when every last thing's bin done, then an' not before, tha's when you paint a boat's name on the bow, for all to see. But seein' as it's you – well, then –' a pause for a notional roll of drums – 'I'm goin' to call this here boat the *Lady Sylvie*. What you say to that?'

I had nothing to say to it. I burst into tears. Tears of joy, gratitude, love. And a dreadful fear at the pit of my stomach that I was being bribed to steal.

*

The nail stall, that Saturday, was doing tremendous business. The Indian was kept on the hop, taking money, making change, listening to requirements and producing the exact nail for the job. If he really couldn't speak English he seemed to have no difficulty understanding it. His bloodshot eyes were everywhere.

As the only female in the vicinity of the stall I felt sufficiently conspicuous already, without taking into consideration my only too questionable behaviour. There was, after all, a limit to the number of times you could circle a pile of nails full of a wide-eyed childish curiosity without giving rise to suspicions. I had pinpointed Chicken's sixteen-pennies almost at once – a cluster of fat little bags leaning against a foot of the trestle. The price of each was marked in black ink, the figures formed in a foreign way, but readable. Only too readable.

3/3.

I had wandered away from Maud and her mother with an air of innocence calculated to put Maud on her guard if she hadn't been taken up with Christmas shopping. As I circled the nail stall yet again I kept a weather eye out for them. Something – you never could tell – might bring them up to the Rag and Bone at the very instant I was stretching out my hand to filch one of those little bags marked 3/3.

'And what d'you think you're doing?' In my imagination I could hear Maud's voice echoing round the Market Place, ringing bells in the police station. It was no good. Nellie Smith was right. I wasn't the type. I couldn't do it.

Bitterly ashamed at having let Chicken down, at proving unworthy of his trust, I left the clatter and chatter all about me and went home. I took a knife out of the cutlery drawer in the sideboard and ran upstairs to my bedroom. As I passed the drawing-room door my mother called out, 'Is that you, dear?' I said it was and continued on my way.

My goal was the money box which stood on my mantelshelf. It was made of red-painted metal, in the shape of a pillar box. You posted money through the slot where, in a real, lifesize pillar box, you would have posted letters. This money box, I can honestly state, was the only festering sore in a family life which was otherwise harmonious to a degree.

The only way to retrieve money posted through the slot was

via a tiny door in the base, opened by a key which my parents kept in a place known only to themselves and God. What went into the box was what I, in my rebellious way, categorized as no-money: small round objects that superficially looked like coin of the realm – shillings, florins, half-crowns, silver of consequence, no sixpences or threepenny bits – but were in fact without reality. Through the year we were seldom without visitors at St Giles, uncles, cousins, aunts, who hardly ever took their leave without pressing money into my hand.

The catch was that no sooner was the guest off the premises than I was escorted solemnly to my bedroom mantelshelf, there to pass through that rapacious slot every penny I had received as a parting tip. *Clink!* it rang in farewell at the beginning of the year, hitting the metal bottom; the sound dulling as the months passed and the money box slowly filled until, by December, it was an over-fed *clunk!* On the first day of the new year the money box key appeared as from nowhere, the door in the bottom ceremoniously unlocked, the receptacle turned upside down on the dining-room table, and its contents counted.

The sum was astronomical! But did I ever see a penny of it? I did not. A nasty little book with *National Savings* on the outside was produced from the desk drawer, and book, Maud and I despatched to the General Post Office – the local sub-branch being deemed inadequate to the occasion – there to hand the money over the counter in exchange for nothing more than an inked entry and a smudged rubber stamp.

'For your future,' my mother always explained. 'When you're grown up you'll be glad you didn't fritter it away on rubbish.'

Since I had never had any intention of frittering it away on rubbish, I remained persistently sceptical of this far-off consummation, so misty down the corridors of time. And, I may say, I was proved right. By the time I came into my little hoard it meant nothing much. It made no difference to my life one way or another. Whereas, when I was young enough to enjoy it, what gratification might I not have had from such necessities as comics, ice-cream boats and gob stoppers?

And nails for Chicken.

I took the money box from the mantelshelf, sat down with it on my bed, and inserted the knife blade in the slot. I knew I would have no luck with the two-shilling pieces and the half-crowns – they were too thick – but I had once almost got it to disgorge a shilling simply by shaking, so you never knew. Twenty minutes later, the money box looking only too clearly as if somebody had been at it with felonious intent, I threw down knife and box alike, buried my head in the pillow, and gave way to despair.

'And what do you think you're doing?' said a voice at my door, the very words I had imagined her saying in the Rag and Bone Market. Maud came into the room, shut the door, took in the knife and the money box at a glance, and inquired calmly, 'What you need so bad, then, you got to go an' commit burglary to get it?'

If it seemed a little unjust to be accused of burglarizing one's own property, I was in no state to dispute the point. I grabbed at Maud's hand, and sobbed out the sorry story of Chicken's nails.

'You're cracked,' she said, when I finished. 'Whyn't you tell me afore I went out wi' ma? I could 've run to it then. Now I haven't got two sixpences to rub together till next Friday.'

'He asked *me*,' I answered, doleful but proud to have been singled out.

'An' where did he expec' *you* to get three an' thruppence from? Don't answer!' she added quickly, as I opened my mouth to tell her what I felt sure Chicken had had in mind. 'Let me have a think.' She frowned, reviewing the position. Clearly, equally with myself, there was one option she had discarded at the outset, that of saying no. If Chicken wanted his nails, he had to have them. 'Can't have that boat of his sinking to the bottom for want of a bag o' nails, can we? Gimme that knife.'

When she had had no better luck than I at coaxing even one shilling through the slot, let alone three, she gave the brisk little nod which I knew meant that she had made up her mind what to do. She took the box over to the hearth, where poker and shovel, brush and tongs shone brightly Brasso-ed, never used except on the rare occasions when I was ill and had to stay in bed, when the sheer gloriousness of a fire in one's bedroom made one wish never to get quite well again. She knelt down and, after a brief contemplation of the possibilities, selected

[227]

the poker: up-ended the money box and, with one unhesitant movement of the wrist, smashed in the little door in the base.

Returning with the box to the bed, having first meticulously rehung the poker on the little stand which housed the fire implements, she tipped the money out on to the quilt, selected a shilling and a two-shilling piece, and returned the rest to their desecrated cubbyhole.

'You got the thruppence?' And when I nodded, speechless in the face of her magnificent audacity, 'Tha's all right, then.' She put the money box back on the mantelshelf, lying it on its side, so the money wouldn't fall out. 'I always told your ma, keeping it there, one day somebody's bound to catch their sleeve on it, knock it off the shelf afore they could stop it, an' down it'd come like Humpty Dumpty.'

'Oh no!' I cried, transported by love. 'I can't let you take the blame! I'll tell her it was me.'

'You'll do nothing of the kind!' Maud retorted sourly. 'I didn't bring you up to be a little liar!'

I couldn't decide whether to lie to Chicken or not. I wanted him to think me a brave girl, bold enough to have stolen a whole barrelful of nails if he had requisitioned them, not just a measly little canvas bag. I wanted him to know how the Indian had grabbed at me, only I had slipped from his grasp, eluding both him and the Market policemen, who, truncheons drawn, had pursued me the length and breadth of the Market Place, blowing on their whistles, like cops in a Mack Sennett movie. Oh, I had the choice of a dozen scenarios which I had lain in bed that night happily devising and revising.

In the event, to my disappointment, the subject never even came up. I cycled to Salham St Awdry on Sunday morning, and called in at Chicken's cottage before I even let the Fenners know I was there. Early as it was, Chicken was already busy, shaving a piece of wood, the delicate slivers curling off the spokeshave on to the floor. Absorbed in what he was doing, he took the bag of nails with a casual 'Ta' and without even checking that they were the right kind. He chucked the bag on to the workbench.

Deflated, I turned to go.

'Hang on!' Chicken said. He put down wood and spokeshave and came over to me, fiddling in the pocket of his black waistcoat as he came. 'You forgot somethin'.' He took my hand, cupped it into one of his and, with the other, poured into it a rain of sixpences, seven of them in all. 'Have to pay me sodding debts, don't I, or you'll have me up in court. Count 'em if you don't believe me,' he went on as I stood dumbly, looking down at the little pile. 'Don' bother with the change. The thruppence extra's for yer trouble.'

'Oh, Chicken –' I stammered.

'Wha's the matter wi' you, gal? Think I expected you to pick 'em up fer nothing?'

Chapter Twenty-four

THAT Christmas, I didn't see a lot of Salham St Awdry. St Giles was awash with visitors and I had my social duties to perform. Maud went off home on Christmas Eve, not to return until the evening of Boxing Day, during which period Mrs Hewitt, putting aside her washboard and dolly blue, functioned as a well-meaning but far from adequate substitute. I think the gift which gave Maud most pleasure at the festive season was to come back to St Giles after the junketings were over to find what a mess the house had got into, without her.

School broke up a week before Christmas, so that I was able to spend a couple of days going plucking with Mrs Fenner. Awful as the plucking sheds were in summer, it was as nothing to the hell of winter: draughts like icicles down your back; your feet, no matter how many pairs of stockings you crammed into your shoes, stuck to the frozen concrete as if by magnets. And the feathers! It was unbelievable, the number of feathers the well-dressed goose or turkey wore as a matter of course, each one stuck in place with a glue which could have made their fortunes if they had had the nous to market it.

Cold in the sub-zero temperature, hot with aggravation, we pluckers displayed little of the Christmas spirit as we wrestled with those bloody feathers and held our own against the foreman who came round threatening to dock us if we didn't make a better job of getting them out. Actually, we knew he didn't dare, because for once we had the upper hand, the demand for pluckers at that time of year far exceeding the supply. All the gypsy women were up in Norwich selling sprigs of holly and mistletoe, as well as hideous furry toys that bounced up and down on an elastic string and were guaranteed to send an infant hysterical.

The four and sixpence I got for my two days' work I laid out on a Christmas cake which I had heard Mrs Fenner admiring in the village shop window. It looked a picture, covered with white icing, with a fancy frill round it, and a snowman on top. Unfortunately, when Mrs Fenner came to cut it, at teatime on Christmas Day, she couldn't. It was so hard that even Tom, who was the strongest of the family, couldn't make a dent in it. Village shops didn't turn over their stock all that fast, and it must have been a cake left over from the year before, if not the year before that.

But it turned out all right. When Mrs Fenner went back to complain, once the shop opened up again after the holidays, the shopkeeper, a formidable woman, swore that the cake was as fresh as a daisy. However, when Mrs Fenner threatened to hurl the object in dispute at the shop window, and then they'd find out how fresh it was, or wasn't, as the case might be, she gave back the money, which Mrs Fenner promptly expended in groceries, to show there was no ill will.

I arranged with Tom to go and cut some holly for me to take back to St Giles: he was off work early that afternoon. It was, as always, restful to be in the company of one so at peace with the world. The bright blue eyes in the lovely cherub's face looked at every stick and stone as if seeing it for the first time, and finding it wonderful beyond words. The fields glittered with frost, a gossamer mist clinging to the beeches, as we made our way along Back Lane, past the allotments and the cemetery, to where the best hollies stuck up at intervals along the hedge-rows.

Alas, we had left it too late. One plundered tree after the other proclaimed that others had been before us. It was a wonderful year for holly berries. Faced with such plenty, the vandals had been choosy, discarding some branches for others more fructiferous. More upset at Tom's plaintively voiced disappointment than by the shortage of really 'good' holly, I began to gather up some of the rejected pieces strewn about the verges.

'These will do.'

'No, they won't!' The lovely face had become contorted with anger. 'Measly things like that!' Tom snatched the holly out of my hands and threw it on the ground. I knew better than to argue. 'We'll go over by Jackson's,' he declared. 'The best un of all's down over by Jackson's.'

The tree in one of the boundary hedges of Jackson's farm was indeed a nonpareil among hollies. But here again the wreckers had been at work. All the reachable parts of the tree had been gone over with such thoroughness that scarcely a berry remained visible. Only at the top, where a thick core poked through, rather as if a Lombardy poplar were sticking up through the tree's middle, were there trusses of berries too good to be true, and too high up, too difficult for anyone's taking.

I had reckoned without Tom.

'What I tell you?' he shouted, and began climbing.

To watch that dreadful ascent in silence was impossible, yet I was afraid to call out, to shout up that Maud had said positively no holly that year, the way it scratched the wallpaper and the picture frames. I was afraid to call out because, every now and again, emerging and disappearing among the holly leaves, Tom's face showed, transformed with a determination so utter I knew it was deadly dangerous to make a sound. '*Please!*' was all I could mutter, under my breath, praying to anyone who might be listening.

The holly tree did not let its last precious cargo go without a fight. Its branches reached for Tom's old greatcoat, slitting the buttonholes, ripping off the epaulettes, tearing the pockets from their anchorage. Crackling insult, the leaves went for his neck, his eyes, his hands. Blood ran down his face, the same colour as the berries. Into my mind unbidden came a picture from one of my favourite legends: Baldur the Beautiful, killed by a shaft of mistletoe, his blood dripping on to the holly berries, turning them red for all time. It was less a holly gathering than a crucifixion.

Ellie was the only one home at Opposite the Cross Keys. She stopped combing her hair when we came in.

'You got yourself in a fine mess,' she remarked to Tom, before setting to again.

I went through the scullery with him and out to the back, where I pumped some water. There was so much blood in his eyes you couldn't have told they were blue. I was afraid he had been blinded. He bent over the bucket and splashed water over his face and neck until he was wet all down his front. He was in great spirits.

'We got it, didn't we? I reckon you won't find anyone in Norwich wi' holly better 'n that.'

'I'll tell everyone how brave you were to get it.'

He wasn't blinded, and though his face looked flayed, his injuries, so far as I could judge, were superficial. There was no first-aid box at Opposite the Cross Keys, but Tom found an old tube of ointment the vet had once prescribed for Gyp, and he put on some of that, and seemed to find it soothing.

He also found some twine with which he went outside and tied the holly, which he had dumped outside the front door, on to the back of my bike. I watched the leaves and the sharp ends of the branches incising deep lines into the paint of the mudguard, but I didn't say anything.

I felt deathly tired. The sun was setting, low and large and red, itself an outsize holly berry. I wondered where I would find the strength to cycle home before dark. Or after.

I roused myself to say, 'Don't tie it all on. You must keep some for yourselves.'

Tom paused in his task, genuinely puzzled.

'Us?' he said. 'The likes of us don't put up holly.'

I said, 'Christmas is for everyone.'

'Oh ah,' he said, pulling the last knot tight.

I rode back to Norwich painfully, every small rise a mountain slope. All the way, I could hear the holly taking its revenge on the mudguard. By the time I came up to Horsford Point the last ray of the sun was full on the signboard and I saw beyond peradventure that, whatever I might have thought in the past, it read, for then and thereafter, MANN EGERTON FOR CARS and nothing else.

Without getting off my bike, I bowed my head to the victorious Mann, and continued on my way.

Chapter Twenty-five

ONE evening in May I sat in Maud's room in my vest and knickers while she turned up the hem of one of my new school dresses, pale mauve linen with a white collar, programmed with that expensive dowdiness exclusive to schools for the daughters of the gentry. (Eldon House was bourgeois to the core, but no matter: the ideal was all.) In summer, Maud's bedroom, under the tiles, was hot to unbearable: in winter, cold to ditto. In spring it was, to my way of thinking, the pleasantest room in the house with its dormer window giving on to a panoramic view down the hill to the Guildhall and over the roof-tops.

I lounged on Maud's bed with its white honeycomb cover, idly turning the pages of *The School Friend*, waiting for it to be time to try on again. Maud, stitching away in the little embrasure under the window, put her sewing down, got up to push the casement wide. She leaned her forearms on the sill and looked out for a moment, into the soft evening. Immediately her voice burst forth in surprise and alarm. 'Here come my brother Charlie!' Leaning out until I feared her gaunt body would disappear over the edge: 'Charlie! Charlie!'

What on earth could be up? That something was, neither of us doubted for a moment. Charlie never came to St Giles. Yet here he was. Something must be dreadfully up.

Maud flew to the door, pausing only to warn me not to dare to follow without first making myself decent. I heard her afternoon shoes with their louis heels clonking downstairs at untypical speed, noisy on the bare treads of the uppermost storey, quieter on the Turkey carpeting below. I ran to my bedroom, stuck head and arms through the first dress I could lay hands on, and hurried down to the kitchen.

Charlie, very red in the face, was ensconced in Maud's special chair, looking important. Having apparently satisfied herself that nobody was dead or dying, Maud had forbidden further reportage until the demands of hospitality had been satisfied. Bursting with curiosity, I was forced to wait until the kettle had boiled, the tea been brewed, a slice of fruit cake cut and arranged on a flowered china plate, before Charlie was permitted to let us know the purpose of his call.

And what a story he had to tell! First, did we know that Chicken had finished his boat? Maud and I looked at each other. Well, we did know and we didn't. For the last three weeks it had indeed looked finished, bright with varnish, the cabin furnished, to a very spartan specification certainly, but with a kettle and crockery of sorts in the galley, pillow and army surplus blankets on the two bunks covered with red American cloth.

Whatever Maud knew (and it was years before she confided that Chicken had promised her the boat was to be called the *Lady Maud*), I knew that, whatever the outward appearances, it couldn't be finished so long as no name, no *Lady Sylvie*, was to be seen on its bow. Much as I yearned to be thus celebrated, the boat's completion was something I dreaded. I wanted it to go on a-building for ever. I had grown used to that in-curving, out-curving shape enthroned on its blocks like a reigning god. In a sense, though I had had nothing to do with its actual manufacture, I had made it: my longings, my dreams, the muddled aspirations of my growing mind and body were all embodied in that tubby little craft which did indeed – it must have been to PC Utting's satisfaction – look like an enlarged version of a toy Noah's ark. It would have been no surprise to find that the roof lifted off the red-painted cabin to disclose wooden animals you could take out two by two, and a Mr and Mrs Noah looking worried because the dove had not yet returned with the olive leaf in its beak.

So long, then, as the boat remained at Opposite the Cross Keys, anything and everything was possible: St Giles, Eldon House, slotted without friction into life with Chicken by the bank of some Broadland river or – engine or no engine, mast or no mast – sailing down to Rio, rounding the Horn, peering through jewelled water for an opening in the Great Barrier

Reef. But once the boat was gone, and Chicken with it –! My mind refused even to contemplate the possibility.

That very afternoon, Charlie said, when nobody was at home except Ellie, there had been a noise, an explosion, which had brought half St Awdry's out of doors in a panic. Even the Harleys, deaf as a post, both of them, had come out of their cottage at the end of the row to see what was up. The licensee of the Cross Keys, opposite, had been sure an aeroplane had fallen out of the sky. PC Utting wouldn't have been surprised to find it was the end of the world.

In fact, it was the derelict cottage. With the aid of some small explosive charges, artfully bestowed, Chicken had demolished the entire front wall. It hadn't taken much doing, considering its already dilapidated condition, though the dust generated had still caught Charlie in the throat hours later, when he came back from work. Then, the first person to meet him with the news had been Mrs Leach from next door, hysterical because the crash had pitched her Welsh dresser over on to the floor and she didn't have so much as an eggcup left in one piece.

By that time the Fire Brigade had been summoned from Norwich, and men were already shovelling the debris into a lorry. Other workmen were doing some emergency shoring-up of the adjoining walls of the Leaches' and the Fenners' cottages, which were showing a distinct tendency to lean towards each other over the newly created space between. In the Fenners' cottage, the two grandads had fallen off the wall and smashed their glass, that was all.

'All!' Maud echoed, aghast.

Was Chicken safe?

'*He* were all right, the clever ole bugger.' Charlie settled back to his tale. It appeared that, a short while before the explosion, a brewers' dray, drawn by two Shire horses and attended by two large men in leather aprons, had arrived in the village, and pulled up by the pond. The dray had attracted some attention because its owners, Bullards' – the name was painted on the sides – supplied beer to neither of the village pubs. One of the two men slipped nosebags over the horses' heads whilst the other, the driver, sat puffing peaceably on his pipe.

The crowd which quickly collected after the blast was not kept long in doubt of the dray's true purpose. Inside what was left of the shattered cottage, Chicken could be seen, spade in hand, systematically shoving aside the rubble so as to make way for a kind of makeshift trackway which he laid down carefully, in several interlocking sections, all the way from the boat, shrouded in tarpaulins, to the edge of the road. When these preparations seemed to be accomplished to his satisfaction he stepped out into the middle of the High Street, put two fingers to his mouth and whistled – a signal the men on the dray were evidently waiting for. The driver put up a large thumb as evidence that he had heard and understood, his companion removed the nosebags and took hold of the horses' halters. Slowly, the two brought the pair round, and the dray with them; moved slowly back down the road until they came abreast of the ruin, where the manoeuvre was repeated, so that the conveyance finished up facing towards Cromer. The brake back on, the two brewery workers unlatched the back of the dray, and then joined Chicken to help with the next stage.

Slowly and carefully – the track must have been well waxed, for after some initial difficulty the vessel moved smoothly enough – the three of them brought the boat forth into the light of day; and then, its dust protection discarded, drew it up the ramp and on to the wide loading area, where they anchored it with ropes and padding. By this time the onlookers had cottoned on to the object of the exercise, and there were many willing hands to help them get the boat safely cradled. Only PC Utting hung about fretfully, unsure whether there was anything he could properly arrest Chicken for, and apparently coming to the conclusion that there wasn't. When everything was ready for departure somebody raised a ragged cheer. It did the heart good, as old Mr Harley unexpectedly told Charlie later, to see something actually happen in the derned ole place.

Charlie stopped talking and, again, Maud and I looked at each other, our hearts too full for words. What we both wanted, I think, more than anything else, was for Charlie to say goodbye and go, leaving the two of us to work out what the intelligence he had brought was going to mean to us. But Charlie showed no sign of making a move.

On the contrary, his demeanour changed, he seemed at a loss for what to say. But that he had something more that had to be said was only too evident.

Maud demanded, 'Tha's all, is it?' And when Charlie fiddled with his cap peak and didn't answer, sharply: 'What else is there, then?'

What else, indeed!

Stumblingly, Charlie recounted the rest. At the last moment Chicken had gone into Opposite the Cross Keys and emerged with Ellie, an Ellie got up in her cotton dress and long brown cardigan; the straw hat with the poppies on her head, and in her hand a brand-new fibre suitcase crammed, presumably, with her belongings. There being no room on the box for more than two, he handed her ceremoniously up the dray ramp, himself following after, unfolding two canvas chairs he had been carrying under his other arm – one for her, one for himself. The driver's assistant lifted the ramp back into place, bolted it and returned to his seat. The driver gathered up his reins and, with a click of the teeth, set his beautiful beasts in motion. The boat, with Chicken and Ellie, side by side, waving and nodding like royalty to all who saw them on their way, receded up the Cromer road, bound for God alone knew where.

Well, not only God. Somehow or other, the word had got about that Chicken had taken his boat to the Bure, to a mooring a little below Buxton. Mr Fenner, stately on his three-wheeler, had ridden the six or seven miles over there that very evening, to ask what Chicken intended to do to make his daughter an honest woman, to which the answer had been 'Nothing.' Mr Fenner had returned shaken, and retired into his private fog, *Old Moore* open on his knees.

My mother gave Maud a couple of days off to comfort her mother, whilst I – it was half-term, May, the sweetest time of the year – hung about the house wondering who was going to comfort me.

I finally decided that Chicken had had to take Ellie. He had to have somebody to cook his meals, wash his underwear, darn his socks. The fact that Ellie couldn't cook water, seldom, if ever, washed her own underwear, let alone his, and didn't know a darn from a drainpipe did not deter my luxuriant imaginings. Ellie was no more to Chicken than Mrs Hewitt was to my mother – somebody you paid (or, more likely in Chicken's case, didn't) to do the jobs you couldn't be fagged to do yourself.

I couldn't have said, next morning, when I wheeled my bicycle out of the shed, if my intention in riding out to Buxton was to offer myself in Ellie's stead or not. My cooking was probably no better than hers, and I couldn't darn. The prospect of laundering Chicken's smalls did not appeal. Let us say, I went because I went, and leave it at that.

I did not stop at Opposite the Cross Keys, did not even slow down: barely spared a glance for the gaping hole next door. Kept on through Norgate, past the gypsy encampment, the cowslip field, past all that Salham St Awdry meant to me.

At Stratton Strawless I turned right on to the Buxton road, wearying a little as the miles receded under my tyres, but spirits rising despite myself. There was blossom everywhere – in the orchards, in the hedgerows. Even in the shadowy woods blossom drew arabesques upon the gloom. I felt that I could easily bud and blossom myself if I could only get the hang of it.

In Buxton village I inquired at the Post Office for any boat arrived by brewers' dray in the past couple of days. The smiling woman to whom I addressed my inquiry directed me without hesitation. Past the mill, a little up towards Lamas, then take the right and the left and the right again. 'Whenever you find there's a road crossing over, m' dear, take the narrowest one and you won't go wrong.'

I passed by the mill, took the right and the left and the right again, by which time the 'road' had dwindled to a cart track between clouds of cow parsley in full flower, along which I was forced to cycle now one side of the central hump, now the other, according to the disposition of pot-holes. Whichever route the dray had taken, it could not have been this.

I was glad it had not tried to come this way, for its passage would have wrought mayhem among the white lace which fringed the path like a bridal veil. I was really tired by now, so I got down from my bike and pushed it, pleased to move half-submerged among the furrowed stems, at the top of which flower parasols swayed, each petal point like the white satin pumps of a well-rehearsed *corps de ballet*, turned in at precisely

[239]

the same angle. Between the delicate stalks of each umbel, I could see a sky so blue it had to be one more figment of my imagination. I could not think how anyone could be unhappy.

The river took me unaware. No reeds to advertise its imminence, the cow parsley growing almost to the water's edge. The boat, tied to a short stake fore and aft, sat squat and still on the water like a contented duck.

How glad, I thought, it must be to be out of that dark room, off those blocks and on to an element that miraculously yielded to its weight yet at the same time bore it up! It was just the right size of river too – not so narrow as to be unworthy of the name, not so wide as to be unfriendly, the two opposite banks not on speaking terms.

The river took me unaware. So did the couple on the boat's tiny deck. I drew back among the cow parsley before they could see me, lowered my bicycle gently on its side.

I do not think they would have noticed me had I rung my bicycle bell peremptorily, *ting-a-ling!* Ellie in her cotton frock, the front unbuttoned, was sitting on one of the folding chairs, her legs apart, her face up to the sun, eyes closed. She seemed to be purring. Chicken stood behind her combing her hair.

He was dressed as usual, all in black except for his shirt. But – oh horrors! – for once, his cap was off and the awful secret was out. Chicken was bald, his bare white patch in startling contrast to the brown of his face. The fringe of curl which had peeped out so fetchingly from under his cap was all the hair he had.

Down the lacklustre length of Ellie's hair went the ghastly comb. As I watched, Chicken paused in his labours, bent over and kissed the upturned forehead, once and once again. On the bow of the boat I could read its name, painted in blue: *Lady Ellie*.

I picked up my bicycle and mounted, making no attempt at concealment. Chicken went on combing Ellie's hair. I wobbled back down the track, the bike jolting from one pot-hole to the next, moving through a mist of cow parsley which wavered in and out of my tear-blurred vision like grasses seen under water, bending with the current. I bumped along until I was out on the road again, heading for home.

[240]